✓ **W9-BXG-079**

JERRY FALWELL
V.
LARRY FLINT

JERRY FALWELL
V.
LARRY FLYNT

THE FIRST AMENDMENT
ON TRIAL

Rodney A. Smolla

UNIVERSITY OF ILLINOIS PRESS
Urbana and Chicago

Illini Books edition, 1990

© 1988 by Rodney A. Smolla

Reprinted by arrangement with St. Martin's Press

Manufactured in the United States of America

P 5 4 3 2 1

This book is printed on acid-free paper.

Library of Congress Cataloging-in-Publication Data

Smolla, Rodney A.
  Jerry Falwell v. Larry Flynt : the First Amendment on trial /
Rodney A. Smolla. — Illini books ed.
    p. cm.
Reprint. Originally published: New York : St. Martin's Press, © 1988.
Includes bibliographical references.
    ISBN 0-252-06151-9 (alk. paper)
    1. Falwell. Jerry — Traials, litigation, etc. 2. Flynt, Larry — Trials,
litigation, etc. 3. Trials (Libel) — Virginia — Roanoke. 4. Freedom of the press
— United States. I. Title.
[KF228.F35S65 1990]
345.73'0256—dc20
[347.305256]
                                                                        9033682
                                                                        CIP

TO LINDA

Contents

Acknowledgments

The author wishes to thank the attorneys for Larry Flynt, Alan Isaacman and David Carson, of Beverly Hills, California, as well as the attorney for Reverend Jerry Falwell, Norman Roy Grutman, of New York City, for their gracious cooperation. The author also wishes to thank Alexander Wellford, and David C. Kohler, of Richmond, Virginia, with whom the author worked in the preparation of a "Friend of the Court" brief in this litigation.

Preface

I first began to follow the litigation in *Falwell v. Flynt* as a First Amendment scholar looking in on the case from the outside. A few weeks after the final decision of the United States Court of Appeals for the Fourth Circuit was rendered, I had occasion to deliver a speech on the case before a combined group of lawyers, judges, and journalists in Richmond, Virginia. I was approached after the speech by John Stewart Bryan, III, the publisher of the *Richmond Times-Dispatch* and *The Richmond News Leader,* and two of his attorneys, Alexander Wellford and David C. Kohler, about assisting them in the preparation of a "Friend of the Court" brief in the United States Supreme Court. I agreed, and helped to write a brief urging the Supreme Court to reverse the judgment of the Court of Appeals.

It was in my work on the brief that I became intimately familiar with the litigation, and realized that it was a truly remarkable episode in American legal history. While I participated tangentially as an advocate in the case, I have tried to do justice to the full power of both Reverend Jerry Falwell's and Larry Flynt's positions. More importantly, I have tried to tell the story as I felt it ought to be told—not in the voice of a legal scholar but in the voice of an observer of the American scene. The book is intended to be as much an exercise in American Studies as Constitutional Law, for the case was as much a cultural battle as a legal battle, a case in which we as a culture put the First Amendment itself on trial.

—RODNEY A. SMOLLA,
Williamsburg, Virginia,
June, 1988

JERRY FALWELL

V.

LARRY FLYNT

Chapter 1

"**R**everend Falwell, have you seen this?"
The question was put to Jerry Falwell by a reporter as Falwell was leaving a Washington, D.C., news conference in November of 1983. The reporter was brandishing the latest edition of *Hustler Magazine.*

Falwell was in a hurry; he quickly glanced at the cover of *Hustler* in the reporter's hand and shrugged off the question. "That is probably nothing new," he said, walking away.

When Falwell returned that day to his hometown in Lynchburg, Virginia, however, he decided that perhaps he ought to take a closer look. He asked a staff member to buy a current issue of *Hustler* (one cannot imagine Jerry Falwell *himself* in line at the local 7-Eleven with a copy in his hand), and when he got the magazine, he opened it to the front inside cover. Falwell then saw what appeared to be, at its first embarrassing blush, an advertisement for Campari Liqueur, with himself as the featured celebrity endorsing the product! Falwell was stunned. But the initial shock was nothing compared to the wave of disgust he felt as he read the Campari ad more closely. Entitled "Jerry Falwell talks about his first time," it includes a picture of Falwell, an illustration of a Campari bottle next to a glass of Campari on the rocks, and an "interview" in which Falwell describes his "first time":

FALWELL: My first time was in an outhouse outside Lynchburg, Virginia.

INTERVIEWER: Wasn't it a little cramped?

FALWELL: Not after I kicked the goat out.

INTERVIEWER: I see. You must tell me all about it.

FALWELL: I never *really* expected to make it with Mom, but then after she showed all the other guys in town such a good time, I figured, "What the hell!"

INTERVIEWER: But your mom? Isn't that a bit odd?

FALWELL: I don't think so. Looks don't mean that much to me in a woman.

INTERVIEWER: Go on.

FALWELL: Well, we were drunk off our God-fearing asses on Campari, ginger ale and soda—that's called a Fire and Brimstone—at the time. And Mom looked better than a Baptist whore with a $100 donation.

INTERVIEWER: Campari in the crapper with Mom . . . how interesting. Well, how was it?

FALWELL: The Campari was great, but Mom passed out before I could come.

INTERVIEWER: Did you ever try it again?

FALWELL: Sure . . . lots of times. But not in the outhouse. Between Mom and the shit, the flies were too much to bear.

INTERVIEWER: We meant the Campari.

FALWELL: Oh, yeah. I always get sloshed before I go out to the pulpit. You don't think I could lay down all that bullshit *sober,* do you?

Located below the "interview" is an additional paragraph purporting to tout the merits of Campari:

Campari, like all liquor, was made to mix you up. It's a light, 48-proof, refreshing spirit, just mild enough to make you drink too much before you know you're schnockered. For your first time, mix it with orange juice. Or maybe some white wine. Then you won't remember anything the next morning. *Campari. The mixable that smarts.*

The ad ends with the catch-line "Campari. You'll never forget your first time."*

This page in *Hustler*'s November issue is listed in its table of contents (yes, *Hustler* has a table of contents) as "Fiction. Ad &

*The reader may wish to refer to the appendix of this book, which contains a facsimile of the *Hustler* ad.

Personality Parody." At the very top of the ad, following the title "Jerry Falwell talks about his first time," a small asterisk appears. At the bottom of the page, the asterisk is repeated with a disclaiming footnote that says, in relatively fine print: "Ad Parody—Not to Be Taken Seriously."

Jerry Falwell, however, took it quite seriously—"As seriously," he said, "as anything I have ever read in my life." Falwell was outraged. "I think I have never been as angry as I was at that moment," he said. "I somehow felt that in all of my life I had never believed that human beings could do something like this. I really felt like weeping." Instead of weeping, however, Falwell commenced a $45 million lawsuit against *Hustler* and its publisher, Larry Flynt.

The lawsuit *Jerry Falwell v. Larry Flynt and Hustler Magazine* is destined to be an American classic. It is one of those few cases selected each year for resolution by the United States Supreme Court, but the majesty of a final decision by the Supreme Court is only a small part of what makes the case *Falwell v. Flynt* one of the most extraordinary legal battles in recent memory. The case was at once high moral drama and farcical passion play, a tragicomic mélange of bombastic lawyers, contemptuous witnesses, and scathing cross-examinations. The case became much more than a battle of lawyers over the legal consequences of a dirty joke. It was also a cultural battle: Presenting to the Supreme Court deep conflicts reaching into the very soul of the American First Amendment tradition, the case involved a battle over the very nature of free expression in a pluralistic society, a battle over competing visions of American life.

The jurors saw Falwell spin out before them his entire vision of a morally rejuvenated America and heard conservative North Carolina Senator Jesse Helms take the stand as a character witness to praise Falwell as one of the greatest living Americans. The jurors also came to know Larry Flynt "up close and personal." They saw Flynt, in deposition testimony, stubbornly refusing to use Falwell's correct name, insisting instead on calling him "Farwell." And they heard wild exchanges between Flynt and Falwell's lawyer, Norman Roy Grutman.

"To save a lot of time," they heard Flynt say, "why don't you just ask them questions direct, so we can get to the meat of things."

"Well," Grutman responded, "I'm trying. I have to do—"

"I'm talking about Farwell fucking his mother," Flynt interrupted.

"What's that?"

"Let's talk about Jerry and his mother. Just get right to the meat of it."

"Talk about whom?"

"Jerry Farwell."

"And his what?"

"And his mother, about him fucking his mother in the outhouse, you know, let's just get—"

"Well, I'm going to come to that in a moment. You know that I'm here for that purpose."

Many other witnesses appeared in the trial, but Falwell and Flynt jointly held center stage, and their performances dominated the case. The trial was the sort of political and cultural drama that periodically plays itself out in American courtrooms, reminiscent of Tennessee's Scopes "Monkey Trial" of 1925 or the battle between Abbie Hoffman and his cohorts against Judge Julius J. Hoffman and Mayor Richard J. Daley in the "Chicago Seven" trial, which arose from the violence at the 1968 Chicago Democratic National Convention. The drama was heightened by the personalities of the two principal trial lawyers—Norman Roy Grutman for Falwell and Alan Isaacman for Flynt. Grutman bombarded the jury at every turn with righteous indignation at the horrible, sleazy sinfulness of Larry Flynt. Isaacman fought back valiantly, against all odds, desperately trying to achieve the litigation upset of the century, a victory for Larry Flynt and *Hustler Magazine* against Reverend Jerry Falwell in Roanoke, Virginia, only a short distance from Falwell's Lynchburg, Virginia, home.

The wild circus of a trial in Roanoke was followed by an appeal to a federal appellate court, the United States Court of Appeals for the Fourth Circuit, and finally by a decision in the nation's highest tribunal, the United States Supreme Court. These appellate decisions took the raw, violent confrontations of the trial and distilled from them several of the most profound freedom-of-speech questions ever decided by American courts, questions that reach to the very heart of the type of nation we want to be.

For many Americans, it is inconceivable that the First Amendment could be intended to protect *Hustler Magazine* and the type of crude, mean-spirited attack Flynt launched against Falwell. Surely, they think, *Hustler* is beneath the dignity of the First Amendment. Surely, freedom of speech is not an absolute license for licentiousness. Flynt's coarse speech is nothing but excrement, a form of moral pollution fouling the cultural environment.

For other Americans, *Hustler* is the quintessential example of what ought to be protected by the First Amendment. Tolerance is often nothing but indifference.[1] It is easy to defend freedom of speech when the speech is bland, polite, and civilized. Tolerance is only meaningful when the speech is jarring to mainstream sensibilities—when it attacks God and Country, when it is violent and vulgar. Like the pilots in Tom Wolfe's *The Right Stuff,* who strain their planes to the breaking point to "test the envelope," Larry Flynt and *Hustler* constantly push us to the outer limits of our tolerance. If we are really to be a pluralistic and open culture, this reasoning goes, we must be willing to embrace all speech, even speech at the extremes, for it is only by such toleration that we give meaning to the ideal of an open society.

One of the wondrous complexities of the American legal tradition is that these fundamental philosophical disputes are never decided by judges in the sterile abstractions of the ivory tower. Lofty legal principles must withstand the practical crucible of litigation, a hot acid-bath of competing legal strategies, lucky litigation breaks, pragmatic rulings from trial judges, dramatic courtroom confrontations, and the common-sense intuitions of juries. In a landmark case rubber meets the road, theory is pressed against fact, abstract philosophical and legal principle is leavened by the human side of the law.

Falwell v. Flynt is not a pretty sight. Viewer discretion is advised. Yet, it is a true "only in America" story, a case worth savoring in all its deep philosophical resonance and in all its bizarre dramatic detail.

Chapter 2

A central strategy in Jerry Falwell's plan of attack against Larry Flynt was to stage the lawsuit as a cataclysmic American contest between Good and Evil. Falwell and Flynt were cast like stern, uncompromising characters from the writings of Nathaniel Hawthorne or Herman Melville, with Falwell representing the puritanical American quest for an orderly and decent society committed to moral principle and Flynt representing all of the violent, dark, free-wheeling, erotic impulses of the human heart.

Falwell and Flynt actually have a great deal in common. Both come from rural hill country—Falwell from the western mountains of Virginia, Flynt from the mountains of Kentucky. Both men are ambitious; both men are naturals in the art of commanding media attention; both men are in their own way great American success stories.

Just how deeply do these common traits run? The lawsuit offered an invitation to plumb Falwell's heart and the often surreal depths of Larry Flynt's mind. Could it be that Falwell and Flynt were selling different versions of the same thing? Does Flynt peddle the quick, evanescent fix of superficial sex? Does Falwell peddle the spurious security and certainty of superficial fundamentalism? Are both men money-changers in the American Temple, pushing pseudo-salvation to the gullible? These questions were raised by both sides.

On the surface, both Falwell and Flynt certainly seem to be hustlers—at least in the innocent, Pete Rose, "Charlie Hustle" sense of the term—passionately seeking converts to their worldviews, propagating their versions of truth through multimillion-dollar empires. Does the lawsuit reveal that Flynt and Falwell are also both hustlers in the cynical, snake-oil sense? Or did both men demonstrate, through their resolute insistence on total litigation victory, that this war was real? Perhaps Falwell and Flynt are not frauds, but true believers, hustling radically different versions of the American dream.

For Jerry Falwell, Flynt's version of that dream had become a nightmare, a freakish, degenerate surrender to all the evil, indulgent excesses in the American character. Falwell had taken his American energy and become America's Minister, channeling his exuberance into building the nation as a shining city on a hill.[1] Flynt had taken that same robust American energy and become America's pimp, tempting the nation to become a perverse, sleazy city on the make. From Jerry Falwell's perspective, his life's work was proselytizing for God; Flynt's was prostituting for Satan. In the early stages of the litigation, Flynt seemed almost anxious to play the satanic role.

As Falwell went to war against Flynt, his first step was to whip his troops into a frenzy and build a litigation war chest. On November 15, 1983, shortly after Falwell first saw the Campari ad in *Hustler,* Falwell's conservative political lobby group, Moral Majority, Inc., sent out two mass mailings, both signed by Falwell. The first mailing was sent to some 500,000 "rank and file" members of the Moral Majority. It described the *Hustler* parody, but did not include an actual copy. Falwell asked for contributions to help "defend his mother's memory" in court.[2]

A second mailing was sent to approximately 26,900 Moral Majority "major donors." For the major donors, Falwell brought out the major artillery: The mailing included a copy of the Campari ad, with eight of the more offensive words blacked out. Falwell went right for Larry Flynt's jugular; the letter to the major donors says in part:

> Sane and moral Americans all across our nation are outraged by how much these pornographers are getting away with these days. And pornography is no longer a thing restricted to back-alley bookshops and sordid movie houses. Now pornography has thrust its ugly head into our everyday lives and is multiplying like a filthy plague. Flynt's magazine, for example, advertises pornographic telephone services

where, for a fee, men or women will engage in an obscene phone call with you!

   . . . Cable pornography with its "X"-rated and triple "X"-rated films can bleed over into a regular cable system right into your own living room. . . .

   And there, in my opinion, is clear proof that the billion-dollar sex industry, of which Larry Flynt is a self-declared leader, is preying on innocent, impressionable children to feed the lusts of depraved adults. For those porno peddlers, it appears that lust and greed have replaced decency and morality.[3]

To fight this billion-dollar sex industry, the letter explains, would take money:

   As you know, legal matters are time-consuming and expensive. There are lawyer's fees and court costs to consider, not to mention the personal time and energy I must devote in these next trying weeks and months. . . .

   Will you help me defend my family and myself against the smears and slander of this major pornographic magazine—will you send a gift of $500 so that we may take up this important legal battle?[4]

Three days after these pitches by the Moral Majority, Falwell sent out yet a third mailing, reaching some 750,000 persons, this time under the auspices of the *Old Time Gospel Hour,* the corporate sponsor of Falwell's religious television and radio programs. This mailing stressed the need for contributions to keep Falwell's television and radio stations on the air so that they could effectively continue fighting the good fight against porno-pushers like Flynt:

   I was ready to cut another 50–100 stations—when someone showed me a full-page liquor advertisement which appeared in the November issue of *Hustler Magazine*—a pornographic tabloid.

   When I saw it—I decided that, in a society containing people like Larry Flynt, the *Old Time Gospel Hour* must remain on the air—on every station. . . .

   I am not a quitter. That is why I have established the *Old Time Gospel Hour* SURVIVAL FUND. . . .

   Please help with this SURVIVAL FUND. Your gift of $150 can make a great difference.[5]

Falwell also used his *Old Time Gospel Hour* television program to display the ad during several nation-wide broadcasts, attacking Flynt and *Hustler* and preaching the need to stamp out pornography. In just the first thirty days following these efforts, the Moral Majority received over $45,000, and the *Old Time Gospel Hour* over $672,000, all earmarked for Falwell's legal crusade against Flynt. No one knows for certain how much the anger whipped up over the *Hustler* ad increased the general donations to the Moral Majority and to Falwell's various religious ministries.

Larry Flynt was surely galled to see his attack on Falwell used as a fundraising device by the Moral Majority and Falwell's ministries. Never backing down from a fight, Flynt had *Hustler* run the Campari ad parody a second time, in its March 1984 issue. To add insult to injury, *Hustler* even turned around and sued Falwell in federal court in California for copyright infringement in distributing copies of the ad parody! Falwell, the theory went, had copied *Hustler*'s ad parody without *Hustler*'s permission and used it to generate nearly a million dollars in profit. *Hustler* lost its copyright infringement case; the court held that even though Falwell had clearly used *Hustler*'s copyrighted material as a fundraising device, such exploitation of the ad was a legally permissible "fair use," since Falwell's purpose was also to engender moral outrage against his enemy and elicit monetary support for the war he was about to undertake.[6]

The copyright infringement suit, however, was merely a sideshow to the real battle in a federal court in Virginia.

Chapter 3

L awsuits are inevitably shaped by the personalities of the lawyers involved, and *Falwell v. Flynt* is no exception. The colorful, clever, and fiercely competitive lawyers hired by Falwell and Flynt together personify those qualities that drive America's love-hate relationship with the legal profession.

Americans are at once enchanted and put off by great lawyers. The image of the lawyer as an avaricious manipulator, an ambulance-chasing shyster, an amoral gun-for-hire, a mouthpiece for gangsters, or an intellectual point-man for capitalist robber barons has always been balanced by the counter-image of the lawyer as a member of a learned profession, a seeker of truth, an officer of the court, a defender of civil liberty, a catalyst for social progress, a statesman and diplomat, a wise counsel for restraint against the passions of the mob and the moment, a tireless warrior in the ongoing human struggle for justice. For every lawyer who wrote laws to hold slaves in bondage, there were lawyers who fought for emancipation; for every lawyer who engineered the subjugation of women, there were lawyers who pressed for sexual equality; for every lawyer who defended the sweatshop, there were lawyers who litigated reform; for every lawyer who betrayed the nation during Watergate, there were lawyers who pursued the orderly channels of due process to rid the nation of corruption. America's love-hate affair with the bar is nicely summed up in a favorite story of Abraham Lincoln's, one of the law's patron saints. Lincoln had decided to stop at the local tavern the evening before he was to try a case. Many of the other lawyers in town were already at the tavern, huddled around a huge fireplace, discussing the next day's trial. "A very cold night," said the innkeeper.

"Colder than hell," Lincoln replied.

Another patron asked, "You've been *there,* too, Mr. Lincoln?"

"Oh, yes," smiled Abe, "and it's just as it is here. All the lawyers are nearest the fire."

Jerry Falwell chose as his attorney one of the most colorful trial lawyers in America, Norman Roy Grutman, of the law firm Grutman, Miller, Greenspoon, Hendler and Levin in New York. Grutman was born and raised in New York City. He attended the Horace Mann prep school, and then went to college at Yale University, where he worked on the *Yale Daily News,* and won the Gardner White Memorial Debate, Yale's highest forensic honor. He graduated Phi Beta Kappa from Yale in 1952 and finished his law degree three years later at Columbia University. At Columbia Grutman established his potential as a superstar by winning the law school's prestigious Laurence S. Greenbaum First Prize for advocacy. Grutman became a skilled trial lawyer. "I began trying cases in the world described in Tom Wolfe's *Bonfire of the Vanities,* " Grutman explains. He became head of the litigation department in a large New York firm, and then left to start a firm of his own. Grutman has a commanding presence. With a melodious basso voice and a rotund Sydney Greenstreet bearing, he can dominate a courtroom.

Jerry Falwell's desire for a top-flight trial lawyer was certainly understandable. But his choice of this particular top-flight lawyer was at least a little remarkable. For Grutman had become famous as the attorney for none other than pornographer Bob Guccione and his slick, skin-filled *Penthouse Magazine.* Falwell, of course, was absolutely entitled to the lawyer of his choice. But there was more than a little irony in the fact that much of the money sent in to Falwell's coffers by all those faithful little old ladies from the Bible Belt and those Moral Majority major donors was funneling its way in legal fees to a lawyer who had made his career working for Bob Guccione. It was a sort of Baptist-to-*Penthouse* Iran-Contra connection.

According to Grutman, Falwell actually used the money he solicited to fight Flynt for his ministries, and financed the litigation himself. Grutman also insists that he took the case primarily as a matter of principle, and at a financial sacrifice, for he could not charge Falwell his full customary fee rate.

Falwell actually met Grutman through a prior lawsuit Falwell had filed against *Penthouse*.[1] Falwell had granted an interview to two freelance journalists, who, in turn, sold the interview to *Penthouse*. From *Penthouse*'s perspective, of course, it was not exactly that its readers were hanging on every word that Falwell had to say. (Who believes "I don't buy *Penthouse* for the pictures, but for those insightful interviews with people like Reverend Jerry Falwell"?) What *Penthouse* had to gain from the interview was the impish scandal value of putting Jerry Falwell's words and photograph in its magazine. The *Wall Street Journal* snidely remarked that "Everyone's atwitter this week over the fact that an interview with Reverend Jerry Falwell, head of the Moral Majority, is appearing in *Penthouse*, the lurid girlie magazine."

Falwell figured he'd been had, and he sued. According to Falwell, the reporters never indicated that they planned to sell the interview to *Penthouse* and even assured him that they did not represent any pornographic magazines. The reporters countered that they were freelancers, who had gotten the interview from Falwell fair and square, with no conditions for where it would appear. Falwell claimed that *Penthouse* was "exploiting me financially and spiritually." Bob Guccione responded that Falwell was a "liar" and "hypocrite."

Penthouse's lawyer was Norman Roy Grutman, and he set out not just to beat Falwell but to punish him for having the gall to take *Penthouse* to court. "This is a media event contrived by the Reverend Mr. Falwell," Grutman gleefully said, "an admitted public figure who craves the limelight."

The *Falwell v. Penthouse* case was tried before federal Judge James C. Turk of the United States District Court for the Western District of Virginia, the same judge who later presided over Falwell's suit against *Hustler*. Grutman did all he could both to win his case in court and to embarrass Falwell publicly. Not unlike Larry Flynt's later fetish for mispronouncing Falwell's name, Grutman called his opponent "Foulwell" on national television. "After having called the magazine a lot of things," Grutman said to the press, "they expect to walk away unbloodied." That would not do for Grutman, and he counterpunched Falwell ruthlessly, attempting to bloody him at every opportunity. At a press conference after a hearing in the case, Grutman pointed to Falwell and sneered, "Ye shall know the truth, and the truth shall make you free." The reporters present roared with laughter, and Falwell could only reply lamely, "God will get the last laugh."

But in the end, it was Grutman, not God, who laughed last on this one. *Penthouse* won the suit. A celebrity might grant an interview to a journalist with certain strings attached, such as a contract between the reporter and the interviewee that the interview could only appear in *Esquire* or the *Christian Science Monitor.* But when a celebrity grants an interview at large—when he gives an interview to a freelance reporter with no such strings attached—then the reporter is free to sell to the highest bidder.

Judge Turk quite astutely identified what Falwell was really after in his suit. In his decision ruling in favor of *Penthouse* he observes, "Stated succinctly, Reverend Falwell does not approve of *Penthouse* magazine. He contends that the appearance of the interview was inconsistent with his ministry." What Falwell objected to was not the substance of the interview (which was, after all, his), but the mere fact that it appeared in *Penthouse.* Falwell was worried that the interview might give rise to the mistaken implication that Falwell approved of *Penthouse,* or was willing to lend his name to *Penthouse*'s sales. As Falwell himself later explained, "My complaint was not based upon its appearance as far as accuracy, but rather my association in a magazine that might increase and enhance sales of that magazine. I did not want a pornographer to ever make a dollar off Jerry Falwell." But Judge Turk notes that the mere fact that Falwell "may not approve of publications such as *Penthouse* or may not desire *Penthouse* to discuss his activities or publish his spoken words, does not give rise to an action cognizable under the law. The First Amendment freedoms of speech and press are too precious to be eroded or undermined by the likes and dislikes of persons who invite attention and publicity by their own voluntary actions."

Falwell may have felt his hand forced in bringing the suit by his own prior criticisms of President Jimmy Carter for an interview Carter had given to *Playboy.* Why, however, should Falwell object to seeing his words in *Penthouse,* if his words were not distorted? If you want to make conversions and save souls, you've got to go where the sinners are—and what better place than *Penthouse* to find souls in need of saving? Even Falwell seemed eventually to see the point. The *Penthouse* interview, he later observed, may actually have done more good than harm: "In all honesty," Falwell said, "a number of people who read that interview, which was reported accurately, have come to know Christ as their savior through reading that interview, and one of them gave two million dollars to Liberty Baptist College two years ago, because he read that interview and came to be one of my supporters."

The most important lesson Jerry Falwell learned from his suit against *Penthouse*, however, was how to pick a good lawyer. When the time came to find a real courtroom warrior to do battle with Larry Flynt, who better to pick than Norman Roy Grutman, a man who would not be afraid to take off the gloves and punch it out with the down-and-dirty Flynt, toe to toe? There was no sense in filing a lawsuit just to lose it; Falwell needed a winning lawyer on his side, and Grutman was the best man for the job. If this was to be a lawsuit for Jesus, it was high time Jesus won.

For all the logic in his choice of lawyer, however, there was no escaping the irony of it all, an irony compounded even more by the embarrassing fact that among the many victories Grutman had notched for *Penthouse* there is a case that seems to resemble closely Falwell's suit against Flynt. That case, *Pring v. Penthouse,* [2] had arisen, like Falwell's suit against *Hustler,* from a crude sexual parody.

In its August 1979 issue *Penthouse* ran an article it described as "humor," entitled "Miss Wyoming Saves the World." Set at a Miss America contest in Atlantic City, the article depicts the exploits of a fictional beauty queen named "Charlene," who enters in the contest as Miss Wyoming. Charlene is a baton twirler. In the story, Charlene is depicted as about to perform an act in the pageant when her thoughts wander back to an incident from college. She remembers performing fellatio on a Wyoming football player, an act that mystically caused him to levitate. Once on stage, Charlene begins to simulate fellatio on her baton, a performance that stops the orchestra. Charlene does not make it to the finals of the competition, but she nonetheless thinks she has a "real talent." While at the edge of the stage watching the finalists answer questions, Charlene's mind again wanders, this time over how she might answer one of the "poise and intelligence" questions. Charlene fantasizes about how she could "save the world" with her real talent, "performing" with the "entire Soviet Central Committee," "Marshall Tito," and "Fidel Castro." Charlene would be the ambassador of love and peace. Charlene then begins to perform fellatio on her coach at the edge of the stage, as the audience applauds the new Miss America. This fellatio also causes her coach to levitate. The story ends with the television cameras leaving the image of the new Miss America to focus on Charlene and the sight of her coach floating in the air.

Despite the obviously fictional nature of this *Penthouse* sexual fantasy, the article drew not one but two separate lawsuits against the magazine, one by Ms. Kimerli Jayne Pring, who was the real

Miss Wyoming of 1978, and the other by the Miss America Pageant itself. A New Jersey federal judge dismissed the suit brought by the Miss America Pageant, but a federal court in Wyoming permitted Ms. Pring to pursue her suit against the magazine for libel.

Pring was represented by the well-known trial lawyer, Gerry Spence.[3] (Spence had been the lawyer for the family of Karen Ann Silkwood in its suit against Kerr-McGee, among other famous cases.) *Penthouse,* as usual, was represented by Grutman. At the time the *Penthouse* article was published, Pring was a senior at the University of Wyoming. She had been selected "Miss Wyoming" in 1978 and had attended the Miss America Pageant in Atlantic City. She was an accomplished baton twirler, having won the Wyoming baton twirling championship in each of six years and the National Baton Twirling Championship in 1977. She had won the title of Miss Majorette of Wyoming four times and was runner-up in the 1977 Majorette of America contest. She had been a contestant and participant in numerous other pageants and competitions, including the Miss U.S.A. Beauty Pageant, the Wyoming Miss University Contest, and the Miss Black Velvet Contest. She was Miss Wyoming at the thirty-third National Sweet Corn Festival.

Ms. Pring claimed that the sexually promiscuous baton twirling Miss Wyoming known as "Charlene" in the *Penthouse* story would be understood by readers as referring to her and that the "net effect" of the article was to create the impression "throughout the United States, Wyoming and the world," that she committed fellatio on a Wyoming football player and also upon her coach "in the presence of a national television audience at the Miss America pageant." She further alleged that the article also created the impression that she "committed fellatio-like acts upon her baton at the Miss America contest." Grutman argued vociferously that Pring's suit was based on nothing more than her "egocentric distaste for the magazine." Grutman defiantly challenged the trial judge, "What is there that can support a claim against the article, this brummagem trumped-up claim, when it is not about her, and when she knows it is fiction?" Grutman even went so far as to suggest that there was an artistic connection between Kimerli Jayne Pring's voluptuous breasts and Wyoming's Grand Teton mountains. "It was the artist's own creative imagination," explained Grutman, "that led him to conceive the idea of somehow relating the beauty and majesty of the Grand Tetons—which in French means 'big breasts'—with the fictional sexual exploits of the beauty pageant contestant."

When he took Pring's deposition, Grutman made it abundantly clear to her that her lawsuit against *Penthouse* would be no ice cream social or sweet-smiling beauty pageant. It would be rough business; if Pring thought the article in *Penthouse* was distressing, she hadn't seen nothin' yet. During the deposition, for example, Grutman pursued the issue of the story's fictional character, showing no inhibition in his questioning.

"Now, you understand," he asked Pring, "from that language, what is described is that after having received his blowjob and ejaculating, the man in the story is levitating. Isn't that what the story is saying?"

"Yes, sir," replied Pring.

"Now, Miss Pring, in the real world, do you know or have you ever heard of anyone who could ever levitate?"

"No, sir."

"Whether connected with a blowjob or otherwise?"

"Correct."

Grutman did not actually handle the trial—he turned that work over to a Denver attorney, Tom Kelley, one of the best media lawyers in the country. A Wyoming federal court jury returned a verdict against *Penthouse* of $1.5 million in compensatory and $25 million in punitive damages, ranking as one of the largest libel jury verdicts in history.

But Grutman and Kelley managed to get the jury award overturned by a close two-to-one vote in the federal Court of Appeals. *Penthouse* thus came within a single vote of the dubious honor of having been saddled with the largest libel award ever to be affirmed on appeal. Although it handed the magazine a narrow victory, in its general tone the Court of Appeals' decision is sharply critical of *Penthouse,* describing the story as "a gross, unpleasant, crude, distorted attempt to ridicule the Miss America contest and contestants." The article has "no redeeming features whatever." The decision states, however, that "although a story may be repugnant in the extreme to an ordinary reader, and we have encountered no difficulty in placing this story in such a category, the typical standards and doctrines under the First Amendment must nonetheless be applied." And then in one of the more candid and revealing statements that any court has made in such a suit, the court states that "The magazine itself should not have been tried for its moral standards." The First Amendment, the court determined, could not tolerate the jury's staggering verdict because no reasonable reader could have understood the story as anything but fantasy and fiction. Charlene's ability to cause others to levitate through the act of fellatio was obviously fantasy, as was the fact of performing simulated fellatio on her baton during the pageant on national television.

The decision exonerating *Penthouse* drew a sharp dissent from one of the three appeals judges. The article, he argues, contains an admixture of fact and fiction: "I consider levitation, dreams, and public performance as fiction. Fellatio is not." The judge then maintained that the jury quite properly punished *Penthouse* for conveying the impression that Ms. Pring engaged in fellatio, stating that it "has long been recognized as an act of sexual deviation or perversion" and that it falls "within the crime of sodomy, which civilized people throughout the world have long condemned."

This view, however, failed to carry a majority. Norman Roy Grutman had accomplished what he was best at, winning. Looking back at the suit, his opponent Gerry Spence sums it up: "Norman Roy Grutman . . . was cunning, crafty, and tough. He would do whatever was necessary to win. His style was to attack straight on—everybody and everything—relentlessly. He gave no quarter until his opponent was subdued, prostrate, and begging for mercy, and—having none—he gave none."

Grutman did not handle Jerry Falwell's case against Flynt and *Hustler* alone. Lawyers, like nuns, tend to travel in pairs. Grutman was assisted principally by a younger colleague from his firm, Jeffrey H. Daichman. Daichman had graduated from the New York University Law School, where he had been managing editor of *The Law Review*. Grutman relied on Daichman and other lawyers in his firm for assistance throughout the case.

Larry Flynt's lawyer was Alan Isaacman. Isaacman was born in Harrisburg, Pennsylvania, in 1942, went to college at Pennsylvania State, and graduated from the Harvard Law School in 1967. After law school he was a law clerk for federal district judge Harry Pregerson in California. (Pregerson is now a federal court of appeals judge.) He then worked as a deputy federal public defender in California and in private practice in a number of Los Angeles law firms. Isaacman developed a reputation as an excellent trial lawyer in both civil and criminal cases. He became head of the litigation department at the Beverly Hills law firm Cooper, Epstein and Hurewitz. His reputation as a top-notch litigator brought him a number of high-visibility clients, particularly from the entertainment world. He represented Lionel Richie in copyright infringement cases, Jerry Lewis in an antitrust case, and Rock Hudson in a negligence suit. One of his biggest cases was a securities and mail fraud suit brought against David Charnay, Isaacman's client, and Howard Hughes, Chester Davis, and Robert Maheu, in which the defendants were alleged to have manipulated the price of stock in the Air West Corporation to enable Howard Hughes to force the sale of the airline.

No client, however, ever brought Isaacman more attention or legal business than Larry Flynt and *Hustler Magazine.* For years Isaacman criss-crossed the United States defending Flynt and *Hustler* in lawsuit after lawsuit.

Isaacman's right-hand man in his work for *Hustler* was a bright young lawyer in his firm named David Odell Carson. Carson has impressive credentials. He earned a bachelor's degree from Stanford, with Distinction in History in 1973, and stayed at Stanford an extra year to earn a master's degree in history. He was a graduate student in international relations at the Fletcher School of Law and Diplomacy at Tufts University and then went to Harvard Law School, where he graduated cum laude. Before joining Cooper, Epstein and Hurewitz (Isaacman's firm), Carson had worked in the State Department, for the Massachusetts affiliate of the American Civil Liberties Union, and for an environmental group in Massachusetts. He started as an associate at Cooper, Epstein and Hurewitz in 1981 and in 1986 was promoted to partner. Although Isaacman played the lead role for Flynt and *Hustler* in the Falwell case, Carson did a huge amount of the work, including the examination of witnesses and the making of arguments at trial and the preparation of legal briefs and memoranda.

Isaacman has an informal, unpretentious style. He often has an impish twinkle in his eye and a slight grin on his face, as if he is sending you the message "practicing law can be fun, if you relax a little." There is a boyish insouciance about him, a sort of Huck-Finn-goes-to-law-school quality, that is effectively disarming. Isaacman is *Hustler's* ideal lawyer because he doesn't look like you would imagine *Hustler's* lawyer would look—he's too much of a regular guy; you can't conjure up any impressions of sleaze or evil about him. He doesn't even subscribe to *Hustler.*

Chapter 4

G rutman's first task was to file the complaint against *Hustler* and Flynt. The complaint is the formal legal document that initiates the lawsuit and sets forth the plaintiff's allegations against the defendant. Grutman filed his complaint on Jerry Falwell's home turf—in the United States District Court for the Western District of Virginia.[1] The case was tried in Roanoke, before Chief Judge James Clinton Turk. Turk, a native of Roanoke who had graduated from nearby Washington and Lee University Law School, is the same judge who presided over Falwell's suit against *Penthouse,* when Grutman was Falwell's adversary instead of advocate.

Three separate grounds for recovery are alleged in Falwell's complaint. The first claim is that the defendants had appropriated Falwell's name and likeness for purposes of "advertisement or trade" without Falwell's consent. The second count in the complaint is libel. The defendants, it alleges, had made the false and defamatory statements that Falwell "commits illegal, immoral, and reprehensible acts, that he is an alcoholic and that he is insincere and hypocritical in his work as a fundamentalist minister." These statements, the complaint alleges, were intended to expose Falwell to "public hatred, contempt, aversion, and disgrace and to induce an evil and unsavory opinion of him in the minds of the community." The complaint explains further that Falwell's "effectiveness as a fundamentalist minister is based on trust and confidence in his morality, honesty, and sincerity, which trust and confidence is directly threatened by defendants' accusations of criminality, immorality, and insincerity." The final count in the complaint is labeled "intentional infliction of emotional distress." In publishing the Campari ad, it alleges, the "defendants acted willfully, intentionally, recklessly, and maliciously, and their conduct was outrageous, extreme, and intolerable in that it offends generally accepted standards of decency and morality." The publication of the ad allegedly caused Falwell "severe emotional anguish and distress."

The complaint ends with a plea for relief in the amount of $45 million in damages. It is signed "Respectfully submitted, Reverend Jerry Falwell" by his legal counsel. The names of three attorneys appear on the complaint for Falwell; listed first are Norman Roy Grutman and his assistant, Jeffrey H. Daichman. An attorney from Lynchburg, Howard H. Rhodes, Jr., signed the complaint as local counsel assisting Grutman and Daichman. (Like Grutman and Daichman for Falwell, Isaacman and Carson for Flynt had also obtained the assistance of local Virginia counsel, Arthur P. Strickland of Roanoke.) The lawsuit had formally commenced. War had been declared.

Chapter 5

Alan Isaacman and David Carson made the general strategy of the defense clear very early on. Cutting across all of the sophisticated legal arguments that were developed by the defense was one overriding theme: "C'mon, Reverend Falwell, loosen up—can't you take a joke?" The Campari ad is not meant to be taken seriously, the defense claimed, and is so outrageous and ridiculous that no one *could* possibly take it seriously. This is not the stuff of which lawsuits are made!

To make a plausible argument that the ad is a joke, of course, required that the defense be able to explain exactly what the joke is. What is supposed to be so funny? The defense claimed that the humor works on two levels, one a parody of Campari Liqueur advertising, the other a satire of Jerry Falwell. (The province of "parody" is language; a text of some kind is what is parodied. The province of "satire" is morals and manners; someone's behavior or attitudes are satirized. Thus the *Hustler* ad parodied the Campari ad and satirized Falwell.)

Campari is a distinctive, bittersweet Italian liqueur and strictly an acquired taste. To convince consumers to give Campari a fair trial, a Madison Avenue advertising agency hit on a clever campaign in which famous celebrities would talk about their "first time." The celebrity interviews in the ads are ostensibly about their first encounter with Campari, but the racy double entendre is sexual—Campari, like sex, gets better with practice.

The ads ran from 1981 to 1983 in magazines as various as *Life,
Cosmopolitan, People, Playboy, Newsweek, Money, Vogue, Tennis,*
and *The New Yorker.* They feature celebrities such as Geraldine
Chaplin, Elizabeth Ashley, Tony Roberts, and Jill St. John.

In one ad, Elizabeth Ashley describes her "first time" as "on the
red-eye from L.A. to New York." She says she wondered, "Is this
it? Is this what all my friends are raving about?" But, as she explains,
she later gave it a second try, and "The second time was wonderful.
And now I just love it; there are so many interesting ways to enjoy
it." The catch-line for Ashley's ad is "Campari. The First Time Is
Never the Best."

Similar ads were run with other celebrities. Tony Roberts's first
time is at a beach party with "an exotic woman in a red sarong," who
tells him after the experience, "You'll acquire a taste for it, Tony.
Most men do." Jill St. John's first time seems better than most. It
is in a sidewalk café in Rome ("I'm basically an outdoorsy type of
person") with the stuntman of her movie film crew. "It's not the kind
of thing you try once and then forget about," St. John explains. "I've
gone out with some outstanding men, and they knew one or two new
ways to enjoy it. I prefer 'The Exotic.' That's Campari with grapefruit juice." St. John's ad ends with a twist slightly different from
those of Elizabeth Ashley or Tony Roberts: "Campari. You'll Never
Forget Your First Time."

Hustler's November 1983 front inside cover was made up to look
exactly like those sexy Campari ads—with the punch line being that
instead of the likes of Elizabeth Ashley, Tony Roberts, or Jill St.
John, the *Hustler* Campari parody features that great American sex
symbol himself, Reverend Jerry Falwell.

When the advertising agency for Campari saw the *Hustler* ad
parody, it was as shocked as Falwell. It reacted instantly to protest
the parody of its $3 million campaign, stating in a letter to Flynt that
"We note with great shock and dismay your use of Campari's trademark and demand you cease and desist immediately."

The satire communicated by the ad, claimed the defense, involves
the farcical juxtaposition of Falwell, the great American moralist,
with the outrageous actions of having sex with his mother in an
outhouse and getting drunk before preaching on the pulpit. Here the
defense attempted to draw a distinction between what is *said* and
what is *communicated.* The literal statement may be that Falwell is
an incestuous drunk, and that statement may be communicated with
an intensity essentially equivalent to saying, "Falwell, you are a

motherfucker!" But what is actually communicated by the ad is not the factual assertion that "Falwell is a drunk who has sex with his mother," nor the verbal insult "Falwell is a drunken motherfucker," but rather the political and religious commentary: "Falwell is a hypocrite."

But if this is believable, if what Larry Flynt really had in mind was to call Falwell a hypocrite, then why didn't he choose *that* word— "hypocrite"—rather than such nice turns of phrase as "Campari in the crapper with Mom," or "I always get sloshed before I go out to the pulpit," or "You don't think I could lay down all that bullshit *sober,* do you?" Flynt's only possible response was that the packaging of the thought cannot be extricated from the substance of the thought. For Flynt, nothing says it better than "Campari in the crapper with Mom"—the medium here is truly the message. The sanitized phrase "Falwell is a hypocrite" doesn't quite make it, because, if truth be told, "Falwell is a hypocrite" is *not* all that is being said. The subliminal message in Flynt's ad satire is more biting, more along the lines of "Falwell, you are a hypocrite, and I hate your guts and all you stand for."

Chapter 6

Beneath the preliminary maneuvers of the lawyers, a momentous philosophical conflict was already beginning to ferment. Do we in America really want a wide-open, unregulated marketplace for free speech? Or is every great nation required at some point to regulate speech in order to insure that it does not degenerate into formless, valueless chaos? If a nation is to be a true community, must there not be some consensus on basic values? And does not such a consensus require that certain forms of speech, no less than certain forms of behavior, be taboo?

Even those Americans who do not find Jerry Falwell's fundamentalism palatable as a guide either to religious or political truth may have felt that it was important that Falwell win his lawsuit over Flynt. One does not need to be a card-carrying member of the Christian Right to fear the disintegration of all moral standards in American society. For such people, it was not so important that Falwell win as that Flynt lose. Larry Flynt stands as the best available evidence of where a wide-open, standardless, uncensored culture finally leads.

The popularity of Allan Bloom's recent book, *The Closing of the American Mind,* [1] is a barometer of how strongly contemporary Americans fear the destruction of our moral gyroscopes. Bloom argues that indiscriminate freedom is pernicious. The marketplace-of-ideas metaphor in modern freedom-of-speech thinking tends to elevate open-mindedness above all other public values. But in a milieu in which the only enemy is the person not open to everything, Bloom asks, how are shared goals, visions of the public good, and meaningful social contact any longer possible? If we are forced by the First Amendment to sublimate the sublime in the name of tolerance, how will we ever take control of our own destinies? From this perspective it is wrong to celebrate freedom of speech for its own sake, for the same reason that it is wrong to celebrate openmindedness for its own sake: Such libertine reveling leads to a moral relativism in which everything is tolerated, even intolerance. Rather than a cohesive nation with a shared sense of the promise of American life, we become an atomistic confederation of selfish individuals. To tolerate Larry Flynt's malicious speech is seen as a return to a world of all-against-all in which ignoble savages such as Flynt are permitted to peddle their nasty and brutish messages to anyone with three bucks to spend on a copy of *Hustler Magazine.* Is that what the First Amendment is all about?

The defense, of course, argued that tolerance for *Hustler is* what the First Amendment is all about. H. L. Mencken once said, "The whole drift of our law is toward the absolute prohibition of all ideas that diverge in the slightest form from the accepted platitudes, and behind that drift of law there is a far more potent force of growing custom, and under that custom there is a national philosophy which erects conformity into the noblest of virtues and the free functioning of personality into a capital crime against society." Was *Hustler* being pursued merely for nonconformity? Or is some minimal conformity necessary in a cohesive culture?

The philosophical schism represented by *Falwell v. Flynt* is, however, ultimately even deeper than a dispute over the meaning of freedom of speech. Jerry Falwell and Larry Flynt did not just disagree on the meaning of the First Amendment. It is more profound than that. For Falwell and Flynt it is really not the same First Amendment, not even the same Constitution.

Falwell's entire intellectual universe is grounded in the faith that truth exists and is knowable. He is fond of attacking "secular humanism." When one listens carefully to the content of that attack, however, it becomes apparent that it is driven by hatred for a far more powerful enemy: the moral relativism that permeates all aspects of modern American thought. Fundamentalism is the antithesis of relativism. Relativism is a threat to the fundamentalist's whole being; it eats at God's universe. God's will and word are absolutes and, as revealed in holy scripture, are unerring and

binding on all men. "In the beginning was the Word," begins the
Gospel of St. John, "and the Word was God." If man is made in
the image and likeness of God, then the purpose of man's law
must be to strive for the image and likeness of God's law. For
Jerry Falwell, law exists to make men moral; law is an instrument
of truth. For Jerry Falwell, the United States Constitution, America's supreme secular law, must also be America's supreme moral
charter. The Constitution, like Scripture, is a source of truth—
though constitutional truths are more mundane and imperfect
than scriptural truths because the framers did not have the advantage of direct divine revelation. But the *functions* of scriptural
truths and constitutional truths are, for the fundamentalist, essentially the same. They serve as moral anchors in our collective
quest for salvation.

In this fundamentalist scheme of things the First Amendment
guarantees of freedom of speech, freedom of the press, freedom of
association, and freedom of religion are not properly understood as
constitutional declarations that in matters of conscience anything
goes. Certainly for the fundamentalist anything does not go. It is
impossible for the fundamentalist thinker to believe that the framers
could possibly have intended the Constitution to be understood as
a morally nihilistic document. America was founded as a moral
beacon spreading forth its light to save a corrupt world. The Founding Fathers self-consciously set out to concentrate the American
mind on this vision of destiny. The First Amendment cannot be
perverted to mean that the nation must tolerate ideas repugnant to
the Constitution itself and the moral truths it embodies. The First
Amendment, in this view, is sacred because it is essential to collective
self-governance. But only constructive speech is essential to self-
governance. There is no value in destructive speech. Speech that is
patently immoral cannot contribute to moral perfection. *Hustler*'s
parody, in the words of Larry Flynt's own testimony, is about Jerry
Falwell "fucking his mother in the outhouse." To the fundamentalist
mind this is the antithesis of morality; it bears no plausible relation
to constructive self-governance; it should be treated as utterly beyond the protections of the First Amendment, as a constitutional
pariah and outcast.

Larry Flynt's position, on the other hand, is tied to an "absolute"
of a radically different nature—not absolute moral truth, but absolute freedom to reject the view that any absolute truth is possible. For
Flynt the only absolute is absolute freedom of speech, at least when

that speech presents no physical threat to anyone. When the only objection to speech is that it is obscene, indecent, or disgusting, it is untouchable to censors.

It is against this legal and cultural backdrop that the nitty-gritty of the litigation started, as the lawsuit began slouching toward Roanoke.

Chapter 7

A mericans may debate whether the First Amendment is meant
for Larry Flynt, but no one will deny that he desperately needs
it. If Larry Flynt at times seems a bit crotchety toward his lawyers,
he may be excused, for they consume a major part of his business
overhead. Larry Flynt is a defense lawyer's dream: wealthy and
always in trouble. Flynt has been prosecuted for sodomy, obscenity,
and contempt charges and has been sued hundreds of times for what
he prints in *Hustler.*

Larry Flynt was in trouble again for the first crucial battle of the
suit brought by Jerry Falwell, his pretrial deposition. Flynt had been
sentenced to prison in the federal correctional institution in Butner,
North Carolina, for contempt of court. (The conviction for which he
was serving time in Butner was later reversed on appeal.)[1] It was one
of the worst periods in Flynt's life. Flynt's publishing empire was his
identity: To cut at it was to cut at his life. But he was losing multimillion-dollar verdicts for libel and invasion of privacy at a breathtaking
pace. Because he was in prison and because he was too erratic and
affected by drugs and pain from his paralysis to manage his affairs
intelligently, his companies were being taken away from him and
placed in the hands of conservators. Flynt was in a pathetic condition
for his deposition. He was in pain, paralyzed, unkempt, bearded,
ridden with bedsores, and handcuffed to his hospital gurney. Like a
trapped and wounded grizzly bear, he was ready to strike out with
bitter hate and paranoia against everyone—against his brother,

Jimmy Flynt, for trying to take over his empire (Jimmy Flynt was the appointed conservator), against the law for not catching the assailants who shot him and left him paralyzed for life years before, against his own lawyers for plotting against him, and, most of all, against Bob Guccione, publisher of *Penthouse,* Jerry Falwell, head of the Moral Majority, and Norman Roy Grutman, whom Flynt perceived as the lawyer who did the hatchet work for both.

The deposition was videotaped, and, when later shown to the federal jury in Roanoke, emerged as the single most important piece of evidence in the trial. In the room were two lawyers for Flynt—David Kahn, his corporate counsel, and Alan Isaacman, his trial attorney, several prison officials, and Flynt's nemesis, Grutman. The doors opened, and Flynt was rolled in on the gurney.

Flynt entered the room with his verbal motor already running, greeting his antagonist by saying, "Well, Mr. Grutman, I thought you'd never shut up."[2]

Grutman knew instantly that he wanted everything recorded for the record. He ignored Flynt's greeting and said, "Videotape on, please. Are the voice levels satisfactory?" Grutman then instructed the court reporter to administer the oath to Larry Flynt.

"Can you raise your right hand?" the court reporter asked.

"No, they're cuffed," Flynt replied.

"Do you solemnly swear that the testimony you are about to give is the truth, the whole truth, and nothing but the truth, so help you God?"

"No, not 'til you take the cuffs off."

This exchange set the stage for what was to come. Larry Flynt was simply not about to cooperate until certain things were resolved his way. His lawyer, Isaacman, insisted that Flynt's handcuffs be removed during the deposition so that the setting would be as normal and as neutral as possible. Grutman was willing to cooperate by having the videotape camera shoot Flynt only from the shoulder up so that the handcuffs would not be visible. Isaacman agreed to this arrangement.

Isaacman then insisted that, if Flynt needed a break for medical attention at any time, he be permitted to take it. Flynt interposed, claiming that in fact he needed a break every twenty minutes to do a brief series of exercises known as "depressions" to help blood circulation in his legs. Grutman was again accommodating. "If he needs his twenty-minute rest periods," he said, "we'll give them to him."

Flynt was still not quite satisfied. He claimed that he had a severe bedsore that had not been dressed that morning and that he really needed to be lying on his side. He did not want to start until his bedsore was attended to. Furthermore, he wasn't satisfied with the deal that his handcuffs would remain on but be off-camera. Grutman grew impatient. He decided to plunge ahead. Flynt could have his medical complaints attended to during the first break, in twenty minutes.

"Mr. Flynt, the oath has been administered to you," said Grutman.

"You don't have to call me 'Mister.' I came up through the ranks, Mr. Grutman."

"Mr. Flynt, the oath has been administered to you; you heard the oath. Do you swear to tell the truth and nothing but the truth, so help you God?"

"No."

"You do not? All right. Will you tell me, sir, please, whether you will affirm to tell the truth, the whole truth, and nothing but the truth?"

"No. I will never affirm to tell the truth as long as these handcuffs are on, Mr. Grutman. Now, if you will call Judge Larkins, the senior judge in this district down here, and I've got his home phone number in my room, Judge Larkins will issue an order to take these cuffs off."

"Mr. Flynt, do you know that you are scheduled pursuant to the order of Judge Turk to give evidence in this case today?"

"Yes, I'm fully aware of that."

"And you've given evidence in depositions before, have you not?"

"I certainly have."

"I take it that you have no religious objection to taking any oath, is that correct?"

"I'll swear on anything, Mr. Grutman, to get these cuffs off. I'll declare you God, but I ain't talking to you with them on. Now, you can stand there and talk 'til the cows come home, but I ain't answering no questions with these cuffs on."

Grutman became exasperated. He accused Flynt of trying to avoid giving testimony. Flynt denied it. Grutman asked Flynt if he realized he was bound by the rules of the federal court to cooperate. Flynt said he understood that. Grutman tried to start again.

"Mr. Flynt, what is your full name?"

"Christopher Columbus Cornwallis I. P. Q. Harvey H. Apache Pugh. They call me Larry Flynt. And all those historical figures."

"Are you known as Larry Flynt?"

"No. Jesus H. Flynt, Esquire."

"Have you ever called yourself Larry Flynt?"

"Used to, but it was spelled with an 'I' then. 'F-L-I-N-T.' Now it's 'F-L-Y-N-T.' I have two birth certificates."

"Were you born in Kentucky?"

"No."

"Have you ever served in the United States Navy?"

"Hmm—I'm not sure."

"Have you ever lived in Dayton, Ohio?"

"No, I was hatched in Dayton, Ohio."

"While you were in Dayton, Ohio, did you ever work in the nightclub business?"

"Huh?"

"Did you ever work in the nightclub business in or around Dayton, Ohio?"

Flynt did not answer; he just picked his nose. Grutman decided to meet grossness with grossness: "Let the stenograph record reflect that Mr. Flynt has just picked his left nostril and placed on the floor some of the mucus that had coagulated there," he said.

Isaacman objected to Grutman's remark. "You have a videotape of what's going on, so it's not necessary for you to—"

"I understand that," Grutman interrupted, "but we have a stenographic record."

"—so it's not necessary for you to state everything that is in view of the steno—of the videotape operator," Isaacman finished his objection.

Grutman continued on. "Did you ever publish a magazine called *Bachelor's* or *Bachelor's Beat?*"

Flynt refused to answer.

"Do you understand the question, sir?"

Flynt shook his head "no."

"You do not? Do you wish to pretend that you don't understand the question?"

Flynt nodded "yes."

"Do you know where you are?"

Flynt shook his head "no."

"Do you know what day today is, Mr. Flynt?"

Again, Flynt shook his head "no."

"Do you know who the man is to whom you pointed earlier and who you said knocked out your tooth last night?"

Another headshake.

"Are you determined, Mr. Flynt, to make a mockery of this deposition?"

Flynt nodded "yes."

"Do you wish to pretend that you don't understand my questions?"

Flynt first nodded "yes," then shook his head "no." About this time, Flynt's lawyers had to be wishing they had *Star Trek* technology and could scream "Beam me up, Scotty! Get us outa here!" Flynt was turning a deposition about a parody of an advertisement into a parody of a deposition. The parody of a parody had a certain perversely amusing quality of its own, but it could be deadly to Flynt's legal interests. The morning wore on, Flynt obstinate, and Grutman becoming convinced that Flynt and his lawyers were determined to make the whole proceeding, as Woody Allen might put it, a mockery of a sham of a charade of a travesty of a mockery of a travesty of a sham.

Alan Isaacman tried to calm his client down by getting Grutman to let Flynt have whatever immediate medical attention he needed. But it was Flynt's show, and he was not about to be of much help to anyone, including his own lawyers.

Isaacman said to Grutman that Grutman was unfairly attacking his motives—that all Isaacman wanted was medical attention and a fair deposition for Flynt.

"Shut up a minute, Alan," Flynt interrupted.

But Isaacman continued, "And if he requests medical attention, like any witness he ought to be allowed to have it, and I say he should have it."

At that point Grutman asked Flynt, "Do you know who that man is talking?"

"He's an idiot."

"Do you know who he is?"

"He's an idiot."

"Do you know his name?"

"I've tried to fire him ever since he's been here."

"Do you know his name? You called him 'Alan' a moment ago."

"Yes, Alan Graham. He's the guy with the sex tape. I got a bedsore needs to be changed, and I need some medication, you know. Now, if you want to get the medication for me, change my bedsore, and put me in the soft cuffs here so I can do a depression, I'll proceed.

But if you're going to treat me like a fool, I'm going to act like one."

"No, Mr. Flynt, we're going—"

"Mr. Grutman, you and I don't have a problem. Our problem is sitting right over there, two of them." Flynt interrupted, pointing to his lawyers. "And you know the difference between them? One's a wet snatch, and one's a dry one."

"Whom are you referring to?"

"Mr. Kahn and Mr. Isaacman."

"I thought you told me you didn't know his name."

"I don't know him."

"You called him 'Alan Graham.' "

"I don't know him. They're all the same."

"You know who I am, don't you?"

"Yep. You're an asshole."

"So you've said in your magazine. Not once, but several times, right?"

"Yeah."

Isaacman couldn't let this continue. His client was off the deep end, and Grutman was exploiting the chaos for all it was worth. And no one was really getting anywhere. Isaacman objected to the colloquy. He tried to get the video camera to show Flynt's bedsore for the record, and he tried to get Grutman to let Flynt have his medical attention. Isaacman, Grutman, and Flynt went round and round. At one point a medical attendant named Bob Kaiser came into the room, and, over Isaacman's strenuous protests, Grutman tried to take Kaiser's sworn deposition to determine whether or not Flynt was lying about his need for medical help. Flynt protested, saying to Grutman, "I thought you came to take my deposition, you asshole, you."

But Grutman would not be stopped from deposing Kaiser. Kaiser stated that Flynt did have a bedsore, which had not been dressed that morning, but that the neglect of the sore was Flynt's own fault—Flynt had refused medical attention and breakfast that morning.

Grutman seemed satisfied; he asked Kaiser to remain in the room in case Flynt genuinely did need medical help. Kaiser agreed. Before Grutman could turn back to Flynt to continue his attempt at questioning, however, Flynt decided to play lawyer himself. Flynt, who was supposed to be the witness, began to cross-examine Kaiser, who had nothing to do with the case at all. Flynt turned out to be a lot better at lawyering than witnessing.

"Now, wait a minute," Flynt said, "I have something. Mr. Kaiser, when you dress my bedsore, what you always do is you measure it, and you put it in the log to see if it's getting worse or better?"

"I don't always do that," said Kaiser.

"But if you don't, you instruct some of your people to do it?"

"I can't do—"

Flynt interrupted, "You instruct your people to do it on the day shift because that's when they provide most of the care. Now, you've already taken the oath, Mr. Kaiser. Did you measure the bedsore today?"

"No, sir."

"Why not?"

"Because you refused treatment for it."

"What kind of treatment did I refuse, Mr. Kaiser?"

"You made the statement that you didn't want anything done except a bath, and that's exactly what you got."

"Did I tell you why I made that statement?"

"I don't recall that you did."

"Would you think about it?"

"I don't recall if you told me why."

"You have no recollection whatsoever?"

"No, I don't."

"Do you know if I had breakfast this morning or not, Mr. Kaiser?"

"No, you didn't. You refused breakfast."

"Do you know why I refused breakfast?"

"No, I don't know why you refused breakfast."

"Have I had an enema today, Mr. Kaiser?"

"No, sir, you haven't. You also refused that."

"Why did I refuse the enema?"

"You said you weren't eating, so you didn't need an enema."

"Why did I say I wasn't eating?"

"You didn't say."

Control of the whole proceeding was ebbing away from the lawyers and being transferred to Flynt. Grutman tried to cut off Flynt's questioning. "All right, Mr. Flynt," Grutman began.

"You're the one who put him under oath," Flynt interrupted Grutman, "Now shut up."

"Now—"

"Objection?" said Flynt.

"Look, Mr. Flynt—"

"Mr. Kaiser will you dress my bedsore while I'm here, and put the soft cuffs on, so we can proceed?"

At this point, all hell broke loose in the deposition, and for several minutes there was a complete breakdown of the judicial process. Grutman tried to order Kaiser not to answer any more questions. Isaacman protested, claiming that it was now *his* turn to question Kaiser. Grutman rebutted him, saying "No, you will not divert the deposition."

"No, no, no, no, no. You—" started Isaacman.

"Leave if you like. I'm going on with my deposition," Grutman cut him off.

"We're all going to leave," said Isaacman. "You interrupted it to take examination from him, and I insist on the right to examine this witness."

"Mr. Isaacman, this is utterly irresponsible."

"No, you're irresponsible."

"You and your client—"

"No, you're irresponsible by doing it, Mr. Grutman."

"You and your client have obviously determined to turn this into a circus or some kind of a freak show."

"You're turning it into a circus. You are, and I'm going—I do not tolerate this."

At this point, Flynt chimed in again, stating that he refused to answer any questions until he got his medical care. "Now, I may be crazy," Flynt said, "but I ain't stupid, Mr. Grutman."

"I think you're neither."

Grutman tried to continue the deposition, but Flynt steadfastly refused to answer questions. "Listen, Mr. Flynt—" Grutman started.

"No, you listen to me, asshole. This ain't your domain. This belongs to him," said Flynt, referring to the medical attendant. "Now, shut up."

"Please, Mr. Flynt—"

"And if my language offends you, then, you leave. Now, goddamnit, I'm talking."

"Mr. Flynt—"

"Shut the fuck up. I'm sorry, ma'am."

"Mr. Flynt—"

"Now, Bob, will you dress my bedsore?"

It was all over. A technical knockout. Referee stops fight. Grutman threw in the towel. He was getting nowhere. Flynt was not going to change his mind, so Grutman changed his tactic. He would let Flynt have his medical attention, allow the circus atmosphere to subside, and try again.

The deposition came to a temporary halt as Larry Flynt's medical needs were attended to.

Chapter 8

If it was the strategy of Norman Roy Grutman to cast Larry Flynt as the Antichrist in the morality play *Falwell v. Flynt,* Grutman could not have found in Flynt a more willing actor. Flynt seemed to be playing Falwell's foil not just willingly, but with enthusiasm. Perhaps it was because hatred of all Jerry Falwell stood for had long since been the consuming obsession of Flynt's life.

Like some frenzied Thomas Sutpen, the central character in William Faulkner's *Absalom, Absalom!,* Flynt left the Kentucky mountain sharecropper's existence in which he was raised to take America by storm on his own terms. He lied about his age and joined the army at fourteen. By the age of twenty-one, Flynt had already declared bankruptcy once and been married twice. He worked at a General Motors plant for a while, and then finally began to ease into his true vocation, opening up a string of "Hustler" strip-joint bars in Ohio. *Hustler* magazine had its genesis as the internal newsletter for the bars. When Flynt took the magazine to major league status, its circulation skyrocketed in just four years to over two million, with annual profits of over $13 million. Among his extravagancies in celebrating his success, Flynt had a statue made memorializing his loss of virginity—as an eight-year-old boy to a chicken on his grandmother's farm.

Hustler carved its own unique niche in the porno market by combining the slick-paper appearance of *Playboy* and *Penthouse* with no-holds-barred raunchiness. *Hustler* is Flynt personified—

flamboyant, tell-it-like-it-is smut with no pretense to serious redeeming social value. The whole ethos of *Playboy* and *Penthouse*, in which sex masquerades as art, literature, and a sophisticated lifestyle, is hypocritical and repugnant to Flynt. Flynt delivers the "real thing"—sex and hate and perversion unvarnished by any claims of taste or respectability. If as a culture we are what we eat, the success of Flynt in catering to the appetites of his constituency is a guide to our times. *Hustler*'s political lampoons come in such forms as crass cartoons about Chief Justice Warren Burger's sex life, Betty Ford's breast cancer, and its regular feature column, "The Asshole of the Month." Its advertising campaigns make such boasts as "Hustler, the magazine nobody quotes." No theme is too sickening for *Hustler*; its principal editorial criteria are to avoid respectability at all costs and never to lose touch with the instinct for the nauseous. *Hustler* regularly features scenes about excrement, mutilation, bestiality, rodents, dismemberment, and bondage.

Hustler is not just a parody of *Playboy* and *Penthouse,* it is a parody of itself. In *Playboy* and *Penthouse* the breasts are usually large; in *Hustler* the breasts are often enormous, to the point of being grotesque. Flynt once claimed, "There's more reality in *Hustler* than in anything you read." In 1983 *Hustler*'s circulation was about two and a half million per month in the United States. The "pass-along readership" and the sales in secondary and foreign markets may, according to the trial record, have pushed the total monthly readership as high as twenty million.

Flynt ventured for a while into straight journalism, acquiring weekly papers such as *The Atlanta Gazette, The Plains (Georgia) Monitor,* and *Ohio Magazine.* Flynt also runs less hard-core pornographic publications, such as *Oui* and *Gentleman's Companion.* The Flynt Distributing Company is a lucrative, diversified magazine distributing operation, with hundreds of titles, ranging from knitting to soft-core porn to motorcycling. It has even distributed *The New York Review of Books.*

Throughout his rise to success, Flynt was accompanied and helped by his wife, Althea. Althea Flynt was born in Marietta, Ohio. When she was only eight, her father shot and killed her mother, her grandfather, and her mother's best friend and then turned the gun and shot himself. At the age of seventeen, Althea was hired by Flynt as a go-go dancer in his Columbus, Ohio, nightclub. Five years later, she married Flynt. The Flynts made no secret of their sexual appetites. Althea was bisexual, and she enjoyed selecting lovers for her husband. He once boasted that he made love to fifteen women a week—most of them chosen by Althea.

In the spring of 1987, Althea Flynt died at the age of thirty-three. She had become addicted to Dilaudid, a morphinelike painkiller, when Larry Flynt began taking the drug after an assassination attempt left him paralyzed and impotent. Althea was found dead in a bathtub at the Flynt mansion, apparently having taken an overdose of drugs. It had previously been rumored that she had AIDS. The death was ruled accidental. Larry Flynt was reportedly distraught and grief-stricken over her death, but appeared to handle the situation reasonably well.

In the fall of 1977 Larry Flynt went through a religious conversion experience. Evangelist Ruth Carter Stapleton, sister of Jimmy Carter, convinced Flynt to renounce his evil ways and accept Christ as savior. Flynt, not unlike Jerry Falwell, had perfect recall of the moment when he first saw the light. The moment came while cruising at forty thousand feet in a chartered jet somewhere between Denver and Houston. "It was powerful and awesome," said Flynt, in the great American tradition of Jonathan Edwards. "There I was, representing the pits of what is wrong in our society, and it happened. I'm not ashamed that I cried for God." Flynt had spent time with Stapleton's family in their Fayetteville, North Carolina, home, and the Stapletons had, in turn, visited Flynt at his mansion in Columbus, Ohio. They had talked about religion and sexual repression, and apparently religion had won. Althea Flynt, however, seemed to grasp the big picture more acutely. "The Lord may have entered your life," she warned, "but $20 million just walked out of it."

During his ill-fated "religious period," Flynt turned *Hustler* into a screwball mixture of sex and religion, a schizophrenic, porn-again, sex-for-Jesus grab bag of dildos and crucifixes. "I'll be a hustler for the Lord," proclaimed Flynt. Perhaps Flynt saw religion and pornography as variations on the same hustle. "I read somewhere that 98 percent of the people believe in God," he said. "There aren't that many people who believe in pornography." In any event, the juxtaposition of sex and salvation did not sell. Whether Flynt was counting on all those fallen ministers with lust in their hearts or all those prostitutes and pimps secretly longing for saving grace, the combination of ingredients just didn't make it. Americans prefer their obsessions pure. Flynt eventually renounced his conversion.

In an interview for *Vanity Fair* given to Bob Colacello, Flynt elaborated on his theology:

If you don't quote me on anything else in your article, quote me on this: *Matthew* sixteen, verse eighteen, okay? "I say also unto thee that thou art Peter, and upon this rock I will build my church." Peter was his cock, the rock meant he had a hard-on and church was his philosophy—life is supposed to be one big orgasm! And there's only one commandment: Do unto others as you would have them do unto you —but do it *first*. [1]

Slamming a Bible shut, Flynt continued:

This is the biggest piece of shit ever written. It's been fucked with since the beginning of time. Religion's done more harm than any other single idea; every war since the beginning of time was the fault of religion. I mean, ask the Jews what they think about religion. And try to find a Jew that's not gonna vote for me.

Here's the January issue. You see, I had Jesus made publisher, an' then I had Him endorse me for president. He says that in two thousand years neither He, the Holy Ghost, or the Father has ever endorsed a political candidate. Now is the time to do it. An' we dispel rumors that He was gay. He said, "Look, jus' cause I hung around with twelve men doesn't mean I was gay, 'cause I was fuckin' Mary Magdalene at the time. . . ."[2]

In 1978 the event that most profoundly changed Flynt's life took place in a tiny town in Georgia. Flynt was on trial in Lawrenceville, Georgia, for publishing obscenity. Copies of *Hustler* had turned up for sale at Stan's Superette in Gwinnett County, Georgia, and the prosecutor had decided to bring charges. There was no particular hysteria in Gwinnett County over *Hustler*; the obscenity charge was actually a mere misdemeanor. The town of Lawrenceville was so peaceful during the trial, in fact, that Flynt gave his bodyguard the day off. "*Hustler* is satire," Flynt testified in the morning. "It is one big put-on." Flynt's testimony was actually going well for a change. Perhaps *Hustler* was just a big joke; perhaps the jury would really believe that.

Flynt wandered out for lunch with one of his lawyers, Gene Reeves, Jr., to the V and J Cafeteria, where he had two glasses of grapefruit juice (he was on a new health-food diet). On the way back to the courthouse after lunch, two bursts of gunfire suddenly rang out. Flynt was hit in the abdomen. He fell to the concrete face first, screaming for help. His attorney Reeves was also hit in the stomach and arm. Flynt was rushed by paramedics to the Gwinnett Hospital in critical condition. Surgeons removed much of his intestine in emergency surgery and his spleen in a second operation. Flynt was then transferred to the Emory Hospital in Atlanta, where surgeons removed a bullet lodged near his spine. But severe damage had been done: The bullet had cut spinal nerves. Flynt was paralyzed permanently from the waist down and from then on had to endure years of pain and endless rounds of surgery. When she learned of the shooting, Ruth Carter Stapleton rushed to his bedside in Atlanta. "I believe in miracles," she said. "I just thank God he's alive." The assassin got away, and no one has ever been charged with responsibility for the shooting. There were early reports of two men speeding away in a getaway car, but the only physical clue that turned up was a spent .44 magnum cartridge.

Rumors began circulating immediately about who was behind the shooting. Top nominees included the Ku Klux Klan, outraged at Flynt's outrageousness, or the Mafia, protecting its turf as one of America's principal purveyors of sex for profit, or mysterious agents working for the murky cabal of conspirators, who were really behind the assassination of John F. Kennedy and who feared that Flynt's pet project of investigating that assassination was getting perilously close to the truth. (Flynt was fascinated by the Kennedy assassination. He took out full-page ads in major newspapers offering $1 million for information leading to the arrest of Kennedy's assassins. He even hired assassination aficionado Mark Lane to work as an editor at *Hustler.* Lane flew to Flynt's bedside from Los Angeles as soon as he learned of the shooting.) Flynt himself stated that "I feel the attempt on my life was a direct means to stop the questions I was asking in my publications about the JFK assassination. I have my own theories on who shot me and why the FBI hasn't done more."

The shooting left Flynt in chronic severe pain, which he fought for years with enormous quantities of drugs. The pain was finally alleviated by a surgical procedure that severed nerves to his legs; but the operation left him without bowel or urinary control.

In the years after the assassination attempt Flynt tended to be reclusive. He continued to receive frequent death threats and remained ensconced in his Bel Air mansion, never emerging without bodyguards. Day-to-day management of *Hustler* was left largely to his wife, Althea. Flynt's reclusiveness, however, did not prevent him from constantly grabbing the limelight as America's Barnum and Bailey of smut.

One of his most infamous episodes involved the trial of auto magnate John Z. DeLorean, who was accused of conspiring to import $24 million worth of cocaine. Flynt acquired videotapes made by the FBI during its undercover investigation and released copies to 60 Minutes executive producer, Don Hewitt, and to a reporter for KNXT-TV, the CBS station in Los Angeles. The tape made for stunning television. In it DeLorean is shown meeting with reputed cocaine traffickers. He seems thrilled as a suitcase containing some fifty-five pounds of cocaine is opened before him. "It's better than gold," DeLorean says, fingering one of the snow-white packets of powder. He later raises a champagne toast: "This is to a lot of success for everyone."

Flynt also played for the press an audio recording that he purported to be the voice of John DeLorean saying he wanted no part of a drug deal. Ordered to appear in court with the audio tape, Flynt announced publicly that he would resist a subpoena with bodyguards and guns. Flynt did concede that "if they send a whole army, I guess I've got no choice." Predictably, the federal government reacted in force, sending federal marshals to Flynt's mansion to arrest him for contempt of court—one of Flynt's pet crimes. Flynt relished the attention. "Larry Flynt had one opportunity to be a martyr," he said, in reference to the 1978 assassination attempt. "If anybody is going to put a bullet in me, I want the whole world to be watching." Flynt tweaked the law and the press by adding, "If any of you want to know if this is a publicity gimmick or not, yes, this is a publicity gimmick, and thank God that all of you fell for it."

Flynt ran for the Republican nomination for president of the United States in 1984. His running mate was Russell Means, the Native American activist, who in 1964 participated in an attempt to reclaim Alcatraz Island in San Francisco Bay for Native Americans, and in 1973 was made famous for leading an armed takeover of the village of Wounded Knee, South Dakota, where the United States cavalry massacred more than 350 Native Americans in 1890. Only in America can a country boy from Kentucky with a grade school education run for president with the campaign slogan "A Smut Peddler Who Cares." Flynt's platform was simple—the exposure of hypocrisy and elimination of those repressive forces that stifle American civil liberties, particularly sexual freedom. His campaign announcement states:

I hereby announce my candidacy for the Presidency of these United States of America. On February 28, I will enter the New Hampshire primary as a Republican. I am running as a Republican rather than as a Democrat, because I am wealthy, white, pornographic, and, like the nuclear-mad cowboy, Ronnie Reagan, I have been shot for what I believe in. . . . If elected, my primary goal will be to eliminate ignorance and venereal disease.[3]

Another of Flynt's political stunts came in 1983, when he mailed five copies of *Hustler* to every member of the United States Congress. In an accompanying letter Flynt explained that he wanted the members to be "well informed on social issues." More than 260 members of Congress complained to the Postal Service—enough to make it jump. The Postal Service attempted to stop Flynt's mailings, invoking a federal law that allows individuals to stop mailings they find "erotically arousing or sexually provocative." (Does this mean that the members of Congress were erotically aroused by *Hustler*? Or were they just "sexually provoked"?) Flynt kept on mailing *Hustler* to the squeamish members of the Senate and the House, and the Postal Service finally sued Flynt to stop him. The Postal Service lost. A legislative house, Federal Judge John H. Pratt ruled, is not a home. Under the Constitution, which guarantees every citizen the right to "petition government for redress of grievances," members of Congress must tolerate diverse views and vigorous debate, even from the likes of *Hustler*. "As elected representatives of the people," according to Judge Pratt, "they cannot simply shield themselves from undesirable mail in the same manner as an ordinary addressee."

Not all of Flynt's political activity is farcical, however. When the Defense Department refused to allow American journalists to accompany the United States forces during the invasion of Grenada, imposing a two-day blockade on all news concerning the invasion other than the truth according to Ronald Reagan and Caspar Weinberger, virtually all elements of the mainstream American press rebelled. It was Larry Flynt, however, who actually took journalistic sword in hand and filed suit against the government, claiming that the First Amendment guarantees the media a right of access to combat areas, at least when the presence of journalists poses no imminent security risks. Flynt lost the case on the grounds that the case was "moot"—by the time it reached the court the restrictions had been lifted. But Flynt had demonstrated his willingness to fight the good First Amendment fight on an issue really more dear to CBS or *The New York Times* than to *Hustler*: the principle that in a democratic society government should not be permitted to censor the free flow of information regarding the gravest decisions any nation can ever face—decisions over war and peace. When the United States invades another nation, Americans should have the right to honest, independent news accounts of the invasion, so that they may judge for themselves whether such an extraordinary national act was justified.

Flynt once compared himself to America's first great secular prophet, Thomas Paine. "I share the same philosophy as Thomas Paine," he said. "I don't wanna kill fascists, I wanna kill fascism. When Paine went to France to help 'em form their government, when he became part of the French convention, he voted against beheadin' the king. He says, 'I don't wanna destroy the monarch, I wanna destroy the monarchy.' I'm sayin' the same thing today. There's nothin' that hasn't been said before; it's jus' been said different, that's all. . . . This country has got to develop so people stop feelin' guilty over the concept of obscenity and sin, 'cause it defies definition."

"The fight to protect the First Amendment has become an obsession with me," Flynt once said. "I plan to continue this battle until pornography is not a political buzzword." This was the Larry Flynt that Norman Roy Grutman was struggling to question in a federal prison in North Carolina.

Chapter 9

Larry Flynt had finally gotten his medical care. Grutman hoped that by letting Flynt get his attention, he would finally become more cooperative. The strategy worked. Flynt came back into the room and began to answer Grutman's questions freely.

Flynt proceeded to give one of the most vulgar, phantasmagorical, and self-destructive depositions in legal history. His answers were a stream-of-consciousness fantasia of disgust for Jerry Falwell, hatred for Norman Roy Grutman, and utter contempt for the normal rules of rational discourse, the judicial system, and anything resembling mainstream American values. Larry Flynt pressed to its outermost limits the First Amendment to the United States Constitution.

Grutman started in with a conciliatory gesture. "If I ask the captain to remove your handcuffs," he asked, "will you give me a real deposition?"

"Yes," answered Flynt.

"Captain, would you please remove his handcuffs?"

The prison official, Captain Sivley, removed Flynt's handcuffs.

"Are they going to stay off if I behave?" asked Flynt.

"Unh-hunh," said Captain Sivley.

"You know what he told me? He said they'd stay off as long as I behaved."

"Well, that's encouraging," said Grutman.

"Okay, and if you misbehave, you know what's going to happen?" Flynt asked Grutman.

"They'll put them on me, of course, right?" said Grutman, now willing to play along with Flynt's game.

"Exactly," said Flynt. Although he was willing to cooperate now, Flynt was not quite ready to abandon all impishness. He began to send and receive "radio signals."

"Mr. Flynt—" began Grutman.

Flynt interrupted, "Bravo November, bravo whiskey."

"Mr. Flynt—"

"Eleven Bravo."

"Mr. Flynt—"

"They know what that means, Bob. Can you give me an ETA on it?" Flynt spoke into his imaginary radio.

"Mr. Flynt, may I have your attention?" insisted Grutman. "Now, you told me that if I had the cuffs removed, you'd give me a real deposition."

"All right, go ahead."

The deposition finally began in earnest. Flynt was sworn in again, and this time he played it straight, swearing to tell the whole truth. Grutman took Flynt through many of the basic facts of Flynt's life, winding its way through such highlights as his opening of a house of ill repute in Kentucky. After shutting down a nightclub in Ohio, Flynt explained, "I opened up a whorehouse in Newport, Kentucky."

"And did you use the proceeds from the bordello to help finance your going into the *Hustler* magazine business?" asked Grutman.

"Hmm—no, I didn't."

"How long did you run the bordello in Kentucky?"

"I didn't run it; I just financed it."

"Did you know at the time that you did it that that was an illicit or illegal business?"

Isaacman interrupted: "I'm going to object to that. That's an irrelevant question, and I instruct the witness not to answer that."

But Flynt answered anyway. "It wasn't illegal for me, because the only thing I did was just loan a friend some money and told him to have a good time. I didn't—"

"Did you know that the friend was using that money to finance a whorehouse?" interposed Grutman.

"Unh-hunh. Of course I knew it."

Grutman explored the complex interlocking corporate relationships among Larry Flynt's various publishing, distributing, and holding companies, painting a portrait of Flynt as the kingpin of an expansive sexual empire. No matter how many layers of corporate insulation may have surrounded Flynt, however, he clearly ran the show at *Hustler* and made no attempt to hide that fact.

"Were you the person who made policy in those years for *Hustler* magazine?" Grutman asked.

"Better believe it," answered Flynt.

"And everything that was published in *Hustler* magazine in those years was material that at least had to be submitted to you for final approval, isn't that true?"

"Everything that has ever went in *Hustler* should have had my approval, and anything that went in that did not have my approval—the son of a bitch is either dead, got the shit kicked out of him, or he's out of a job."

In Flynt's mind the only people connected with *Hustler* who ever gave him any flak were his own lawyers, including David Kahn, who was in the room with Flynt at the deposition. Flynt explained to Grutman how Kahn had frustrated Flynt's efforts to write a damaging article about none other than Grutman himself.

"I wanted to say certain things in an article that I wrote about you," Flynt told Grutman, "and that son of a bitch took it out of there because it was libelous. There wasn't a word of it libelous, and he knew—he knew. He just took it out of there because he knew you would sue at the drop of a hat, that's all. The only problems that I've ever got have been caused by a lawyer. Now, remember that."

Grutman was interested in Flynt's reference to libel. He tried to get Flynt to admit that he knew a great deal about libel from books, from prior lawsuits, and from his lawyers. Isaacman tried to stop any inquiry into Flynt's conversations with his lawyers, claiming attorney/client privilege. Flynt quickly put his own macabre spin on the business.

"The discussion that I'm talking about didn't take place with any lawyer," Flynt claimed. "It took place with John Fitzgerald Kennedy, former President of the United States."

Grutman ignored the reference to Kennedy and began to zero in on the actual production process leading to the publication of the ad parody. His first step was to try to pin Flynt down on exactly where Flynt got his idea about Falwell having sex with his mother.

"Have you ever met Reverend Falwell?"

"Ah, no, I have not."

"Have you ever met any of the members of his family?"

"No, I have not."

"Is anybody within your immediate circle of friends a person who is personally acquainted with Reverend Falwell or his family?"

"Yes."

"Who's that?"

"My ex-wife."

"Mrs. Barr?"

"No."

"What's her name?"

"Peggy Jean Abney."

"Where does she live?"

"Jacksonville, Florida."

"And what is the nature of the relationship that you say she has with Reverend Falwell or the members of his family?" asked Grutman.

"She subscribes to his philosophy, and she's profoundly religious," said Flynt.

"And she believes that Reverend Falwell is a good person, correct?"

"Hmm, she believes more than that. She believes he's the real one."

"I take it that that means that she has an affirmative, strong, and supporting admiration for Reverend Falwell, is that correct?"

"She likes Oral Roberts better, because Oral Roberts' Christ was nine hundred feet tall. I'm not sure how tall Jerry's is. But, she's— she accepts the Judeo-Christian ethic, Mr. Grutman, to be more serious about answering your question."

"In any event, Mr. Flynt, do you have any information that Reverend Falwell ever committed incest with his mother?"

"Yes."

"You do have that information?"

Flynt nodded "yes."

"Who provided that information to you?"

"Captain Joe Sivley, Bureau of Prisons."

"Pardon?"

"Captain Joe Sivley, Bureau of Prisons."

"He told you that Reverend Falwell had incest with his mother?"

"Ah, no. Lieutenant White did, Lieutenant White works in Springfield. Okay? And Lieutenant White also works for the Bureau of Prisons."

Grutman decided to question Flynt on his actual involvement in publishing the ad. Referring to a typewritten script of the ad copy, he asked Flynt about the various approval initials contained on the script. One set of initials was "B. H.," referring to one of *Hustler*'s editorial people, Bruce Helford. Who was Bruce Helford, Grutman wanted to know?

"He's Jesus H. Christ, Esquire," Flynt explained.

"You mean the person carried on the masthead as 'Jesus H. Christ, Esquire,' is really a man named Bruce Helford?"

"Yes."

"Fine. Did you think that was an amusing idea?"

"Yeah, I thought it was."

Other initials on the script indicated approval of the legal department and the copy department at *Hustler*. Grutman then turned to the initials "L.F."

"What did the 'Okay, L.F.' mean?" asked Grutman.

"It means they could take it to the bank," said Flynt. "It means that it was going to run in all my magazines, every month, every week, any time I wanted it to run."

"You mean you wanted this to have wide circulation?"

"Yes, sir."

"Was there—did you read this over before you wrote 'Okay, L.F.'?"

"Yes, sir."

"Did you have any knowledge specifically yourself that Reverend Falwell had ever had intercourse with his mother?"

"At that time, no."

"Mr. Flynt, when you put your signature 'Okay, L.F.', did it occur to you that the average, ordinary person who didn't commit incest with his mother would be offended, would be angered by such a suggestion? Did it occur to you, sir?"

"No."

Isaacman interrupted, "I'm going to object on that."

Grutman kept questioning. "Did you think, Mr. Flynt, that making such a suggestion was amusing?"

"Yes."

"In other words, you think that it's funny to say that somebody has committed incest with his mother, right?"

Again Isaacman interposed, "I'm going to object to that. That's argumentative, and it mischaracterizes what appears in this parody of an ad."

But Isaacman was overruled by his own client. "I think it's hilarious. Shut up, Isaacman."

Isaacman tried to slap Flynt back into line. "No, I'm making my objection."

"Do you recognize, Mr. Flynt, that committing incest is, among other things, a crime?"

"Pardon?"

"Do you know, or did you know when you approved by putting your 'okay' on what you thought was this hilarious text, that you wanted in every magazine that you published, the notion that committing incest was a crime? Did you know that?"

"No, no, I did not know it was a crime."

"If you had known it, would have you published it anyway?"

"Yeah, probably."

"Is that because you are indifferent to the consequences of publishing things about people which may not be true, if you accuse them of a crime?"

Isaacman tried to object again. "That's an argumentative-type question."

Flynt was still obstinate. "That's an argumentative—how in the world can I answer if you don't shut up, Isaacman?"

"From your study, or your interest in the law of libel as it affected publishers, did you know that it was—what did you know as to whether a publisher had the right to publish a statement which was false about somebody committing a crime?" Grutman asked.

"I'm objecting," said Isaacman. "It's irrelevant. The question is whether it was an intent to be a true statement or was intended to be a parody, that's the question."

Flynt just ignored his lawyer and let it all hang out. "I don't care, Mr. Grutman. I didn't care, Mr. Grutman."

"You didn't care?"

"Didn't care then, and don't care now."

"Okay. Do you care, Mr. Flynt, about hurting the feelings of people about whom you write things in your magazine?"

"Yes."

"I object," said Isaacman. "That's—it's an irrelevant question."

"You do?" Grutman asked again.

"Yes."

"Fine. Did it occur to you—and since you read this document, which is Exhibit One, rather Exhibit Two, the text before it was published—that, among other things, Reverend Falwell's mother is likened to a whore? Did you remember that?"

"I object to that." Isaacman jumped in. "That mischaracterizes the document."

Flynt answered, unperturbed. "Yes, I think."

"Well, you've read this over, haven't you, Mr. Flynt?"

"Yes."

"All right. Let's go down—"

Flynt interrupted, "You got to be a good whore to be a good mother, Mr. Grutman."

"Was your mother a whore?"

"Yes, she certainly was. She was a good one, too."

"Did you care whether or not, Mr. Flynt, whether or not the statements contained in Exhibit One were true or not?"

"Not really."

"Did you make any effort to ascertain whether they were before you published it?"

"Yes."

"What efforts did you make to ascertain whether the statements contained in Exhibit One were true or not before you caused it to be published?"

At this point, Flynt decided to give Grutman a little lecture on "where he was coming from." "Well, I met with Mary Calderon Waseka, and Masters and Johnson, Morton M. Hunt, Dr. James Prescott, who helped design and build this prison here. And I know a lot about, you know, behavior modification, and I know a lot about the origins of violence, where they came from, and that our inability to deal with our religious convictions was largely rooted in our inability to deal with our sexual perversion. But, as you and I both know, one man's perversion might very well be another man's marriage. And, to get right to the point and answer that question so you could more clearly understand where I'm coming from everybody knows I had a relationship with Ruth Carter Stapleton, but nobody knows what that relationship was. And I'll tell you what it was."

This was really getting to be too much for Grutman. He tried to bring Flynt back to reality.

"Please, Mr. Flynt," interrupted Grutman.

"I think it's very important."

"To answer my question?"

"Yes, to answer—"

"As to what—"

Flynt interrupted, "You asked—you asked if I had done any research. You may not have used those words, but you asked if I had looked in—to obtain any kind of evidence before I—"

"As to the truth of what you published about Reverend Falwell in this ad?"

"Yes," Flynt said. But he was determined to finish his dissertation. "And I'm telling you that what I did was an awful lot of research, because every college campus that I ever spoke on, there was, you know, Gloria Steinem Dykes passing out flyers, you know, accusing me of every ill that society embodies, and I was really concerned if *Hustler* in any way, or magazines like it, had any harmful effect on the consumption, whether it be—by what sex, or children, or animals, or whatever. I had my own opinion, and I knew that it wasn't harmful in any way, but I felt that I needed to convince the government so that we might do away with the concept of obscenity. So, what I did was I researched the sexual behavior, attitudes, and values of people like Mr. Farwell. I called them the Farwellians of the world. And I had the support of the federal government in doing this research because they all work for me. Some of them lost their jobs, like Dr. James Prescott when he wrote the article on child abuse for *Hustler,* but he didn't care, because he found another one. And when Ruth Carter Stapleton came to me, it was part of my research program, and she says, 'Mr. Flynt, you're going to have to say, "Bring Jesus into your life." ' And I told her, I says, 'Ruth, bring George or John inside you, and it'll feel just as good.' And I opened up a copy of *Hustler,* and she says, 'Oh, my God.' And I says, 'What you're doing, the inner healing that you're talking about is nothing more than sexual healing.' Marvin Gaye sang about it, and a lot of people sing about it, you know, whether it be George Jones, Boy George, or whatever. Now, you asked the question, and I'm demanding the time to answer it, and it's got to do with our sexual values. And I am telling you that that is what it's all about. Boy, you crawled out of one and you been trying to crawl back in one ever since, and eventually you're going to realize that. And most of the people that work here in the B. O. P. already know that, and they already know that a few people's got to drink out of a commode over there with some cigarette butts and shit in it, and it ain't going to be me."

Grutman, having let Flynt have his way for a while, tried to nail him down to specifics. What exactly was his proof that Falwell had committed incest with his mother? Flynt claimed that he had an affidavit signed by three different people from Lynchburg, Virginia. Grutman was incredulous. He accused Flynt of making the whole affidavit story up. Flynt denied it. The document did exist. If the affidavit was real, Grutman wanted to know, where was it and who were the witnesses who signed it? Flynt spun out a bizarre tall tale, eventually claiming that the affidavit was back in his prison cell. What did this affidavit actually say, Grutman demanded? "Do these witnesses say that his mother had intercourse with him and they observed it?"

"Yes."

"Where did they say that it occurred?"

"I believe they said it occurred in Missouri, but I'm not sure. We'll have to check the document."

"Does the affidavit indicate how these boys who saw this were able to have observed this incident taking place?"

"Yeah, they were watching."

"Where were they watching from?"

"Through the window of the house."

"And they could see into the outhouse?"

"No, this happened—this—the first time was in the outhouse, okay, with the picture, you see. And he was only masturbating. The next time, he was a little older, and it was in—it took place in the house."

"So these boys, who saw him masturbating with a picture of his mother in the Sears and Roebuck catalog, are the same people who saw him having intercourse with his mother, right?"

"Two of them are. The other one—"

"Don't you think that stretches credulity just a little further than anybody would swallow it?"

"What's credulity?"

This last question by Larry Flynt may well have been one of the most honest and revealing responses in his whole fantastic performance. What's credulity? It's doubtful that at the time of his deposition Larry Flynt really knew.

Like a clever boxer feeling out his opponent, bobbing and weaving, dancing and jabbing, Grutman continued to circle his adversary. Grutman was steadily gaining Flynt's measure. Grutman would move in on an issue, score his points, and then retreat out of harm's way as Flynt flailed back in wild flurries. Grutman's punches began to land more heavily as he started pounding in on Flynt's mental attitudes toward Falwell. Flynt had claimed that he had gotten the information about Falwell's incestuous proclivities in 1978. If Flynt really had the goods on Falwell as early as 1978, Grutman demanded to know, why did Flynt wait until 1983 to publish the story?

"I was waiting to settle a score," explained Flynt.

"Oh, to settle a score?"

"Unh-hunh."

"You mean you were trying to get even with Reverend Falwell?"

"Yeah."

"Has Reverend Falwell, to your knowledge, Mr. Flynt, ever made any personal remarks about your mother?"

"Hmm, no, but he did about my father, and that's no difference."

"Has he ever made any remarks about your personal sexual practices?"

"Yes."

"What do you say Reverend Falwell has said about your personal, private life?"

"He says it's abominable."

"What you personally do with Althea is abominable, he has said?"

"Hmm, my conduct is abominable, he says."

"Okay. Now you said a moment ago that you were waiting to even a—settle a score with him, is that correct?"

"Unh-hunh."

"When you use that phrase, does that mean you were trying to get even with him?"

"Yep."

"So I take it from that, or those several answers, that when you published this, this was not intended to be a parody. It was intended to be the publication of the truth, right?"

"Objection," said Isaacman, "It's argumentative, and it speaks for itself."

Sticking to his pattern, Flynt ignored his own lawyer and answered anyway. "Yes. I didn't even want to put the word 'parody' on there."

"Who made you do that, if anybody?" asked Grutman.

"That asshole sitting over there," said Flynt, referring to his lawyer David Kahn.

" 'That asshole' you'll have to identify for the record," noted Grutman.

At times, Grutman was content to let Flynt punch himself out in wild flights of imagination. When Grutman asked Flynt where the mysterious documentation for his allegation had gone, Flynt's lawyers indicated that they had never heard of any such proof.

"What you need," Flynt lectured his own lawyer, "is a copy of the letter that Richard Nixon wrote to Cardinal Cooke asking what he was going to do about the tuition tax credit on parochial schools, and you'll find a copy of that letter in the file, and you'll also find a copy of the New York Police Department's report when John Lennon was murdered, and they went to Ronald Reagan to ask for a comment. And he was in Cardinal Cooke's apartment, teaching Cardinal Cooke how to bite the big one. You'll need a copy of that police report from the New York—"

"What do you mean 'teaching Cardinal Cooke to bite the big one'?" asked Grutman.

"It's called 'Bravo Eleven,' and you don't have a high enough security clearance to talk about that."

"Well, what do you mean, Mr. Flynt?"

"Well, I if the captain will let me explain it to you, I will."

"Nobody's preventing you from explaining it, so tell us, what does 'bite the big one' mean?"

"I have to have a radio, or a cord, or something. That's up to the captain. If he wants to get—if he gets a line—if the captain's got a box up there, if he brings it in here, I'll talk to Reagan on the phone."

"Okay. Now, Mr. Flynt— "

"Okay? Now, he's got a radio out there that he lets me use. If he'll bring it in here, I'll let you talk to Ronald Reagan. Now, you understand what I'm saying? And I ain't crazy."

Grutman then asked the not-crazy Flynt about who had actually composed the parody. It was put together by a committee, Flynt explained.

"And who was on the committee?" asked Grutman.

"Ah, Stephanie Ross, Greg Ross, Steve Sesadian."

"Anybody else?"

"Ah, yeah. Billy Idol, Yoko Ono."

"Yes."

"And David Lee Roth and Ted Nugent."

In addition to this rock-'n'-roll hall of fame, Flynt claimed that Congressman Larry McDonald and Jimmy Carter had also helped in putting the parody together.

Grutman asked Flynt about the incident in 1983 in which Flynt screamed obscenities at the justices of the Supreme Court in the midst of an argument in a case involving Flynt. Did Flynt remember being there, Grutman asked?

"You bet your sweet ass I was there," Flynt said.

Isaacman tried to get Flynt not to answer questions about the incident, but Flynt shouted Isaacman down. Not only was Flynt proud of his conduct in the Supreme Court, he threatened to repeat the performance.

"I called them nine assholes, one token cunt, and I forgot to remind them that eight of them were pricks." said Flynt. "And I'm going to go back and do it, once more, with style."

Flynt then lectured Grutman, with a relish, on the distinction between class and style. "You see, there's a difference between class and style," he said. "Mr. Grutman, you've got class. And I've got style." Flynt then threatened, "And before we ever get to the courthouse, you're going to know the difference between the two."

Flynt's antipathy for Falwell's religious convictions clearly formed a major part of his motivation in launching his attack on Falwell. His response to questions concerning religion were among the most vicious in the deposition.

"Do you have an aversion or antipathy to organized religion?" Grutman asked.

"You better bet your sweet ass I do," said Flynt.

"And to the Bible?"

"Goddamn right I do."

"Have you ever said, speaking of the Bible, 'This is the biggest piece of shit ever written'?"

"You're goddamn right I did."

"Is that really a personally held conviction of your own?"

"You're goddamn fucking right it is."

Isaacman, sensing disaster, tried to intervene. "I'll object. It's irrelevant."

Grutman continued. "Do you believe that, because of your aversion to the Bible and organized religion, that gives you license to hold up to ridicule and scorn leaders of religious movements?"

"You're goddamn right."

"Objection," said Isaacman. "It's irrelevant. It's argumentative."

"Free expression is absolute."

"It's absolute? Including the dissemination—"

"Unequivocally."

"Fine. Does that include, Mr. Flynt, disseminating things about the private lives of religious leaders?"

"Objection," claimed Isaacman again. "It's irrelevant."

As always, Flynt still answered. "You're damn right."

Flynt was allowed to expand somewhat on his philosophy of life. While crude, this was probably the most cogent part of his testimony. "I don't think the government, or you, or me, or anyone belongs in someone else's bedroom," Flynt explained. He then elaborated on his own secret war against child pornography. "What we got to stop doing is we got to stop fucking with the kids, you know. You understand what I'm saying now? I mean, you adult faggots can do anything you want to up there at Time, Inc., in New York. We don't really care. But, when you mess with the kids, we got a special place for you, down here at the Rock, you know. And it's over in mechanic services, with Doolittle. And they'll take a shiv to your fat ass."

Grutman reminded Flynt that he was under oath.

"Yes, I'm testifying under oath," admitted Flynt. "And I have a secret plan to win the war on obscenity and stop the molestation of children. And the way you do that is to keep Jerry Falwell off the air. Give him a pack of seed corn and send him to Israel and let him tell them what thou hath said. Let him learn to live on the West Bank and eat his manna and his corn. And he should take all the John Birchers and the niggers with him, too."

"Mr. Flynt," said Grutman, "do you agree that there is a difference between contending vigorously, in a sort of debate, with people who have different ideas, and arguing about one concept, as against another, in distinction from making personalized attacks on the private lives of people with whom you disagree?"

"Mr. Grutman—"

Isaacman cut Flynt off. "Question is ambiguous and—"

"Shut up, Isaacman," said Flynt. "Mr. Grutman—"

"I'm making an objection," said Isaacman.

"I understood his question," insisted Flynt. "It wasn't vague. It wasn't vague."

"Please answer it," said Grutman.

"Look, I'll answer this question the way you ask it."

"Right."

"The truth is an absolute defense. And if it offends you or Jerry Falwell, then the two of you have a mental problem, not me."

Flynt was moving in circles. He was again taking the preposterous position that he had actual proof of sexual misconduct by Falwell. He claimed to have a photo of Falwell having coitus with a sheep. "I tell you I have got a photograph of Jerry Falwell masturbating," Flynt said. "And I've got a photograph of him fucking some young girl," he continued. "And no one has the right of taking the individual liberty of sticking their sexual organ in some child's mouth. Now, there's a big difference between civil rights and individual liberties. And you should learn the difference. I mean, an individual liberty is something I'd like to do right now—take a shit right on top of your head. But, now, civil rights is what these assholes over here are doing to me now. They're violating my civil rights, by making me stand here and ask you to insult my intelligence."

"I understand that as a champion of children, you said what you did," said Grutman. "But, do you think that, with respect to adults, you can say anything that you want about their private sexual activities, whether it's real or fancied, or not?"

"Yes."

"No matter how horrible it may be to the average, ordinary person?"

"Yes."

Grutman may have been the master pugilist, scoring heavily with each barrage of bodyblows against Flynt, but was he completely satisfied with the way the deposition was going? Flynt's answers were self-destructive, to be sure, but they were becoming almost *too* self-destructive—if the deposition kept going as crazily as it had been, there was a danger the court could throw the whole thing out on the grounds that Flynt was insane at the time. Grutman at times seemed personally frustrated at Flynt's flippancy. But Grutman was himself a master actor, and may have been feigning frustration for effect. Grutman was scoring technical legal points in spades, but, in some strange, subterranean sense, Larry Flynt often seemed to be winning the personal fight between them. Grutman's punches were scoring points with the judges, but they were not making Flynt hurt internally. Flynt was actually enjoying the questions—enjoying them so much that he constantly shouted at his own lawyer to stop interfering. Punching at Flynt was like punching a pillow: He just absorbed each blow with his mocking, corpulent mass, responding with a combination of unrepentant candor, crude humor, and surreal fantasy.

"I put it to you, Mr. Flynt, that you are making this up. You had no proof of any such thing," Grutman said during one exchange.

"You wanna bet?" replied Flynt testily.

"I'm asking you now."

"If I ain't crazy, why would I make this up?"

"Because, Mr. Flynt, you're an utterly irresponsible, arrogant, truculent, demented, deranged person." Grutman could string out a list of pejoratives with the best, but no matter how much he hated Flynt, he couldn't seem to make him hurt, and Flynt would not stop laughing at him. Flynt had a smart-ass response ready for anything. Grutman asked, for example, about Flynt's proof of Falwell's drinking.

"He drinks a little wine. Nothing wrong with that," replied Flynt.

From a legal perspective, however, Grutman was getting everything he could possibly hope for from Flynt. Grutman was able to get Flynt to make two critical concessions. The first was that Flynt hoped that *Hustler* readers would treat the Campari ad *not* as parody but as conveying actual truth about Falwell.

"Mr. Flynt," Grutman asked, "I take it, then, from what you're telling me, that this publication about Reverend Falwell and Campari was not intended to parody or exaggerate anything, but to convey the truth. Is that right?"

"Yes, sir," replied Flynt. Indeed, said Flynt, he had been against putting in the disclaimer, "Ad Parody—Not to Be Taken Seriously," because he *wanted* the ad to be taken seriously.

Flynt's second concession was even more devastating. Grutman had been picking and poking at Flynt's motivation throughout the whole deposition. He finally led Flynt through a series of questions that firmly nailed down the issue of intent.

"Do you recognize that, in having published what you did in this ad, you were attempting to convey to the people who read it that Reverend Falwell was just as you characterized him, a liar?"

"He's a glutton."

"How about a liar?"

"Yeah. He's a liar, too."

"How about a hypocrite?"

"Yeah."

"That's what you wanted to convey?"

"Yeah."

"And didn't it occur to you that, if that wasn't true, you were attacking a man in his profession?"

"Yes."

"Did you appreciate, at the time that you wrote 'Okay,' or approved this publication, that for Reverend Falwell to function in his livelihood and in his commitment and career he has to have an integrity that people believe in? Did you not appreciate that?"

"Yeah."

"And wasn't one of your objectives to destroy that integrity, or harm it, if you could?"

"To assassinate it."

In getting these admissions from Flynt, Grutman had achieved as much of a victory as he could hope for, even if it lacked the satisfaction and catharsis of making Flynt squirm. Flynt's answers to this series of questions, particularly his brazen admission that he had deliberately set out to "assassinate" Falwell's character, emerged as one of the most influential pieces of evidence in the case.

Lest anyone think Flynt's attack on Falwell was some freakish aberration in an otherwise respectable publishing career, Grutman ended the deposition with a flourish, taking Flynt through a whole series of gems from *Hustler*'s past. Before it was over, everyone was offended. Had Flynt once written that "I have always thought this nation's courts were deserving of contempt?" Yes, he had. Had Flynt published an article featuring Norman Roy Grutman himself as "Asshole of the Month"? Yes, he had. Had Flynt republished the article about Grutman in a publication called *The Best of Hustler*? Yes, he had. Had he published "An Interview with John F. Kennedy's Cock"? Yes, he had. Had he published a photograph showing what appeared to be Ronald and Nancy Reagan in bed, with Nancy Reagan in a position where it appeared that a man was having anal intercourse with her, while the president was sitting there smiling? Yes, he had. Had he published articles describing Jerry Falwell, as well as other members of Falwell's Moral Majority, as "Assholes of the Month"? Yes, he had. Had he published a cartoon with the caption, "Supreme Court Chief Justice Warren Burger, begging Jerry Falwell for a blow job"? Yes, he had. Had he published a cartoon showing an old lady sitting in a rat-infested apartment, in ragged clothes, with dog food in a can, a naked lightbulb above her impoverished surroundings, writing a letter that reads, "Dear Jerry Falwell, I want to thank you for the inspiration and comfort your television broadcasts give me. I am enclosing the remainder of my social security money to help you keep up your fine work, as I know you need it"? Yes, he had. Had he published a cartoon showing a patriarchal figure sitting in a chair labeled "God" saying, "Send someone down to see Falwell; tell him to get off his power trip"? Yes, he had. Had he published a cartoon showing the devil sitting at an executive's desk, talking into a speaker phone, saying "Send Falwell in here. I want to see the look on the fucker's face"? Yes, he had.

Flynt remained completely unrepentant. Did he, Grutman asked, publish a cartoon in which Ronald Reagan and Jerry Falwell were shown participating in pagan sexual orgies?

"Unh-hunh," said Flynt.

"Is that true?"

"That's a cartoon."

"I see. But it was intended to hold the President and Reverend Falwell up to ridicule, wasn't it?"

"No, contempt."

"Contempt. Scorn?"

"Truculent."

"Obloquy?"

"*Parlez-vous français?*" asked Flynt.

"*Je parle le français mieux que toi.*" replied Grutman.

"*Oui, je veux vais coucher vous, avec vous*—I'm sorry, it's rusty, Jesus Christ, it is rusty."

Grutman turned to some of Flynt's exaggerated threats to others.

"Mr. Flynt, have you ever asked to have Frank Sinatra assassinated?"

"Yes."

"Did you ever ask to have Kissinger assassinated?"

"Yes."

"Did you ever plan to blow up the Supreme Court of the United States?"

"Yes."

The deposition ended in bile and bitterness.

"Now, something else I want the record to reflect," said Flynt. "These sons-of-bitches told me if I behave, they'd take me back over there, they'd take these cuffs off. That goddamn nigger took me back over there and put them on. And I'll tell you why, before we get through with these depositions."

"Don't refer—"

"He's a fucking nigger. And if my fucking words offend you or him, either one, you can all suck my dick."

"They offend me. Yes."

"Well, fuck you, motherfucker. Now, you got any more questions?"

Flynt's clown act was beginning to evaporate; perhaps Grutman was finally getting to him. Flynt's hatred was now coming through as raw undistilled venom with not even the faintest pretense of humor or irony.

"I didn't want to physically hurt you," said Flynt. "I wanted to hurt you mentally, boy."

"Do you realize, Mr. Flynt, that you can injure people by inflicting mental suffering and disturbance on them that will cause pain that is as great or greater than physical suffering?"

"You're goddamn fucking right. And you're all going to be on your knees before we finish here."

Flynt was so consumed with disgust for Falwell and Grutman, however, that he could no longer maintain the distinction between infliction of emotional distress and physical attack.

"And it will be physical pain," said Flynt, "because after what I've been put through and after my leg getting broke, I'm no longer settling for psychological pain. You and Mr. Farwell and the rest of the 'Farwellians' have to crawl to New Orleans, 'cause I'm the real one."

"Okay. And you want to inflict physical pain on us?"

"Yes. Torture."

"And mental pain?"

"Yep. An eye for an eye, and a tooth for a tooth. Except I say fuck it, you know. A man messes with my leg, his head comes off."

"You suggest Reverend Falwell messed with your leg?"

"I'm saying Reverend Falwell messed with my cock, and that's enough. He kept me in pain for six years."

"In what respect did Reverend Falwell mess with your penis?"

"Cause Reverend Farwell ordered—"

"Ordered what?"

"—my assassination in Georgia."

This was too much for Grutman. "You know, Mr. Flynt, you expect us to take you seriously about this. There are about a half-a-dozen people that you have accused of being responsible for your being physically injured in 1978."

Flynt lamely tried to link Falwell with all the other superstars in his rogues' gallery as the architects of his assassination attempt. The effort impressed no one.

Flynt and Grutman had been fighting each other for hours, in one of the most mean-spirited confrontations between lawyer and witness in legal history. Flynt had acted more as if he was under anesthesia than oath. Grutman had scored a crushing victory on the legal merits. But despite the flashes of unvarnished contempt at the end of the proceeding, Flynt had also scored a personal victory of sorts. He had remained true to Larry Flynt. He had not broken. He hated Jerry Falwell's guts. He hated Norman Roy Grutman's guts. He hated the guts of half of America. He proudly vented that hatred, with no self-censorship and no apologies to anyone. "Because," as Grutman put it to Flynt, "as far as Larry C. Flynt is concerned, whatever he wants to do, he's going to go ahead and do it. The devil take the hindpost."

Chapter 10

F lynt's deposition was an orgy of hatred for Jerry Falwell. But could that hatred translate into a victory for Falwell in the trial? The general "can't you take a joke, Jerry?" theme of the defense was exquisitely simple. But the specific details of Flynt and *Hustler*'s responses to each of the three counts in Falwell's complaint were much more complicated. *Hustler*'s dirty little joke was only one page long, but it implicated one of the most convoluted and confusing bodies of law in contemporary legal practice—the interlocking theories of libel, invasion of privacy, and infliction of emotional distress that serve as the principal vehicles for modern lawsuits against publishers and broadcasters.[1] As the lawyers for both sides made final preparations for the trial, they had to puzzle through the intricacies of these legal theories as guideposts for their litigation strategies. As that great legal theorist Yogi Berra once put it, "If you don't know where you're goin', you're gonna wind up somewhere else."

Falwell's action for libel involved the oldest and most venerable legal theory. For Jerry Falwell, of course, libel is not just unlawful—it is a sin. "Thou shalt not bear false witness against thy neighbor," the commandment pronounces, and the Book of Proverbs counsels that "a good name is more to be valued than great riches."

Reputation is a sacred commodity in the Anglo-American cultural tradition.[2] "Who steals my purse steals trash," teaches Shakespeare, but a good name is the "jewel of the soul"; and "he who flinches from me my good name robs me of that which not enriches him and leaves me poor indeed." At the time of Alfred the Great the penalty for libel was to cut out the slanderer's tongue. Civilization is now more advanced; modern juries reward money as the remedy for injured reputations, using their own mystical alchemy to turn tarnished images into hard currency. A good name may be more to be valued than great riches, but if a good name has been besmirched, great riches will do.

Libel is actually defamation through the written word; its twin is slander, spoken defamation. To be libelous a statement must lower someone's reputation in the eyes of the community, by asserting a false fact about the person. A libel, in short, is a lie.

As one might expect, however, lawyers could never rest easily with so simple a legal principle as "Thou shalt not bear false witness." The almost perverse ingenuity of the legal mind has insured that when this seemingly straightforward moral command finds its way into a modern American courtroom, it becomes a legal fog almost as impenetrable as the sinister shroud looming over the London Court of Chancery in Charles Dickens' *Bleak House*.[3]

Much of the chaos in the contemporary law of libel comes from the fact that it is an amalgam of state common law (lawyers often refer to traditional state laws as "common law") and federal constitutional law principles emanating from the First Amendment. In a landmark 1964 decision entitled *New York Times Co. v. Sullivan*,[4] the United States Supreme Court began to place First Amendment restrictions on the power of states to award damages to plaintiffs in libel trials.

The New York Times case grew out of a paid advertisement in the *Times* by the Committee to Defend Martin Luther King. The advertisement attacked southern racism and police brutality aimed against Dr. King and others struggling for racial justice in the South during the early 1960s. An Alabama jury had awarded a Montgomery police commissioner, Mr. L. B. Sullivan, $500,000 against *The New York Times* for libels allegedly contained in the ad.

The Supreme Court overturned the jury award on the grounds that it violated the First Amendment. Justice William Brennan was the author of the Court's opinion. Commissioner Sullivan, Justice Brennan reasoned, was a member of the government, and thus to criticize Sullivan was largely to criticize the government itself. If the First Amendment had any settled core of meaning, it was that citizens should be free to speak out against the government and its officials without fear of prosecution for "seditious libel"—slander

against the state. Indeed, a hallmark of totalitarian regimes throughout history has been the stifling of dissent by making it unlawful to
criticize the existing order. Seditious libel, the Court was saying, has
no place in American life.[5]

This does not mean, however, that public officials should be left
utterly without remedy when their reputations are attacked. An
official may still recover in a suit for libel, the Court ruled, but only
if he or she can prove with "clear and convincing evidence" that the
defendant published the libel with what the Court called "actual
malice." This term "actual malice" in *The New York Times* case
unfortunately turned out to be a terrible choice of words, for the
"actual malice" the Court had in mind had nothing to do with actual
malice. In ordinary English usage, malice is a synonym for hate—
it connotes spite, malevolence, ill-will, and vengeance. The law of
libel, as it existed in most states prior to *New York Times,* used this
juicy, old-fashioned type of malice as the trigger for permitting juries
to award "punitive" damages—damages over and above those
needed to compensate the plaintiff for injury, designed to punish the
defendant for reprehensible behavior and to deter such evil conduct
in the future.

The Supreme Court's definition of "actual malice" in *New York
Times,* however, has nothing to do with the old common-law definitions of malice, but rather deals solely with the state of mind of the
defendant in relation to the truth or falsity of the story. The Supreme
Court thus defined actual malice as "knowledge of falsity" or "reckless disregard" for truth or falsity. The Court made it quite clear, in
New York Times itself and in subsequent cases that the "reckless
disregard" standard is not to be confused with personal malice or
hatred nor with run-of-the-mill negligent mistakes. To be reckless,
the press has to be more than sloppy or stupid—it has to harbor
subjective doubts about the truth or falsity of the story and then go
ahead and publish anyway.

In ensuing years the Supreme Court decided a number of cases
that refined the First Amendment principles first articulated in the
New York Times decision. The most important of these refinements
was the Supreme Court's extension of the "knowing or reckless
falsity" standard for actual malice beyond the realm of public *officials* to include public *figures* as well. Many public figures exert an
enormous influence on American life, an influence often every bit as
important as that wielded by public officials. In a 1974 case entitled
Gertz v. Robert Welch, Inc.[6] the Court held that public figures should

be required to meet the same actual malice burden as public officials. Public figures, the Court reasoned, usually have access to the press and therefore have the opportunity to engage in "self-help" by publicly counterattacking when they are defamed. (Jerry Falwell's mass mailings and his use of the *Old Time Gospel Hour* to counterattack Flynt are examples of this rationale in action.) The Supreme Court in *Gertz* further reasoned that public officials assume a greater risk of being exposed to defamation as part of the price for their increased fame. The Faustian bargain made for power and glory diminishes protection from the slings and arrows of outrageous fortune; if you can't stand the heat of the fire, stay out of the kitchen.

The Court held that private figures, on the other hand, are often helpless in the face of an attack by the media and cannot be said to have voluntarily assumed greater risks of reputational damage in exchange for entry into the public arena. A private plaintiff, the Court held, can recover on a showing of fault less than actual malice—mere negligent behavior by the press would suffice.

The *Gertz* decision to subdivide the First Amendment universe according to the public or private status of the plaintiff has gotten mixed reviews over the years. Some have argued that *Gertz* gives too much protection to the press. Public figures like Carol Burnett or Wayne Newton or Joan Rivers (all recent libel plaintiffs)[7] do not contribute meaningfully to our self-governance as a nation, one argument goes, and it is unfair to subject them to the same legal tests applicable to public officials such as Police Commissioner L. B. Sullivan or General William Westmoreland. To criticize an army general or police commissioner for matters arising from their conduct in office may be so close to criticism of the government that our concerns for seditious libel make the actual malice standard wise. But how can stories about Burnett or Newton or Rivers ever be seditious? Furthermore, although some public figures may have access to other media channels to try to counter the libelous story, such access is often illusory, and the vigorous denial often does not travel as far or communicate as effectively as the original attack. Many people reflexively assume that where there's smoke, there's fire; "categorical denials" often seem routine and lame, about as effective as Tommy Smothers sheepishly protesting, "Oh, yeah?"

The *Gertz* decision has also had many detractors who claim that it does not go far enough to protect free speech values. Many important news events concern private figures. When the news story involves a question of public interest, the argument goes, the press should not be shackled by the fear that a private figure participating in these events could later successfully sue because the press reportage had been negligent. The level of First Amendment protection should be pegged to the importance of the story, not the people involved. Furthermore, the importance of the story should not be linked to politics alone. It is too narrow a conception of the First Amendment to treat only political speech as worthy of special protection. Statements concerning arts and entertainment, science, sex, and religion should all be regarded as part of the same First Amendment family. All these topics are vital to social life, and all deserve spirited constitutional protection in a robust and open society.

Despite these critiques of *Gertz,* however, the case has continued to serve as the governing framework for modern libel law. Today, the actual malice standard still applies only to public officials and public figures. If *Gertz* is a judicial compromise, it is a relatively stable one. In Jerry Falwell's case, *Gertz* clearly requires that he prove that *Hustler* and Flynt acted with actual malice, for Falwell is the quintessential American public figure. Falwell, in fact, is one of the best examples of a plaintiff for whom the *Gertz* assumptions are completely valid. For although Falwell is not a public official, his influence on public policy has been extraordinary—that influence, in fact, is precisely what drove Larry Flynt to attack him. Falwell had access to the media to fight Flynt back and was surely no thin-skinned shrinking violet unused to being lambasted in connection with his religious and political ministry. This meant that Norman Roy Grutman's first task in attempting to establish his libel claim for Falwell had to be to prove that Flynt and *Hustler* published with actual malice—actual knowledge of falsity or reckless disregard for the truth.

As the lawyers shaped their strategies in the case, however, the actual malice question began to take on a perplexing cast. This was no ordinary libel case. Larry Flynt's deposition makes it clear that he was dripping with "old-fashioned" malice. But was there *New York Times* "actual malice"? What does the phrase "knowledge of or reckless disregard for falsity" mean in the context of an ad describing Jerry Falwell having sex with his mother in an outhouse? In a superficial sense Flynt and *Hustler* had, of course, acted with knowledge of falsity, since they never really believed that the ad's statements are literally true. But if the real message of the ad is not literal, but symbolic, if it is along the lines of "Falwell is a hypocrite and we hate you," then to speak of "knowledge of falsity" is nonsense, for that message is neither true nor false—it is simply opinion.

This theme, yet another variation on the "can't you take a joke?" defense, became one of the most critical questions debated in the trial. Libel requires a misstatement of *fact*. An expression of opinion does not qualify. Grutman had to brush with meticulously fine strokes. He had to make the ad appear outrageous enough to get the sympathy of the jury, outrageous enough to convince the jury that *Hustler* must have known it was false, and outrageous enough so that Falwell did not come off as a thin-skinned wimp for suing. Yet at the same time Grutman had to refrain from making the ad appear so outrageous that it would be perceived as being incapable of being understood factually and thus be dismissed as mere opinion. Falwell's libel suit was this far from a sure thing, for the ad may have been too outrageous to be libelous.

If Grutman at times seemed a flashy, flamboyant, riverboat gambler, he was nonetheless like many good gamblers possessed of shrewdness beneath the show. Grutman knew how to cover his bets. He had protected himself in the complaint against Flynt by suing under two back-up theories, "appropriation of name or likeness" and "intentional infliction of emotional distress."

The first of those back-up theories required Grutman to navigate some extremely murky legal waters. Over the years American courts have recognized four different species of invasion of privacy. The first, "intrusion," involves some invasion of the solitude of another — such as a "peeping Tom" peering through the bedroom window. If Larry Flynt really had hired someone to spy on Falwell inside an outhouse, this tort of intrusion might have existed. But since the event was sheer fantasy, this theory was clearly not available to Grutman.

The second species of invasion of privacy, "publication of private embarrassing facts," involves making public some intimate detail of an individual's life that reasonable people would regard as no one else's business. For public officials, celebrities, and persons swept into newsworthy events, the press may be permitted to publish intimate facts that would otherwise be regarded as private—such as Jim Bakker's liaison with Jessica Hahn or Gary Hart's relationship with Donna Rice. The publication of private embarrassing facts theory was also clearly of no use to Falwell, since *Hustler* had not published any actual facts at all—the events portrayed in the ad never happened. Even if they had happened, this theory would have been of no avail to him because such incestuous behavior by a leading minister would qualify as newsworthy, and the ostensibly private behavior would thus be treated as fair grist for the public mill.

The third branch of modern invasion of privacy law is known as placing a person in a "false light in the public eye." This "false-light," invasion-of-privacy tort is a very close relative of libel, and in many cases the two are virtually identical twins. False-light invasion of privacy is essentially a watered-down version of libel: Whereas libel requires that there be a false statement that actually causes an injury to the victim's reputation, the false-light theory permits recovery even when the accusation does not actually lower the victim's reputation in the eyes of the community but merely portrays the defendant falsely in a manner deemed highly offensive to an ordinary reasonable person. Unlike the first two notions of invasion of privacy, this third false-light theory could have been attempted by Grutman. He chose not to try this approach, however, apparently deciding that there was too much overlap with the libel count. Since one of the primary thrusts of the plaintiff's complaint was that the Campari ad did, in fact, injure Falwell's reputation, there was no perceptible usefulness in bringing in the false-light count.

Grutman's final option under invasion of privacy is known as "appropriation of name or likeness." (In many states, this cause of action goes by the title invasion of "right of publicity.") Although this is classified as a species of invasion of privacy, in fact what has been invaded is not so much the plaintiff's privacy as his property— the "property" being his own face and name. Celebrities don't sell products for free. A celebrity's name and likeness obviously will often have commercial value. In today's advertising milieu Joe Piscopo, Michael Jackson, Bruce Willis, or Cybill Shepherd may make more from product endorsements than from entertainment engagements. Campari Liqueur, after all, paid Jill St. John, Tony Roberts, and Elizabeth Ashley for their endorsements in the real Campari ads, and if Campari had been so brazen as to stick Jill St. John's picture on its ad and then print a fictional endorsement of her talking about her "first time," she undoubtedly could have recovered for appropriation of her name and likeness.

Grutman decided to try to convince the judge and jury that the same principle was at work in Falwell's case. He pointed out, for example, that the advertising people for Campari had written to *Hustler* and bitterly complained about the ad, claiming that it was an unlawful appropriation of *Campari*'s name and trademark. The potential problem for Grutman, however, was once again the fact that the *Hustler* piece isn't real. Perhaps on first seeing the ad, readers might for a few fleeting seconds think that Falwell is endorsing Campari. But once the interview is read, surely most readers understand that Falwell's name and likeness aren't being used to sell liqueur. Arguably, the only thing Falwell's name was being used to sell was *Hustler* magazine itself, since the parody was part of the entertainment package that the reader was purchasing in the magazine. That, however, is traditionally not the sort of use of name or likeness that qualifies as an appropriation for purposes of trade or advertising. An established line of cases has held that the use of a public figure's picture or name in conjunction with a story about that person did not give rise to a claim against the publication for appropriation. To permit claims in such cases would prevent publishers or broadcasters from using photographs or film footage to illustrate a story. Thus, while Nike must pay Larry Bird before it may use his picture to sell basketball shoes, *Sports Illustrated* does not have to pay Bird to put him on its cover, even though his picture may help sell the issue. And so again, Grutman had a legal theory that did not fit very neatly with his facts.

The gambler had one more card to play, however, and it was perhaps the wildest card in the deck. The tort of "intentional infliction of emotional distress" is a relative newcomer to American law. Historically, courts were reluctant to permit lawsuits based solely on infliction of emotional distress. Because emotional injury is not readily quantifiable and difficult to diagnose objectively, courts were afraid that recognizing the emotional distress tort would open up a floodgate of frivolous or faked claims. Emotional distress is endemic to social life; all of us are constantly inflictors and inflictees. Fearing that the law could not hope to cope with lawsuits stemming from every friction and irritation of life, courts were hostile to such claims.

Throughout the last hundred years, however, courts sporadically approved of lawsuits based solely on the infliction of psychic harm. These cases almost invariably involved monstrously outrageous behavior by the defendant. In some states, indeed, the tort actually went by the name "outrage."

One of the earliest examples of the tort was a nineteenth-century English case, *Wilkinson v. Downton.* [8] The defendant was a practical joker who told a woman that her husband had been severely injured in an accident, causing the wife severe distress. She recovered in her suit for infliction of emotional distress; the comeback "Can't you take a joke?" did not impress the English judges, who thought statements about the death or injury of a loved one no laughing matter. Before long, an entire class of cases developed in England and in the United States imposing liability for erroneous messages announcing a relative's death.

The emotional distress tort evolved to fill a perceived void in the law. It covered situations in which the defendant's conduct was reprehensible and the distress involved was severe, but in which the facts could not be made to fit comfortably into more traditional legal theories. In a Texas case,[9] for example, a black customer was attending a luncheon at a restaurant club when an employee at the restaurant abruptly grabbed the customer's plate and snatched it from his hands, saying that the club did not serve blacks. The black customer sued the restaurant and won on the grounds that the grabbing of the plate from his hands was an offensive contact with his person and thus fell within the technical legal definition of a "battery." While the result was technically correct, it was transparently obvious that the suit was not really about battery. The plaintiff was not suing for a punch in the nose. Rather, the suit was an expression of the plaintiff's outrage at the offensiveness of the racial hatred and insult to human dignity embodied in the racial slur. The case was really an "infliction of emotional distress" theory squeezed into the rules governing battery, a demonstration of the quicksilver ingenuity with which a clever lawyer may press an old tort to do new tricks. The problem with this approach is that the fleeting touching of the plate, itself a trivial harm, became the critical fact opening the door to recovery. The insult and the distress would have been the same if the employee had simply sneered, "We don't serve niggers here!" and touched nothing. Yet, in such a case, no recovery for battery would be allowed.

Sexual harassment situations posed similar problems. If the sexual aggressor touched the victim, then a battery existed. But what if no touching occurred? For a time, the law was sufficiently sexist to dismiss cavalierly mere verbal advances as innocuous, on the logic that you can't blame a man for trying. Some courts were sufficiently sensitive and ingenious, however, to treat such advances as "assaults"—situations in which the plaintiff was placed in reasonable apprehension that a battery would be committed. While the phrase "assault and battery" falls naturally off the tongue as if it were the name of a single offense, in fact the phrase is like "salt and pepper," with two quite distinct components. While a battery is a hit, an assault is a near-miss. Assault was thus one of the law's earliest forms of recovery purely for the emotional distress induced by the plaintiff's behavior—the distress of being a near-victim of physical harm.

In a case involving the Western Union Company,[10] for example, a telegraph operator leaned across the counter and attempted to touch a woman customer's hand, though he never made contact. She had inquired about whether he did watch repairs, to which he responded, "If you will come back here and let me love you and pet you, I will fix your clock." Recovery was permitted for assault, though the true harm was the insult to the customer's dignity in the sexual advance.

Eventually, courts began to drop the pretense of fitting these types of cases into older torts such as assault or battery and became willing to label the suit for what it really was. Liability for infliction of emotional distress was upheld in a wide variety of contexts, including excessive harassment by bill collectors, the mutilation of a corpse, and, in one particularly egregious case, against a hospital when one of its employees displayed to the plaintiff a stillborn child in a formaldehyde jar.

Since Jerry Falwell is a citizen of the state of Virginia and is deemed to have suffered his emotional distress primarily in Virginia, the tort is treated as having taken place there, and the state tort law of Virginia would control the definition of the tort. Virginia courts had established four requirements to satisfy the definition of infliction of emotional distress. Those requirements are that the wrongdoer's conduct be intentional or reckless, that it offend generally accepted standards of decency or morality, that it be causally connected to the plaintiff's emotional distress, and that it cause emotional distress that is severe.

From Norman Roy Grutman's point of view, the intentional infliction of emotional distress theory was originally thrown into the complaint almost as an afterthought, but as the case evolved it increasingly seemed made to order. Surely he could convince a jury that *Hustler* acted intentionally to inflict severe distress upon Falwell, particularly if the judge would allow the jury to view Flynt's wild North Carolina deposition. So, too, he could probably persuade the jury that Falwell was severely upset by the ad. And finally, he had an excellent chance of convincing the jury that depicting Falwell as having had sex with his mother in an outhouse is offensive to "generally accepted standards of decency or morality."

The beauty of the emotional distress theory from Grutman's point of view is that it is not beleaguered by many of the nagging questions that surround the libel and appropriation of likeness claims. While the libel and appropriation claims might founder on the defense that no one could have taken the ad satire seriously and that its primary message is really a statement of opinion, there is nothing in the history of the emotional distress theory to indicate that it matters whether or not the statements are a joke or an opinion. Unlike libel, for example, the emotional distress theory is not concerned with truth or falsity.

If Grutman's invocation of the emotional distress count was ingenious, it was also highly experimental, for the use of the tort of intentional infliction of emotional distress against publishers or broadcasters was a relatively new idea. As part of a flood of litigation aimed against the media in the 1980s, creative plaintiffs' attorneys had begun to supplement more traditional claims for libel and invasion of privacy with claims for intentional infliction of emotional distress. Only a handful of those cases had ever reached the stage of an appellate court opinion, however, and the sparse precedent was highly ambiguous.[11] The momentous issue looming behind the tort of intentional infliction of emotional distress was whether it was constitutional when applied to distress induced by a media publication. If the First Amendment placed limits on the law of libel, what limits did it place on recovery for emotional distress?

There were a few recent cases involving sexually oriented satire. In a 1987 case entitled *L. L. Bean, Inc. v. Drake Publishers, Inc.*[12] the United States Court of Appeals for the First Circuit held that the First Amendment permitted *High Society* magazine, which features adult erotic entertainment, to parody L. L. Bean's catalogue in a two-page article entitled "L. L. Beam's Back-to-School-Sex-Catalogue."

In *Dallas Cowboys Cheerleaders, Inc. v. Pussycat Cinema, Ltd.*[13] the United States Court of Appeals for the Second Circuit upheld a preliminary injunction prohibiting the Pussycat Cinema in New York from exhibiting the movie *Debbie Does Dallas.* The movie depicts Debbie, a high school cheerleader, who had been selected to become a "Texas Cowgirl." To raise the money to get to Dallas, Debbie and other cheerleaders perform sexual services for a fee. In the movie's final scene, Debbie dons a uniform strikingly similar to that worn by the real Dallas Cowboys Cheerleaders and performs various sexual acts while clad in the uniform. The movie was advertised as "Starring Ex-Dallas Cowgirl Cheerleader Bambi Woods." Bambi Woods, who played Debbie, never was a Dallas Cowboys

Cheerleader. The theory on which the real Dallas Cowboys Cheer-leaders managed to enjoin *Debbie Does Dallas* is trademark infringement.

These cases, however, did not involve the emotional distress theory, and there was very little guidance from any other decisions on whether an emotional distress recovery could be permitted if a libel count failed. Nothing quite like the Falwell case had ever sur-faced before; American courts had yet to decide whether damages could be rewarded just for hurt feelings arising from the content of this type of speech.

As Supreme Court Justice William Brennan once observed, how-ever, "To experienced lawyers, it is commonplace that the outcome of a lawsuit—and hence the vindication of legal rights—depends more often on how the factfinder appraises the facts than on a disputed construction of a statute or interpretation of a line of prece-dents." There would be time enough later for the lawyers to theorize; the immediate battle was over the facts.

Chapter 11

As the trial date fast approached, Alan Isaacman and David
Carson were faced with one fact that loomed above all others
in the case—Larry Flynt's wild performance with Norman Roy
Grutman during his deposition. Isaacman and Carson attempted to
overcome that disadvantage by planning two maneuvers. First, they
would try to get Judge Turk to throw out Flynt's deposition and rule
it inadmissible in the case. Second, they would try to get Judge Turk
to throw out Norman Roy Grutman.

Flynt's lawyers knew, of course, that if the jurors were permitted
to see Larry Flynt's videotape deposition from Butner, the effect
could be devastating. Grutman was sure to introduce the deposition,
or at least the most damning segments of it. Larry Flynt's bizarre
behavior, however, had in one ironic respect been a possible blessing
in disguise. If Isaacman and Carson could convince Judge Turk that
Flynt was out of his mind when he gave the deposition, Turk might
agree to exclude it from the trial on the grounds that Flynt had been
mentally incompetent to testify. They argued that Flynt was in the
manic phase of a manic-depressive syndrome, had broken his leg
only days before, and was on medication. They presented the af-
fidavits of two psychiatrists who had observed Flynt and determined
that he was at the height of his manic-depressive syndrome during
the deposition.

Grutman countered this argument by arguing that Flynt had
merely feigned incompetence "to justify his intentional campaign of

personal vilification." Flynt was capable of turning his bizarre behavior on and off like a faucet; the fact that he was cunning, irresponsible, and deceitful should not render him legally incompetent to testify. Grutman pointed out that both before and after his June 1984 deposition Flynt had been found competent to testify in other judicial proceedings. In a January criminal case he had been found competent to stand trial. On June 26, 1984, only eleven days after his deposition performance, Flynt had been held competent to stand trial and even to conduct his own defense in a case arising from his vulgar outburst in the United States Supreme Court in November 1983, in which he had been dragged away screaming obscenities at the justices.

Finally, Grutman argued, the modern rules of evidence were on his side. There was a time when proof of mental incapacity was deemed a legitimate basis for barring the witness from testifying. The contemporary rules of evidence governing federal courts, however, have substituted a more liberal rule. Now the witness is allowed to testify, and the jurors may take into account their assessment of his or her mental capacity in determining how much weight to attach to the testimony. In cases in which lawyers once argued that the witness should not be heard, they now must argue the witness should not be believed. The judge may totally bar the witness only in the rare case in which the testimony is so off-base that it is no longer relevant to the issues in the case.

Presented with these arguments, Judge Turk at first sided with Flynt. He agreed with one psychiatrist's diagnosis of Flynt as suffering from "manic grandiosity" and judged him irrational and incapable of giving truthful responses. This ruling was probably influenced as much as anything by the visceral shock to Judge Turk's system that viewing the videotape must have created. Larry Flynt looked as crazy as a loon. Turk concluded, "As Flynt could not comprehend the obligation of the oath, and could not give a correct account of events, his deposition of June 15, 1984, must be excluded from the case in chief."

If Flynt's attorneys were dancing in the streets, however, the dance was a short one. Not long after this ruling, on the very first day of the trial, Judge Turk changed his mind and reversed himself. Perhaps he had reconsidered some of the authorities cited in Grutman's brief. If Flynt was too crazy to be credible during his deposition, the jurors, in their common-sense wisdom, could decide that for themselves. Judge Turk allowed the deposition to be played.

Isaacman and Carson next tried to get Norman Roy Grutman thrown out of the case. David Carson filed a motion with Judge Turk to disqualify Grutman, with a supporting memorandum. Carson began his memorandum by reminding Judge Turk that Turk had already had several occasions to observe "and perhaps even enjoy" Grutman's zeal as an advocate for his client. This time, Carson claimed, Grutman had "indisputably crossed over the line separating zealous representation from fanatical disregard for the precepts of professional responsibility and even criminal law." Grutman, he maintained, had bribed a witness and then audaciously memorialized the evil deed by signing a formal agreement attesting to the crime. Flynt's attorneys felt obliged to report this conduct by Grutman to the court, Carson stated, not merely because of its relevance to the case but pursuant to the professional obligation of all lawyers to report violations of the rules of professional conduct.

Carson's case against Grutman arose from the circumstances surrounding the deposition testimony of a witness named Bill Rider, Larry Flynt's brother-in-law. He had been employed by Flynt and *Hustler* for several years as chief of security. He was discharged, however, in 1983.

Rider offered to help Grutman in Falwell's lawsuit against Flynt by providing Grutman with a document that would establish that Flynt personally knew of the contents of the ad before it was published and with a sworn statement that Rider had heard Flynt say at a poker game that he would really "get Falwell" with the Campari ad. Carson alleged that Grutman agreed to pay Rider $10,000 in exchange for Rider's deposition testimony against Flynt and for a draft of the Campari ad parody containing Larry Flynt's initials approving its content. Rider received $6,500 of the total $10,000 payment; the other $3,500 went to his attorney, Don Erik Franzen, who negotiated the arrangement with Grutman.

Describing this transaction as a "sordid deal," Carson tried to convince Judge Turk that the $10,000 was a bribe paid to Rider in violation of federal criminal statutes and canons of professional ethics. Carson further maintained that the $10,000 actually came from Jerry Falwell's funds and was paid under Falwell's auspices.

Carson produced two documents as his "smoking guns." The first was a partial copy of a letter dated June 8, 1984, from Grutman to Franzen, Rider's attorney. A copy of this letter was provided to Carson by Franzen, but with portions blocked out. In this letter Grutman stated to Franzen:

. . . in reference to Mr. Rider's statement to me on several occasions
that he is possessed of information which would conclusively demonstrate my client Jerry Falwell's right to recover against *Hustler Magazine* and Larry Flynt and would establish factually the malice by
Flynt against Falwell, including but not limited to the circumstances
giving rise to the 'Campari Ad,' I am disposed to offer to pay for
investigative work by Mr. Rider that will produce evidence to establish those facts.[1]

Grutman's letter then elaborated, stating that he would place
$10,000 in escrow for Rider,

. . . providing that you can produce to me a statement from Bill Rider
as well as a description of the specific other information and evidence,
including the names, addresses, and other identities of witnesses (such
as those that were at the alleged poker game), whose testimony can
be taken and which testimony will support the facts as Mr. Rider
claims them to be.[2]

Grutman's letter further required that, as "justification for the re-
quested compensation," Rider provide "a description and identifica-
tion of specific documents" establishing the "propositions in
question."

Carson next produced a letter from Franzen back to Grutman,
dated June 14, 1984. Franzen's letter did not beat around the bush.
Franzen decided to just "tell it like it is," laying out point-by-point
exactly what his client Rider would do for his $10,000:

My client has authorized me to make the following offer in connection
with the Falwell/Flynt suit:

1. Bill Rider will, concurrently with delivery of this letter, provide
to you a copy of a document that is probative of the knowledge of
Larry Flynt of the contents of the 'Campari Ad' and his approval of
its publication with such knowledge.

2. Mr. Rider will provide a declaration, in which he will disclose
facts relative to the "Poker Game" probative of Mr. Flynt's role in
the creation of the ad, malice toward Rev. Falwell and knowledge of
the defamatory character of the 'Campari Ad,' and further provide
the names of other witnesses to the same fact.

3. Mr. Rider will be available for a deposition to be videotaped
at a place to be designated by you, on reasonable notice, in Los

Angeles, California, concerning the "Poker Game" and the names, identities, and addresses (if known) of other persons present. For these services, Mr. Rider is to be paid the sum of $10,000.[3]

The letter provided that $5,000 would be paid on receipt of the document and Bill Rider's written declaration of the facts concerning the poker game and that the balance of $5,000 would be paid on the taking of Rider's deposition. It further provided that Falwell would release Rider of any legal liability arising from the Campari ad. At the bottom of the letter was a space for Grutman to sign his assent to the agreement. There appeared in that space the unmistakeable signature of "Norman Roy Grutman, Attorney for Rev. Jerry Falwell."

Carson argued that this arrangement was both illegal and unethical. A federal criminal statute entitled "Bribery of Public Officials and Witnesses" forbids the payment of money "to any person, for or because of the testimony under oath or affirmation given or to be given by such person as a witness."[4] A second federal statute provides that anyone who "directly or indirectly, corruptly gives, offers, or promises anything of value to any person . . . with intent to influence the testimony under oath of such person, shall be guilty of a felony."[5]

Carson also cited the legal canons of ethics. The Virginia Code of Professional Responsibility contains an "Ethical Consideration" stating:

> Witnesses should always testify truthfully and should be free from any financial inducements that might tempt them to do otherwise. A lawyer should not pay or agree to pay a nonexpert witness an amount in excess of reimbursement for expenses and financial loss incident to his being a witness; however, a lawyer may pay or agree to pay an expert witness a reasonable fee for his services as an expert. But in no event should a lawyer pay or agree to pay a contingent fee to any witness. A lawyer should exercise reasonable diligence to see that his client and lay associates conform to these standards.[6]

Both the American Bar Association and the New York Bar have identical provisions.

But had Grutman really violated any of these provisions cited by Carson? If Grutman or Falwell had paid Rider $10,000 to influence his testimony, the criminal and unethical nature of the payment would be indisputable. To pay a witness to lie is bribery, pure and simple. But Grutman had not done that.

What Grutman had done, Carson claimed, was to pay Rider $10,000 for his cooperation in supplying information useful to Grutman's case. The claim was not that Grutman had paid blood money to corrupt Rider's tongue so much as to loosen it up a little.

It *is* permissible to pay an "expert" witness. The term "expert witness," however, refers to someone who testifies in a specialized field on technical matters unfamiliar to the lay person. A doctor may testify as an expert witness in a medical malpractice case to explain a complex surgical procedure; an engineer may testify in a case involving a building that collapses. Bill Rider, however, was clearly not an expert witness. He was an ordinary percipient witness, a witness testifying simply about events he had observed. Carson argued that neither the criminal law nor the ethical canons require that the witness be paid to lie. It is enough to run afoul of them that the witness be paid at all, other than for reasonable travel expenses and expenses incurred through lost work time. The logic of this rule is that any financial payment above actual out-of-pocket costs could influence a witness and that lawyers must avoid not merely outright corruption of the judicial system but any *appearance* of impropriety.

Although Grutman's initial letter said that Rider was being paid for "investigative work," this phrase, Carson claimed, was a self-serving euphemism designed to mask the true *quid pro quo*—money for testimony. The letter sent by Rider's attorney and agreed to and signed by Grutman did not mention "investigative work" but simply called a spade a spade: Rider would receive $10,000 for a document, a written declaration, and a deposition. What "investigation," after all, did Rider have to do? All he had to do was turn over the document and state the facts as he knew them. His deposition lasted only an hour.

Carson ended his attack on Grutman by attaching to his presentation to Judge Turk an appendix listing other examples of cases in which Grutman had gotten into trouble because of his conduct in a case. In a Los Angeles case involving Grutman's defense of *Penthouse,* the defense had been cited by a judge as having "flagrantly and deliberately misconducted itself in reprehensible manners which were calculated to improperly prejudice plaintiffs and improperly influence the jury against plaintiffs."[7] The case arose from a *Penthouse* article claiming that a plush California resort, the Rancho La Costa, "was established and frequented by mobsters." The operators of La Costa sued *Penthouse* for a whopping $522 million. If a libel trial itself can develop a bad reputation, no suit has ever generated a worse one than the La Costa case. It became a circus. After a pretrial litigation period lasting six and one-half years and a trial lasting five months (reportedly generating over $4 million in legal fees on each side), the trial court ultimately ended up ordering a whole new trial. *Penthouse* was defended by Grutman, and the La Costa resort was represented by another of the country's most famous trial lawyers, Louis Nizer. Nizer and Grutman fought bitterly in the case, each constantly sniping at the other both in and out of court.

In a case entitled *Penthouse v. Playboy*[8] the court dismissed *Penthouse*'s suit "where under the direction of Grutman, plaintiff's defiance climaxed a sordid pattern of prolonged and vexatious destruction of legitimate discovery sought by defendant, in which false testimony, material misrepresentations by counsel, and footdragging were used in an effort to prevent defendant from getting relevant records." And in another case involving Grutman against *Hustler,* an Ohio suit called *Guccione v. Hustler Magazine,*[9] repeated condemnations by the trial judge finally caused Grutman to withdraw from the lawsuit for fear of being expelled by the judge. In its June 1979 issue *Hustler* depicted Guccione engaged in an act of anal intercourse, with the caption, "Bob Guccione Discovers Vaseline." A photograph of Guccione's head purchased from United Press International is superimposed on the body of another man performing the act. In a wild trial, both sides ranged far and wide in their attacks. In his testimony, Guccione suggested that Larry Flynt might do anything to him, including future libels on his daughter and mother. Guccione's lawyer, Grutman, put the invitation to stop Larry Flynt more bluntly. Grutman told the jury:

"The law, you will learn, says that it is not Mr. Guccione's need which is relevant, but the necessity, the imperative, crying necessity to put an end and stop to this kind of calumny.

"What would stop Larry Flynt? The lawyer's letter? He paid it no mind. The lawsuit, which was originally commenced, he laughed at. . . .

"Ladies and gentlemen, this man knows nothing except that he will go on doing what he willfully wants to do unless you stop him, and the only way in which he can be stopped, and that is in his pocket book. Those are why punitive damages are essential.

"If you award a verdict against Larry Flynt of several hundred thousand dollars above the several hundred thousand dollars of lawyers' fees already expended to make Mr. Guccione whole, do you think that would stop Larry Flynt, a man who has a cash flow that he admits is more than a million-and-a-half dollars a week? Now, these are sums, I know, astronomical and outside of the experience of almost all of you, all of us, but that is the reality of the bloated Larry Flynt, a man heaped up on his own ill-gotten success. A modest verdict, he will rear back and roar at you and will have gotten away with it, and what will happen next month or the month after to Mr. Guccione, to his mother, to Ms. Keeton, to his children, to President Carter? . . .

". . . To anyone whom he may elect to vent his spiteful, vicious ire upon. That is the focus. How do you stop that man? How do you stop him? I have calculated from the figures which the Flynt organization provided to us that of the magazines which were involved in the publications of the specific evils against Mr. Guccione, Mr. Flynt probably made over $10 million, and I could ask you rationally, as a matter of punitive damages, to stop Mr. Flynt by making him pay back the money that he made on this vile pile of swill."[10]

The jury clearly took this invitation to heart, for it returned with an award calculated to put *Hustler* and Flynt out of business: $1.5 million in compensatory damages and $11 million in punitive damages against *Hustler* and $26 million in damages against Flynt. Guccione's award against *Hustler* and Flynt was reversed on appeal on the grounds that the jury had been motivated by passion and prejudice against Flynt.

Grutman's defense of the misconduct charge was handled principally by Jeffrey H. Daichman, the lawyer in Grutman's firm who assisted him in the Falwell suit. Daichman launched a spirited counterattack. He decried the lawyers for Flynt who, "halos about their heads," tried to cast their attack on Grutman as merely part of their professional obligation to report misconduct. In fact, Daichman claimed, it was a transparent, last-minute strategy to sidetrack the trial and deprive Jerry Falwell of the lawyer of his choice, a tactic that "bespeaks a shameful disregard for the code of professional ethics and the dignity of this court." It was Carson and Isaacman, not Grutman, who deserved rebuke for improperly haranguing opposing counsel. Daichman cited a provision of the canons of his own:

In adversary proceedings, clients are litigants, and, though ill feelings may exist between [them], such ill feeling should not influence a lawyer in his conduct, attitudes, and demeanor towards opposing lawyers. A lawyer should not make unfair or derogatory personal references to opposing counsel. Haranguing and offensive tactics by lawyers interfere with the orderly administration of justice and have no place in our legal system.[11]

According to Daichman, Carson had completely misrepresented the nature of the transaction between Grutman and Rider. Grutman's exchange of letters with Rider, he argued, accurately reflected the parties' best estimate of the actual expenses Rider incurred in connection with his deposition, the value of his critical assistance in the development of proof for trial, and the losses he might suffer by reason of his cooperation and services in the case. The agreement represented an arm's-length transaction, entered into by both parties with the advice and assistance of counsel.

Rider, Daichman noted, played a critical role in the development of Falwell's case against *Hustler* and Flynt. Rider testified under oath that Flynt was among those responsible for the Campari ad and was able to provide a document probative of Flynt's knowledge regarding the ad. Without this assistance, he maintained, Falwell's case against *Hustler* and Flynt would have been seriously jeopardized.

Daichman further argued that Rider incurred "substantial costs and financial losses" in connection with his depositions, his preparation for the depositions, and his general role in the development of proof for trial. Rider "devoted time and effort to the tasks of investigating potential evidentiary leads, discussing the fruits of these investigations with counsel, generally assisting counsel in developing strategies, and planning plaintiff's future course of action."

Daichman essentially dismissed the disqualification motion as a cheap, dirty tactic calculated to derail the case at the last moment. Flynt's lawyers had known of the payment to Rider in September 1984, yet they waited until mid-November, as the trial was fast approaching, to report the incident to the court. "Far from being an inducement to testify," he concluded, "the sums paid to Mr. Rider were clearly reasonable, even modest, compensation for the critical services he rendered."

And so the issue was joined. Carson had cast the payment as

money to induce testimony, well above any actual reasonable expenses Rider could possibly have incurred. Daichman insisted it was an honest, above-board deal reflecting the true value of Rider's services.

It was difficult to predict how Judge Turk would rule. Daichman's insistence that Rider had been paid a fee commensurate with his critical importance in the case was itself dangerously close to a self-damning admission. Witness fees were supposed to be based on the expenses the witness incurred, *not on how important the witness was to the lawyer's case*—for that was what created the risk that the fee would influence the testimony, subtly or not. Perhaps Judge Turk would view Grutman's track record of prior run-ins with courts as incriminating; perhaps he really was capable of impermissibly paying a witness for his testimony. Yet, Judge Turk could just as easily dismiss the payment as a legitimate "arm's-length" transaction reflecting Rider's "investigative" efforts and similarly dismiss the prior incidents involving Grutman as the inevitable judicial flare ups any aggressive attorney will ignite from time to time. Great American courtroom masters from Abraham Lincoln to Clarence Darrow and F. Lee Bailey all had gotten into trouble at some point in their careers while zealously representing clients. If Grutman throws an occasional tantrum, so does Bobby Knight. Better for the trial lawyer occasionally to get slapped with a contempt of court citation (the technical foul of litigation) than to be too timid ever to raise any judicial hackles. But still, a payment of $10,000 for Rider's relatively meager efforts did seem excessive.

In the end Judge Turk dropped back fifteen yards and punted. He ruled for Grutman, but at the same time he delivered a cryptic jab at "attorney misconduct" without ever actually saying that there had *been* attorney misconduct. Disqualification is a "drastic measure which courts should hesitate to impose except when absolutely necessary," stated Turk. "Indeed," he noted, "courts have previously declined to disqualify counsel even though the court had serious misgivings about counsel's conduct, and even though the court found that the attorney had in fact violated the canons of professional ethics." Had Grutman engaged in unethical behavior? Judge Turk declined to be pinned down, ending his ruling with the ambiguous sentence: "Therefore, although the court does not condone attorney misconduct, it declines to dismiss the action or to disqualify counsel for the plaintiff."

Grutman had won the first round in court. The victory was

critical, even if the outcome had never been in serious doubt. The referee had ruled that no low blows were thrown. Grutman was allowed to stay in the fight.

The attempt to disqualify Grutman demonstrates the particularly bitter quality of the *Falwell v. Flynt* litigation. That bitterness had roots in prior cases in which Grutman tangled with Larry Flynt and his lawyers. Other courts in other jurisdictions had witnessed the rivalry firsthand. In yet another *Guccione v. Hustler* case pitting Grutman against Isaacman, this one in New York, the United States Court of Appeals for the Second Circuit begins its opinion with two paragraphs that say it all:

> Publishers of pornography are, not surprisingly, often criticized and scorned and, on occasion, may even be libeled. This libel action brought by Robert Guccione, the publisher of *Penthouse* magazine, is noteworthy, because the alleged libel was authored not by a right-eous crusader against smut but by Larry Flynt, the publisher of *Hustler* magazine. An article printed in *Hustler* in 1983 stated that Guccione "is married and also has a live-in girlfriend, Kathy Kee-ton." In what the District Court for the Southern District of New York (Robert J. Sweet, Judge) characterized as a "grudge match," Guccione sued for libel. The undisputed facts disclosed at the trial revealed that Guccione had been notoriously living with Miss Keeton while still married to Muriel Guccione for thirteen of the seventeen years prior to the article's publication, though he and Mrs. Guccione were divorced four years before the article appeared. Guccione emerged from the fray with a judgment in his favor of $1 in nominal damages and $1.6 million in punitive damages.
>
> We must be careful in cases such as this not to accord either the pornographer plaintiff or the pornographer defendant less protection than would be accorded libel litigants who publish more traditional works of literature or journalism. Bearing that point firmly in mind, we conclude, for reasons that follow, that Guccione's claim fails as a matter of law, both because the statement at issue was substantially true and because Guccione was "libel-proof" with respect to an accu-sation of adultery. We therefore reverse.[12]

Grutman and Flynt had been carrying on these judicial "grudge matches" for years. In the case *Keeton v. Hustler,*[13] involving a libel suit by Kathy Keeton, the vice-chairman of *Penthouse* and Bob Guccione's lover, against *Hustler* and Larry Flynt, Grutman was

Keeton's lawyer in the litigation, which went all the way to the United States Supreme Court.

Keeton claimed that she was libeled in five separate issues of *Hustler,* published between September 1975 and May 1976. She first filed suit against *Hustler* and Flynt in Ohio, where *Hustler* is incorporated, but the Ohio courts ruled that her suit had expired because she had failed to commence it before the Ohio statute of limitations had run out. Keeton's lawyers looked around for another jurisdiction in which to bring the lawsuit and were discouraged to discover that the statute of limitations had run out in every state in the United States except one, New Hampshire, which stood alone with an unusually long six-year limitation period for libel.

Could Keeton, who lived in New York, sue *Hustler* (a publication incorporated in Ohio and based in California) in New Hampshire, a state that seemed at first blush to have little, if anything, to do with the dispute? The usual rule in civil litigation is that a state must have a sufficient level of what courts call "minimum contacts" with a company in order to force it into its courts. Did *Hustler* have sufficient contacts with New Hampshire to be subject to that state's jurisdiction?

Hustler, it turned out, was not exactly what you would call a big seller in New Hampshire. *Hustler* had no offices, employees, bank accounts, or real property in the state. *Hustler*'s only contact with New Hampshire was that its magazine was available for sale there—but sales were relatively miniscule. New Hampshire sales were less than 1 percent of the magazine's total circulation.

In a decision with important implications for the entire media, the United States Supreme Court held that Kathy Keeton could bring her suit against *Hustler* in New Hampshire. In his opinion for the Court, Justice Rehnquist argued that, even though neither Kathy Keeton nor *Hustler* had very much to do with New Hampshire, the fact remained that some copies of *Hustler* had been sold there. Even if none of the New Hampshire citizens who read the allegedly offending articles about Kathy Keeton knew who she was nor cared, they had nonetheless read material that was allegedly libelous. Justice Rehnquist then shifted his analysis of the problem to an entirely new approach: New Hampshire's libel laws, he reasoned, were not merely designed to protect the direct victims of the media; they were designed to protect New Hampshire's readers and listeners from being exposed to falsehood. Rehnquist maintained that libel does not merely safeguard individual reputations; it safeguards the public at large from what is essentially moral and factual "pollution." Thus, "False statements of fact harm both the subject of the falsehood *and* the readers of the statement. New Hampshire may rightly employ its libel laws to discourage the deception of its citizens."

On another occasion, Grutman found himself going against Larry Flynt's empire in a more oblique way, suing Flynt's magazine distributing business. In its May 1980 issue a relatively obscure publication called *Adelina* magazine proclaimed on its cover: "In the Nude from the *Playmen* Archives . . . Jackie Collins." Inside the magazine there are two photographs printed from the movie *The World Is Full of Married Men,* based on the book of the same title by Collins. One of the photos shows a topless woman; the other shows the same woman in a nude orgy scene. The caption accompanying the photos identifies the woman as writer Jackie Collins, with a short article commenting on the increasing willingness of "serious" actresses to appear nude in films.

Jackie Collins wrote the book *The World Is Full of Married Men,* and she wrote the screenplay for the movie, which was directed by her husband, Oscar Lerman. Jackie Collins, however, did not appear in the movie, clothed or unclothed, and she has never appeared nude in public. The magazine had mistakenly identified the anonymous actress who appeared nude in the photos as Collins, when it was not Collins at all.

Jackie Collins sued the publishers and distributors of the magazine, including Larry Flynt's distributing company.[14] For her lawyer Collins chose Grutman.

After a relatively short trial in New York federal court, a jury returned a verdict in favor of Jackie Collins for a whopping $40 million in damages—$7 million in compensatory and $33 million in punitive damages. In analyzing her claim on appeal, the Federal Court of Appeals pointed out that Collins had achieved substantial fame as the author of nine novels. Her books, the court noted, were controversial because of their emphasis on a recurring theme—that there is ubiquitous inequality in the treatment of women relative to men, an inequality that is particularly pronounced in sexual mores. Collins points to the fact, for example, that women appear naked in films and magazines more frequently than men, a phenomenon that she regards as unfair because men have more opportunity to view unclad women than women have to view unclad men. Collins advocates "equal nudes for all."

The court ruled that the magazine piece fell into the category of

newsworthy commentary about Collins and that she could thus recover against the defendants only on clear and convincing proof of
recklessness. Such proof, the appeals court said, was lacking. The
court then chastised the jury for its gargantuan damages award,
stating that: "Putting aside First Amendment implications of 'mega-
verdicts' frequently imposed by juries in media cases, the compensatory damages awarded shock the conscience of this court." The
damages, the court went on, were "grossly excessive and obviously
a product of plaintiff's counsel's appeals to the passion and prejudice
of the jury."

It was, of course, precisely Norman Roy Grutman's passion that
Alan Isaacman and David Carson had most to fear. They had tried
to knock Falwell's star performer out of the box, but had failed. They
were then faced with battling extraordinarily long odds in attempting
to achieve a victory for Larry Flynt against Norman Roy Grutman
and Jerry Falwell in Roanoke, Virginia.

Chapter 12

T he trial date finally came. The jury had been selected. The
lawyers had made opening statements to the jury explaining the
case. It was time to start hearing the evidence. Grutman led off with
his star witness, Jerry Falwell.

If Larry Flynt had turned his witness oath into a defiant tragi-
comedy, Jerry Falwell had no difficulty in serenely taking the witness
stand and swearing to "tell the truth, the whole truth, and nothing
but the truth." Falwell's testimony on the stand was cool, composed,
and, if anything, understated. Grutman led him through the essential
points with relative economy and only a modicum of gratuitous
hype.

Yet Jerry Falwell's testimony was as remarkable in its sweep as
the deposition of Larry Flynt. Falwell managed to explore, quickly
but with pronounced intensity, every important point in *Falwell v.
Flynt.* More significantly, he managed to traverse virtually every
important theme in Jerry Falwell's life as well as all of the subterranean cultural conflicts lurking beneath his battle with Flynt. Falwell
dealt head-on with the suspicion that he is every bit as much a hustler
as Flynt, with the arguments against his mixing of religion and
politics, with his moral agenda for America, and with why Larry
Flynt's behavior is not merely a personal insult to his human dignity
but an assault on that moral agenda. With Larry Flynt as his foil,
Jerry Falwell's testimony put in relief everything that Falwell and
Flynt find disgusting in each other; it was an excursion through the
education of Jerry Falwell.

The testimony conducted by Grutman began by establishing for the record what everyone in the courtroom already knew, that Jerry Falwell was a hometown boy.[1]

"Reverend Falwell, will you tell me first, please, how you prefer to be addressed in this trial?"

"I would just prefer to be 'Mister Falwell.' "

"Very well, Mr. Falwell, will you tell us first when you were born?"

"August 11, 1933."

"Where were you born?"

"Campbell County, Virginia."

"From the time of your birth have you lived most of your life in Virginia?"

"All fifty-one years, with the exception of four years away in college."[2]

Falwell's roots in nearby Lynchburg trace to the town's beginnings.[3] The Falwell family dated back to the founding of Lynchburg in 1757 by John Lynch, a son of an Irish tobacco farmer who established a ferry on the James River. John Lynch and his brother Charles began seizing Tories during the American Revolution and hanging them by their thumbs until they screamed "Liberty forever!" Legend has it that this was the source of the term "lynching." Lynchburg was always predominately Baptist, though it had Quakers from its beginnings and a Catholic church as early as 1843—decades before the first Catholic church was officially instituted in Washington, D.C. It is a town of historical markers and Confederate monuments, a dusty southern manufacturing town, described by writer Dinesh D'Souza as "a conglomeration of rednecks and aristocrats, Southern crazies and Southern belles, white trash and old money."[4]

Falwell's great-grandfather was a slaveholder, his grandfather a landowner, and his father, Carey Falwell, a well-known local businessman in the fuel-hauling, trucking, and bus transportation business. His father had no use for religion; he once counseled Falwell, "Don't be a preacher, son; when a preacher walks into a room, people start acting funny." In 1931, two years before Falwell's birth, two events scarred the life of his father. Carey's younger brother, Garland, high on whiskey and drugs, came shooting his way into a restaurant and chased Carey into a back office. Carey returned the fire, and a load of shot tore through Garland's body above the heart. He died instantly. The same year, Carey's daughter Resha got appendicitis, but the family doctor diagnosed it as pneumonia. Carey distrusted hospitals and did not take the girl to one. Her appendix burst, and she died of blood poisoning. Falwell was always convinced that it was guilt from these two events that drove his father to alcoholism. After heavy drinking bouts, he would always talk about his dead brother Garland and dead daughter Resha. This history also affected Jerry Falwell deeply. "I am not ashamed or embarrassed to speak of sin," says Falwell, "because I have seen its power in my own life, in the lives of my family, and in the lives of most of the people of this planet."

Grutman brought up alcohol early on in his questioning. "Speaking of you as a man, as to your own personal convictions, I address myself to the question of the consumption of alcohol. According to your religious ethics, Mr. Falwell, is drinking alcohol something that you avoid or not do?"

"Since I became a Christian in 1952, I have been and am a teetotaler."

"That means you don't drink alcoholic beverages, is that correct?"

"That is correct."

"Since the time that you became a Christian in 1952 right up until today, Mr. Falwell, is it your testimony that you do not, have not, and will not drink alcoholic and aperitif beverages?"

"That is correct."

"Have you ever sponsored, endorsed, or promoted the advertisement of any alcoholic beverages?

"Never at any time."

"Have you ever taken alcoholic beverages before going into the pulpit to deliver your message or address your congregation?"

"Never at any time."

The Jerry Falwell known to these jurors is in many respects a truly great American. He certainly is all-American, with an attractive combination of spiritual depth and self-made pragmatism, serious fidelity to principles and cantankerous good humor. The people in the Virginia mountains knew that as a kid Falwell had been a little wild, always skirting the edge of serious trouble with pranks and disorderly youthful exuberance. In classic American "boys will be boys" fashion Falwell's early wildness only made him more attractive, for he had turned that energy to constructive use; he had put Lynchburg on the map; he had become the quintessential hometown boy made good.

Falwell has a twin brother, Gene. The two boys were quite different. Jerry, like his father, is aggressive, ambitious, and a natural orator. Gene is easygoing and always quiet. As kids, Gene was bigger than Jerry and dominated their relationship. "We had many fights," Falwell once recalled. "Luckily, my father would stop them, because I would have gotten creamed."

Falwell was a straight-"A" student and was particularly good in math. He thought for a while that he wanted to be a journalist and considered applying to Notre Dame or Harvard for college. He was editor of his high school paper, *The Brookville Bee,* and came to understand the power of the press through the irritation his paper could cause the high school principal. Falwell was also a good athlete, starring in basketball and baseball. He may have made his biggest mark as a youth in Lynchburg, however, as a punky firecracker of a kid, always pulling some kind of stunt.

Falwell's reputation as a merry prankster started early. In grade school Falwell once locked his math teacher in a storage closet, and in high school he once put a live rat in the desk of his Latin teacher. Falwell was barred from giving his high school valedictory address because he had masterminded a scheme for the school's athletes to eat without meal tickets at the dining hall.

As a teenager Falwell hung around with a group of friends in Lynchburg who had some hell-raising tendencies. Falwell was a particularly popular member of the group, not the least because he owned a 1934 aluminum-top Plymouth. He admits that he did a lot of teenage drinking, mostly to be part of the group. On Halloween night in 1949 the Falwell crew set fifty railroad ties on fire on Campbell Avenue in Lynchburg and then diverted traffic down a dead-end street. The blaze got hot enough to ignite the asphalt on Campbell Avenue. "We watched with fascination," says Falwell, "as a stream of fire boiled toward the neighbor's picket fence like hot lava boils from a volcano." The Lynchburg police never caught up with the culprits. Falwell's gang also liked to station one of the puny kids in the group out in front of Lynchburg's Royal Cafe to pick fights with college boys. Just as they would begin to respond to the taunts, about forty members of Falwell's group would descend on the scene for a good old-fashioned brawl. Falwell emphasizes that the fights were never vicious—no knives or guns, just split lips and broken noses. He also likes to note with a laugh that they taught him the importance of superior numbers. (Could these victorious brawls decades before in Lynchburg somehow hold the key to Falwell's later insistence that the holy gospel stood four-square against the ratification of SALT

II?) Falwell still enjoys a practical joke; he's been known to set off a stink bomb in the church choir's airplane before running to his own Commander jet for the next stop on his sermon circuit.

In examining Falwell, Grutman quickly began to get to the emotional heart of the case by leading Falwell into the two most intimate relationships of his life: with his mother and with his God. The two seem inextricably intertwined.

"From the time you were fifteen until you reached majority, with whom did you live?"

"With my mother."

"Would you tell us, please, Mr. Falwell, what was the nature of the relationship that existed between you and your mother?"

"It was a very, very intimate relationship. My father, while a successful businessman who certainly loved and cared for his family, was an agnostic, and his father before him an agnostic. I, therefore, had from that side of the family no religious training. I didn't own a Bible. I was in my second year of college, actually, when I became a Christian. I would say that through the influence of my mother, who was a very godly woman, probably the closest to a saint that I have ever known, I was pointed to Christ."

Falwell testified that his conversion took place on January 30, 1952. (Apparently, whether or not one ever forgets "one's first time," the date of a conversion experience is customarily recalled with pinpoint accuracy.) Falwell had spent two years at Lynchburg College and was trying to decide whether to go into mechanical engineering or journalism, when he "felt a definite calling of God to the ministry." God's calling came via radio airwave, while Falwell was listening to Dr. Charles Fuller, an old-time-religion revival radio broadcaster from California.

Although his agnostic father would not allow Falwell's mother to force the children to go to church, they all observed her lifestyle, and she attended her Baptist Church each Sunday. When she left for church, she would leave the radio turned on to a religious broadcast. One fateful Sunday morning in January of 1952, Falwell listened to Dr. Fuller's radio show and "heard the Gospel of Jesus Christ for the first time, really; the message of his death, his burial, his resurrection," and realized that "all men need to develop a relationship with God through Christ." As Fuller preached that one Sunday morning, Falwell says, "a lump began to form in my throat. And it wasn't the hoecakes or the fatback bacon."

Fuller's show was the preeminent religious radio broadcast of its time. He was on 152 Mutual radio stations across the country and into South America. The show was called the *Old Fashioned Revival Hour,* and Falwell followed both its name and its format in his *Old Time Gospel Hour.* Fuller had an old-fashioned message but a modern understanding of the medium. He didn't thump and rave about hell and damnation but delivered his sermons in a calm, intimate voice. The show always began with the hymn "Jesus Saves" and was a potpourri of praying, preaching, and singing the gospel. Falwell's *Old Time Gospel Hour* eventually came to dwarf its predecessor in its reach and impact, but Falwell remains more or less true to Fuller's low-key style; when he gets worked up at all, it is usually over political and social issues, not fire and brimstone.

Back in January, 1952, Falwell didn't even know whether the radio preacher he was listening to was "Baptist or Catholic or whatever," but he had seen the light, and that light was not just Jesus, but Jesus of the airwaves: "With no religious background, I became convinced that this pioneer in Gospel broadcasting was ringing my spiritual bell."

And, oh, what a bell it proved to be. Falwell first left Lynchburg College and enrolled at Baptist Bible College in Springfield, Missouri. He spent four years there under the tutelage of Dr. John Rawlings, who became Falwell's mentor and teacher for the next thirty-two years. During his first years at the Bible College, Falwell wasn't sure what sort of religious work was really for him; he didn't know whether to try to be a youth worker, a missionary, or a pastor. To support himself in his last year of college, he began to work 180 miles away, in Kansas City, as a youth pastor. It was in Kansas City that he was asked to preach his first message to a congregation. He delivered the sermon and at that moment, "through a pulling-out of the fleece," became aware that preaching was what God wanted him to do.

A twenty-two-year-old pastor, however, does not exactly have churches standing in line to get his services. At first, he planned to go to Macon, Georgia, to help start a church with some friends. After his graduation from the college in Springfield, however, Falwell headed back to Lynchburg, to spend some time with Macel Pate, the woman he was engaged to marry. A small group of people in Lynchburg wanted to start a church and asked Falwell to help. He agreed and never got to Macon.

They rented a small cinderblock building on Thomas Road, only fifty-by-thirty feet, which had originally been owned by the Donald

Duck Bottling Company. Donald Duck had gone defunct, and the fledgling church was able to get the building at a bargain price. It was called the Thomas Road Baptist Church and started off with thirty-five members. The congregation's first job was to scrub the cola off the walls. Falwell was pastor, song-leader, secretary, and janitor. He was paid sixty-five dollars a week—though some of the church deacons thought that was extravagant. For the first several years, the local kids called it the "Donald Duck Baptist Church."

"Donald Duck" proved to be a prodigious success; the flock of the Thomas Road Baptist Church multiplied like the miracle of the loaves and fishes. In the twenty-eight years from its genesis to the Larry Flynt trial it grew to 28,000 members, the second largest church congregation in America. Falwell's electronic ministry came to reach far beyond Thomas Road, however, becoming a veritable empire of evangelism. When his religious broadcasting career first began in 1956, the church purchased half an hour a day on a local station for seven dollars a show, forty-nine dollars a week. By 1985 500 radio stations, 392 television stations, and over 10,000 cable television stations were carrying his daily half-hour program.

Falwell's success is largely the fruit of his enormous energy and indefatigable persistence in propagating his faith. Unlike many broadcast preachers, Falwell believes in making personal contact with his television flock. "You don't really get their support," he explains, "unless you've actually been there." His travel schedule is brutal. His typical day begins at 5:45 every morning and usually does not end until midnight or 1:00 A.M. He travels an average of 400,000 miles a year, with over 1,200 annual speaking engagements. If heaven has a frequent-flyer plan, Jerry Falwell has accumulated more free trips to paradise than he will ever be able to use.

This is the all-American crusader Larry Flynt had dared to desecrate. As Senator Jesse Helms, who had agreed to testify as a character witness, told the jury, "In my judgment, there is no finer citizen than Jerry Falwell. He is easily one of the most dedicated men, not only to his noble profession, but to this country. Words escape me to properly describe what this man means to so many, including me."

Falwell's energies, of course, are not all directed outside of Lynchburg. He has been careful constantly to nurture his hometown ties while establishing his national prominence. A good example of the successful marriage of national impact and local benefits is Falwell's creation of the the Lynchburg Christian Academy and the

Liberty Baptist College. Grutman very nicely paraded these local accomplishments before the jury.

"Our concept was to begin a Christian educational system that would eventually provide for Christian young people an educational program from kindergarten through a Ph.D. in a fully accredited institution. We started kindergarten through grade five," explained Falwell.

"Let's start with kindergarten: where is the kindergarten activity through grade school conducted, and what is the name of the institution?" asked Grutman.

"It is called Lynchburg Christian Academy. It is located in the Thomas Road Baptist Church facilities."

"How many students presently—well, let us say, through November of 1983—were enrolled in the Lynchburg Christian Academy?"

"Approximately fifteen hundred."

"Besides the Lynchburg Christian Academy, was there a school or schools of higher education which you created for advanced learning through the college level?"

"In the fall of 1971, we established what was then Lynchburg Baptist College, now Liberty Baptist College, and we added to that a seminary and an institute and a graduate program since that time."

"Who acquired the land on which Liberty Baptist College is situated?"

"The Thomas Road Baptist Church."

"How large is the land that belongs to Liberty Baptist College at the present time?"

"Forty-four hundred acres."

"How many buildings have been constructed since you created Liberty Baptist College on its campus?"

"Forty buildings in the last seven years."

"In November of 1983, approximately how many students were enrolled at Liberty Baptist College?"

"In the college itself, something over forty-three hundred."

"Do you yourself have some title as a functionary at either the Lynchburg Christian Academy or Liberty Baptist College?"

"I am Chancellor, which is an honorary title."

"Was it your intention, Mr. Falwell, for Liberty Baptist College to stay with only forty buildings and approximately six thousand students, or did you have plans for enlargement and expansion?"

"We purchased the great acreage in order to develop a Christian university of fifty thousand students in our twenty-five-year plan."

"And was such a plan in existence as of 1983?"

"It was."

"Was it your intention to enlarge the college into a university?"

"That is correct."

"Besides the college itself, does the college, or any institution that you are connected with, have other types of education, such as Bible study, which it sponsors?"

"We have a Bible institute and a seminary."

"Has the seminary graduated any ministers or pastors who have gone out in pursuit of their Christian vocation and established churches elsewhere?"

"We have seven hundred graduates from our schools who are now pastoring local churches, many of which they, themselves, started."

Falwell had parlayed his cinderblock "Donald Duck Church" into a vast complex of high-visibility national organizations and had become one of the most influential public figures of his time. If Larry Flynt is behind a maze of interlocking corporations controlling a wide variety of sexually oriented publications and enterprises, Jerry Falwell is very much his religious counterpart. Falwell and Flynt are both, in effect, human holding companies. Falwell is the driving persona behind an impressive array of religious and political entities. However impressive the profit margin for porn may be, morality is no slouch in the American market either. Falwell testified that for the fiscal year ending in June of 1985 the aggregate budget for all of the various ministries he directed was approximately one hundred million dollars.

Grutman led his client through a series of questions concerning the awards and accolades his efforts had won.

"When you left the Baptist Bible College in Springfield, what was the title of the degree that you received?"

"Th.G., that is a Graduate of Theology."

"Now, Mr. Falwell, I am going to ask you about some of the things that you have done since 1956, and I ask you, without seeming immodest, please answer these questions: besides receiving the Th.G. Degree, has there been any honorary degree or degrees conferred upon you since then and, if so, by whom?"

"I have received a number of them. I have received a Ph.D. from the Central University in Seoul, South Korea. I have received a Doctor of Divinity Degree from the Tennessee Temple University.

I have received a number of degrees—Doctor of Letters from the California Graduate School of Theology—but they are all honorary, like curls on the pig's tail. They don't add much to the meat."

"In any event, they attest to what those schools thought of you. Besides those honorary degrees—"

"Your Honor," Isaacman interrupted, "can counsel be directed not to add his own comments?"

"Yes, let's don't add editorial comments," Judge Turk admonished Grutman. "Go ahead, proceed."

"Mr. Falwell, have any other honors been conferred upon you besides those honorary degrees from those institutions of higher learning?"

"Are you speaking of academic honors?"

"Not necessarily academic honors—distinctions, recognitions by various publications of Christian groups."

"The Religious Heritage of America, which is a group headed by persons like Norman Vincent Peale, Clement Stone—many of the business leaders of the country, in 1979 honored me with 'Clergyman of the Year' in America. Food for the Hungry, which is a sort of Red Cross-type humanitarian—international humanitarian program—in '80 or '81, I have forgotten the year, awarded me 'Humanitarian of the Year Award'—awards like that."

It was against this background that Grutman attempted to impress the jury with the monstrous nature of Larry Flynt's ad parody. Flynt was perversely caricaturing the loving relationship between an all-American boy and his saintly mother.

"From the time that you and Mrs. Falwell were married, did your mother continue to play any part in your family life?"

"My mother was very unusual. She would never call our home, unless we called her. She was what some may refer to as an atypical mother-in-law. She was not typical. She never gave advice; you asked for it. I never heard her raise her voice, never heard her use a bad word. My wife and my mother were the closest of friends. Our children, until her death seven years ago at age eighty-two, considered her the number one grandmother in the world."

"Did you continue to maintain the close relationship that you had with your mother such as you described earlier in your testimony?"

"In spite of my traveling schedule, it was a rare week if I did not call her the night before and join her very early for breakfast at her home before flying out to meetings, at which time I would tell her what happened last week, what is going to happen this week, and at which time she just graciously listened while she prepared the meal for me. She was a little better cook than my wife; my wife is better now, but she was better then. But she knew exactly what I liked, and the way I liked it, and once a week I got permission to indulge."

"Did this close time, visiting with and seeing your mother, continue right up until she passed away?"

"It did, indeed."

"When you started your pastorate at Thomas Road Baptist Church, was your mother an active participant or a contributor to the church?"

"She became a charter member the day we opened the church."

"Did she financially support it?"

"She was probably our number one contributor until her death."

"The year she died—what year was that, Mr. Falwell?"

"1977."

"How old was your mother at that time?"

"She was eighty-two."

"Since her death, have you continued to think about her?"

"Just about daily."

"Was her memory precious to you?"

"Of course, my wife and children are my immediate family, and our relationship is as close as any family I have ever known, but I doubt if she were here but what she would say what I am saying, that we probably were as close as a mother and son could be on this earth."

"You have described your mother earlier in your testimony this morning as a woman closest to a saint that you have ever known of any woman you have ever met. Do you remember saying that?"

"And all the people who knew her would say 'Amen' to that."

"I must ask you, Mr. Falwell, in this case, insofar as it relates to this case, concerning some questions about your mother's personal conduct. To your knowledge, Mr. Falwell, was your mother a morally correct woman insofar as her personal life was concerned?"

"Without a blemish."

"By that I mean, was your mother a woman who committed adultery?"

"I would stake my life on her purity."

"Forgive this question, but I must ask it: was your mother anyone who ever committed incest?"

"Your Honor, excuse me, it seems to me that we could certainly stipulate to that," protested Isaacman, trying to break up the momentum of this line of questioning.

"Thanks a lot," said Grutman. "I want the evidence." He needed no favors from Isaacman.

"Let's address the remarks to the court," said Judge Turk.

"I would like to say, Your Honor," explained Isaacman, "that there is no issue in this case, that certainly we will stipulate that his mother was a person of the finest moral character and that she is now deceased and that this really is not necessary."

"Your Honor, this case is—" began Grutman.

"I will let him answer the question," Turk cut him off. "Let's move along."

"Mr. Falwell, specifically, did you and your mother ever commit incest?" asked Grutman.

"Absolutely not."

You don't have to be Perry Mason to realize the effect that this whole line of questioning had on the jury. Yet even the hometown fans must have had some pause. If Falwell was a superstar and basically a nice guy, he was also, they knew, no wimp. He could be tough and unrelenting in his crusading. However rotten Larry Flynt's joke might have been, hadn't Jerry Falwell in some sense asked for it? For Falwell had done the one thing sure to draw heavy fire in American society: He had crossed the border from religion to politics. Surely it was that venture that drew the flak from Flynt. Would Falwell simply have to live with such attacks? Had he crossed the border into a reputational free-fire zone?

This combination of religion and politics formed the next segment of Falwell's testimony, revealing much about what *Falwell v. Flynt* means in the larger scheme of American life.

Chapter 13

"**A** nd therefore, render unto Caesar the things that are Caesar's, and God the things that are God's." Falwell's decision to enter the arena of social and political debate in the United States inevitably weighed on the minds of the jurors. As hot as the fires of hell may burn, American clergy are usually insulated from the fires of vicious attack from members of their own congregations. But no such immunities are granted in the arena of national political debate. If Falwell could not stand the heat of those political fires, should he have stayed out of the kitchen? Falwell and Grutman dealt with those concerns in two stages. First, Falwell vigorously defended his entry into politics as fully consistent with both the First Amendment's principle of separation of church and state and with the fundamentalist Christian religious tradition from which his ministry sprang. Falwell's second step was to demonstrate how, even in the midst of fierce and passionate battles over such wrenching American debates as abortion, gay rights, or pornography, he had never encountered an attack so personally mean and coarse as Larry Flynt's.

Grutman started matters off by questioning Falwell on his influence in American culture.

"In various polls," he asked, "for example, the *Good Housekeeping* Poll, were you included in that poll as an influential American?"

"For the past few years, a number of times," said Falwell. "Last year, second most-admired American behind the President."

"Are you aware of any poll in which *U.S. News and World Report* has ever included you?"

"Each year, I am among the twenty-five most influential Americans."

"Have you written any books, Mr. Falwell?"

"Oh, a dozen or so."

"They have been about what kind of subjects?"

"Most of them about religious subjects, several in recent years on moral and social issues."

The "moral and social" issues alluded to in this last answer, of course, are what really made Jerry Falwell the formidable American public figure that he is. His comment concerning moral and social issues is pregnant with meaning for the lawsuit *Falwell v. Flynt,* for in many ways it is the peculiar mix of politics and religion that both the lawsuit and Jerry Falwell are all about. If Falwell is lord of a vast religious conglomerate, the most significant of the companies in his empire is the Moral Majority, Inc., founded in 1979 with Falwell as its president.

Falwell explained to the jury why a fundamentalist minister from Virginia would spearhead what is clearly a national political, not a religious, organization. As his television and radio ministry grew, he became increasingly aware of the intertwining of religious and political issues in contemporary American life. Falwell, a conservative minister deeply concerned about issues such as abortion and pornography, felt the need to speak out but was faced with both pragmatic and philosophical impediments to addressing such issues from the pulpit.[1] On the one hand, as the line between religious proselytizing and political advocacy became increasingly blurry, Falwell was concerned that tax exemptions for his church ministry could be jeopardized. On the other, as Falwell testified, "It also brought outcries from people everywhere that you were violating the First Amendment, although we saw others doing it who were not getting similar treatment."

Those concerns made it strategically wise to farm out political activism to a satellite organization. The founding of the Moral Majority was seen as an antidote to these problems, for in creating an explicitly political arm and using that political arm as the forum for advancing the social agenda of the new Christian Right, Falwell and his followers could not be accused of breaching the wall of separation between church and state. (Precisely the same concern, a decade later, induced Pat Robertson to resign his ministry on the day he declared himself a candidate for the Republican nomination for President of the United States.)

This concern with the separation of church and state is worth noting, for it is a key to understanding what makes Jerry Falwell tick and why he is so influential in American culture. Like the Nashville country singer who crosses over into mainstream popular music in order to really make it big, Falwell thrust himself onto the center stage of American life as a religious/political crossover artist. If he had stayed within the confines of the Thomas Road Baptist Church and the broadcasts of the *Old Time Gospel Hour,* if he had limited his sermons to witnessing to Jesus and railing on the seven deadly sins, Falwell could never have become a consummate threat to Larry Flynt's being. Falwell's conscious decision to straddle the religious and political worlds is what goaded so many of his enemies, including Larry Flynt.

Flynt's flailing, drug-dazed venom usually came out in the warped epithets "asshole" and "motherfucker"; at his inarticulate best, Flynt occasionally managed a critique as precise as "hypocrite." Flynt's hatred was driven, however, by an intuition shared by many other Americans who would not dream of either associating with Flynt or participating in his personalized, mean-spirited attacks on Falwell, but who nevertheless reflexively blanch at Falwell's easy intermingling of religion, morality, and politics. What lies behind the wild anger of Flynt and the controlled fear of many more temperate Americans? What could be so bad about Falwell's creation of the Moral Majority or Pat Robertson's quest for the presidency?

Falwell revealed in his testimony that he thinks the outcry against his mingling of church and state is largely illegitimate—that it is used selectively against conservative Christians by those who simply do not like the political and social goals of the Christian Right but who have no qualms about mingling religion and politics when their causes are being advanced. "We saw others doing it," he lamented, "who were not getting similar treatment." If Catholics, Jews, and liberal Protestants can freely capitalize on their religious stock in advancing political causes, why are conservative Evangelicals somehow summarily disqualified? He who is without sin should cast the first stone, and his enemies, Falwell suspects, are not truly motivated by some abstract philosophical objection to mixing religion and politics but rather are afraid of just how effective Falwell's particular mix can be.

"Nobody's ever accused the National Council of Churches of

mixing religion and politics," Falwell complained in 1980. "But when old Jerry gets into it, that's violating separation of church and state. The problem isn't violating anything. The problem is that we don't agree with those buzzards—and that we outnumber them."

Among the things that many of the "buzzards" do not agree with is Falwell's position on pornography. Falwell's testimony made it quite clear that he would do everything in his power to stamp out the influence of one particular species of buzzard—pornographers such as Larry Flynt.

"Have you attempted to influence public opinion against pornography?" asked Grutman.

"With every breath in my body," said Falwell.

Chapter 14

P ornography, of course, is only one small part of the picture for the Moral Majority. When it began in the late 1970s, the alliance of the political and religious right was a marriage made in heaven. It had dreams of changing American society across an entire spectrum of social issues. The emerging leaders of the extreme political Right in the 1970s were people like Richard Viguerie, activist for George Wallace and Senator John Tower and the mastermind of mass direct-mail fundraising for conservative political candidates; Howard Phillips, the founder of the Conservative Caucus, an organization of conservative activitists; and Paul Weyrich, director of the conservative group Committee for the Survival of a Free Congress.[1]

These leaders have no religious ties to fundamentalist Baptists— Phillips is Jewish, and both Viguerie and Weyrich are Catholic—but they are clearly linked ideologically. As early as 1974, tentative flirtations between the political and religious Right began to surface. Conservative beer magnate Adolph Coors helped fund voter profile studies in pursuit of a political strategy aimed at attracting the "Christian moral voter." Small pilot efforts in 1976 and 1978 demonstrated the ability of the conservative political and religious coalitions to defeat liberal political candidates. In 1978 they helped unseat Senators Dick Clark of Iowa and Thomas McIntyre of New Hampshire and helped elect Governor Fog James of Alabama. Conservative targets included liberal senators such as Mike Gravel of Alaska, George McGovern of South Dakota, Frank Church of Idaho, John

Culver of Iowa, and Alan Cranston of California. "Christians gave Jimmy Carter his razor-thin margin of victory of 1976," said Colonel Dunnon, of the conservative religious magazine, *Christian Voice.* "We plan to reverse that in 1980."

Evangelists Jerry Falwell, Pat Robertson, and Jim Bakker were all buoyed by the successes. Bakker announced, "Our goal is to influence all viable candidates on issues important to the church." Robertson claimed that "We have enough votes to run the country." Interestingly, Pat Robertson did sound a cautionary note about conservative activism, claiming that "God isn't a right-winger or a left-winger. The evangelists stand in danger of being used and manipulated."

It was Falwell, however, who truly captured the moment. During a 1979 strategy session among leaders of the political and religious Right, Paul Weyrich used the term "moral majority." Falwell, the natural-born preacher that he is, knew a nice turn of phrase when he heard one and seized those magic words as the perfect symbol for the new conservatives. Falwell, Weyrich, and others in their circle fervently believe that the real America is *their* America, but that a cadre of liberal elites running the federal government, the prestige universities, and the national media have managed to impose an immoral agenda on the quiescent majority.

As the success of Falwell's mailings in raising money to fight Larry Flynt attest, Falwell's *Old Time Gospel Hour* prime donor mailing list is one potent fundraising roster. The Moral Majority had set a $3 million first-year budget. Using the *Old Time Gospel Hour* list, the organization raised $1 million in the first month. Weyrich was careful to downplay the Moral Majority's instant impact. "Anybody who thinks this group is going to contribute to a political revolution this election is going to be disappointed." Phillips, however, was more optimistic. "The basic problem, only now being overcome, is to get people involved," he said. "Once that is done, this movement will be formidable."

As he toured the country, Falwell held luncheons for born-again pastors. He urged them to replicate his voter registration efforts. "If there is one person in this room not registered," Falwell told pastors, "repent of it—it's a sin." The order of the day was "Get them saved, baptized, and registered."

His "I Love America" roadshow was like a fundamentalist rock-'n'-roll tour, with a thirty-three member choir and a stage resplendent in American flags. Holding a Bible in the air, Falwell preached:

"If a man stands by this book, vote for him. If he doesn't, don't."
The number of fundamentalist voters registered by these efforts is a matter of dispute. Cautious, relatively "hard" estimates placed the number at two million. Softer figures from the Moral Majority estimate the new fundamentalist voters at between four and eight million. However many million, the numbers are significant. In the 1980 election, the only region of the country with an increase in voter turnout was the heavily Evangelical South.

The Moral Majority, Inc., worked to focus and mobilize the latent outrage felt by many Americans toward the liberal usurpers of power and to restore the United States to moral sanity. All moral comers would be welcome, including right-thinking (in both senses of the term) Catholics, Jews, Protestants, Mormons, and fundamentalists. The only litmus test would be commitment to the proper moral causes. In his 1981 activist manifesto, *Listen, America!,*[2] Falwell makes the agenda clear, ticking off the five major sins of America:

The first is abortion. Falwell argues that our Supreme Court justices in the 1973 abortion case *Roe v. Wade* authorized the killing of millions of babies. "The Nazis murdered six million Jews," Falwell writes, "and certainly the Nazis fell under the hand of the Judgment of God for those atrocities." Christian America, he admonishes, has murdered more unborn innocents than that.

Homosexuality is second. Falwell says that the Bible designates this sin as an act of a "reprobate mind," and "even the ancient Greeks, among whom homosexuality was fairly prevalent, never legally condoned its practice." Falwell warns sternly against giving gays legal status as a legitimate minority group suffering from discrimination, arguing that "If our nation legally recognizes homosexuality, we will put ourselves under the same Hand of Judgment as Sodom and Gomorrah."

America's third major sin is pornography. The $4 billion-a-year pornography industry, Falwell claims, "is probably the most devastating moral influence of all upon our young people." For Falwell, the connection between porn and sinful behavior is obvious: "Sex magazines deliberately increase the problem of immoral lust and thus provoke increased adultery, prostitution, and sexual child abuse." Pornography, argues Falwell, is not a victimless crime; its victims are the "wives and children" left behind in broken homes caused by adultery. (In asserting that pornography's victims are "wives and children," Falwell apparently discounts any lust-driven infidelity by women exposed to pornography.) Pornography, says Falwell, is the "No. 1 enemy against marital fidelity and therefore against the family itself."

Fourth on the Falwell top sin chart is humanism. "The contemporary philosophy that glorifies man as man, apart from God," Falwell wrote, "is the ultimate outgrowth of evolutionary science and secular education." Humanism, claims Falwell, ultimately rests on existentialism, which has become the religion of the public schools. It glorifies the moral neutrality of the popular phrases "Do your own thing" and "If it feels good, do it." This morally corrosive philosophy "has no room for God and makes man the measure of all things."

The final major sin is the fractured family. The Bible pattern of the family (presumably Falwell means the post-polygamous Bible pattern) has been virtually discarded by contemporary Americans. Movies and magazines emphasize physical gratification to the point that love is a forgotten value. Our vocabulary today includes communal, common-law, homosexual, and even transsexual "marriages." This is not, Falwell argues, a move toward "an alternative family lifestyle" but a move toward "the brink of destruction."

Modern Evangelicals agree with the general fundamentalist commitment to the primacy and inerrancy of Scripture and share the faith in spiritual renewal (being "born again") as the central religious experience in Christian life. The Evangelicals are a distinct branch of fundamentalists, however, a branch that tends to eschew the more extreme reflexes of fundamentalism, such as narrow legalistic preoccupation with the scriptural text or bitter separatism. The modern Evangelicals tend to emphasize participation in mainstream American life, displaying a more palatable, less divisive form of fundamentalist exuberance. Bob Jones of Bob Jones University and Jerry Falwell both may be fundamentalists, but Falwell would never be heard preaching Bob Jones's gospel of racial separatism and the Pope as Antichrist.[3]

Falwell has, however, tended to take a low-profile position on race issues. To his credit, he began baptizing blacks in the early 1960s. His Lynchburg Christian Academy is integrated, though only nominally so, with just a handful of black students. "I don't think we've gone after blacks aggressively," he admits.

"When I was a boy in Virginia, in a redneck society, patriotism was just a part of life," explains Falwell. "Whatever was for America was right, whether it was right or not. I had an overdose of patrio-

tism as a boy. I also grew up in a segregated society. I was a segrega-
tionist, and Thomas Road Church was five years old before God
flushed that out of my system. I thought segregation and spirituality
were the same. I would have fought you over saying that I was
prejudiced; I would say it was scriptural. When I first baptized a
black man in this church, it caused quite a ripple. A number of years
after that, Thomas Road Baptist Church, which had always been
patriotic in a redneck way, really became patriotic in the Christian
way. It was through an osmosis by which the Spirit of God, through
the Word of God, taught me that I was wrong and made me willing
to say it publicly. It cost me a lot of friends for a while. That's not
an issue any more, but it was a big issue in this town twenty years
ago. We still have that to overcome with the older black people in
this community who remember Jerry Falwell in that context."

Falwell has distinguished himself as a Zionist through and
through; it is hard to imagine any Christian leader, Protestant or
Catholic, more ardently friendly to Jews. (This has not, however,
necessarily been reciprocated by the Jewish community. His extreme
conservative positions have made him an anathema to many Jewish
voters.) Falwell explains his support for the Jewish community primarily in biblical terms. "I support the Jews," he says, "first, for
biblical reasons; I take the Abrahamic covenant literally." For Falwell tolerance for Jews is essential to America's claim as a shining
city on a hill. To be a chosen nation, America must have compassion
for the chosen people. "God has blessed America, because we have
blessed the Jews," Falwell insists. "God has also blessed America,
because we have done more for the cause of world evangelization
than any other nation. I also support the Jews, because I think
historically the evidence is on their side that Palestine belongs to
them. Legally, they have had the right to be in the land since 1948.
I also support the Jews, because, from the humanitarian perspective,
they have the right to exist, and there are a hundred million neighbors who are committed to their extinction. I also support the Jews,
because they are the only true friends America has in the Middle
East."

Falwell's affection for Jews is so pronounced and so dramatically
visible against the backdrop of the traditionally pervasive anti-
Semitism of conservative southern Christians that he has the rare
luxury of being able to joke about the issue with impunity. At a rally
in Richmond he acknowledged that much of his audience harbored
ill will toward Jews, and then he chided the crowd: "And I know why

you don't like the Jew. . . . He can make more money accidentally than you can make on purpose."

Falwell has preached as a guest before virtually every religious denomination in America—Catholic, Jewish, Mormon, and Protestant. He once said that if he accepted every invitation he receives to preach in a synagogue, he would be preaching in a synagogue every week.

With its ecumenical membership and its agenda of no abortion, no gays, no porn, no existential humanism, and no fractured families, the basic supposition of the Moral Majority seems plausible. Perhaps a too-long-silent majority of Americans *does,* in fact, subscribe to these positions. The genius of this political-religious gospel is twofold. First, it crosses the lines of many religious sects. The Falwell list is a near-perfect recreation of the theological agenda of Pope John Paul II. Conservative Catholics, Jews, Mormons, and Protestants (even nonfundamentalist Protestants) can easily be brought on board this morality train.

Second, the list is not exclusively negative and bitter. While blind conservative prejudice against gays and the old philosophical boogeymen of evolution and existentialism and secular humanism are prominent on the agenda, the Falwellian crusade is careful to simultaneously accentuate the power of love. Fight abortion, because we should love the unborn; fight pornography, because we should love fidelity to spouses and children; fight humanism, because we should love God. In attacking a culture that advises its members to "do it" if it "feels good" and in bemoaning the American preoccupation with physical sex at the expense of deeper love and commitment, Falwell genuinely appeals to a pervasive disquiet in modern culture, sounding themes no longer just extremist and separatist, and he is at once disturbing and comforting. The agenda of the Moral Majority is no longer a fundamentalist harangue; it is a serious appeal to the nation to take hold of its quality of life. The message is no longer "Kill the Commies and the homos"; it is "Come home to family, fidelity, normalcy, God, and love."

Chapter 15

L arry Flynt and *Hustler* were technically on trial in Roanoke only for the Campari ad satire. Inevitably, however, the struggle for the hearts and minds of the jurors tempted Grutman to try to put *Hustler* magazine on trial in a broader sense. Falwell was thus asked whether or not he had appeared in other issues of *Hustler.* Falwell noted that "I have since made it my business through counsel to obtain an issue of every ensuing issue, which I have been in a number of times. As a matter of fact, through counsel, I received previous issues in which I found a very long trial of Jerry Falwell appearances." Many of these other appearances in *Hustler* are every bit as crude as the Campari ad satire.

Grutman showed Falwell a particularly lewd portrayal of Falwell and former Chief Justice Warren Burger. "Did you and Chief Justice Burger ever engage in the kind of conduct that is depicted in the December 1983 issue of *Hustler Magazine?*"

"We have not."

Grutman missed no trick in raising the Roanoke jury's disgust level to maximum heights. He coaxed Falwell into reviewing the various sexual combinations to be found in the magazine, from female-on-female to black-on-white.

"I draw your attention to a few specific things, Mr. Falwell. As you go through this magazine, speaking only about this magazine, does it contain pictures of lesbians?"

"It does."

"Full color?"

"Full color."

"Does it show naked women lewdly exposing themselves?"

"Yes."

"Does it have pictures of interracial sex?"

"It does."

"Does it have advertisements for women offering themselves for sexual experiences?"

"Many."

"Does it contain advertisements for sexual aids and mechanical devices?"

"Yes."

"When you saw your picture on the inside cover of a magazine that contained such contents, how did you feel about that, Mr. Falwell?"

"It would be difficult to describe my emotions, because I have never in my life seen such a despicable array of garbage."

Grutman's mastery of the courtroom stage, however, was nowhere more apparent than his line-by-line dissection of the Campari ad with Reverend Falwell. The jury would not be permitted by Grutman to treat the Campari ad satire as a joke. Each sentence of the ad was taken up in isolation and fingered and fondled to knead out every repulsive nuance, all through Falwell's own testimony. The drama of having Falwell read and reexperience each line added to the courtroom shock value.

"Mr. Falwell, you can read along with Exhibit One, which has been received in evidence—and the jury can see this enlargement which has been placed here as a visual aid. The caption reads: 'Jerry Falwell talks about his first time,' and there appears to be a photograph of you. Do you recognize that photograph?"

"I do."

"Had you ever posed for that photograph?"

"Somewhere."

"But was the photograph when you posed for it somewhere intended to be used for this ad?"

"Absolutely not."

"Did you, Mr. Falwell, give consent for the use of your photograph in this ad?"

"I did not."

"Did you, Mr. Falwell, give consent for the use of your name in this ad?"

"I did not."

"Underneath your photograph, it reads: 'FALWELL,' in all caps with a colon, and then there is some text following it. Do you read that as being words attributed to you?"

"I interpret it that way."

"All right, it reads: 'FALWELL: My first time was in an outhouse outside Lynchburg, Virginia.' Then it says, 'INTER-VIEWER,' in all caps with a colon, and then it reads: 'Wasn't it a little cramped?' Do you read that as sort of a dialogue between you and this interviewer?"

"I do."

" 'FALWELL: Not after I kicked the goat out.' 'INTER-VIEWER: I see. You must tell me all about it.' 'FALWELL: I never *really* expected to make it with Mom, but then after she showed all of the other guys in town such a good time I figured, "What the hell." ' Now, referring to the use of the verb 'make it' in the last citation, according to your interpretation of reading it, Mr. Falwell, did that have a sexual connotation?"

"That is street vernacular for sexual intercourse."

"Next: 'INTERVIEWER: But your mom? Isn't that a bit odd?' 'FALWELL: I don't think so. Looks don't mean that much to me in a woman.' 'INTERVIEWER: Go on.' 'FALWELL: Well, we were drunk off our God-fearing asses on Campari, ginger ale and soda—that's called a Fire and Brimstone—at the time. And Mom looked better than a Baptist whore with a hundred dollar donation.' Did you ever say that?"

"Never."

"Have you ever drunk a Fire and Brimstone?"

"Never heard of one until I read it here."

"Have you ever drunk Campari?"

"Never."

" 'INTERVIEWER,' continuing, 'Campari in the crapper with Mom . . . how interesting. Well, how was it?' 'FALWELL: The Campari was great, but Mom passed out before I could come.' I draw your attention to the last quotation attributed to you and specifically to the verb 'come' in that context; as you read that, Mr. Falwell, what did the word 'come' in that context mean?"

"Again, it is street vernacular for reaching a sexual climax."

"The next citation out of this publication, it says, 'INTER-VIEWER: Did you ever try it again?' 'FALWELL: Sure . . .' Do you see the impersonal pronoun 'it'? The antecedent 'it' refers to what?"

"In my opinion, the sexual relationship with my mother referred to in the previous statement."

"Then it says, 'FALWELL: Sure . . . lots of times, but not in the outhouse. Between Mom and the shit, the flies were too much to bear.' As you read that, Mr. Falwell, 'Sure . . . lots of times,' does that refer to Campari and soda or having sex with your mother lots of times as you read it?"

"Obviously, sex with my mother."

" 'INTERVIEWER: We meant the Campari.' 'FALWELL: Oh, yeah, I always get sloshed before I go out to the pulpit. You don't think I could lay down all that bullshit *sober*, do you?' Did you ever say that?"

"Of course not."

"Do you ever drink Campari before you go to the pulpit?"

"No."

"Or any other alcoholic beverage?"

"Never."

"The word 'sloshed,' do you understand that to be a colloquialism or slang for drunk?"

"Yes."

"Then below that, Mr. Falwell, do you see where there is a little 'c' with a circle indicating copyright. It says, '©1983—imported by Campari, USA, New York, New York, 48 proof Spirit Aperitif (Liqueur).' Then, on the bottom, I draw your attention: It says, 'Campari, like all liquor, was made to mix you up. It's a light, 48-proof, refreshing spirit, just mild enough to make you drink too much before you know you are schnokered. For your first time, mix it with orange juice or maybe some white wine. Then you won't remember anything the next morning.' All bold face: 'Campari. The mixable that smarts.' Then, over to the right is a beautiful photograph of the bottle, orange juice glass with a peel and some ice in it, and then another shorter, rounder glass with some orange and ice in it, tongs and some ice, and then Campari with a little circle around the little 'r' indicating registered trademark, 'Campari,' all caps, bold type, 'You'll never forget your first time.' Then, at the very bottom, in much smaller type there is a teeny-weeny asterisk and it says, 'Ad parody—not to be taken seriously.' Do you see that, Mr. Falwell?"

"I see it."

"When you first looked at it, did you notice that teeny-weeny little type at the bottom?"

"I did not."

"When you read it, did you take this ad seriously?"

"As seriously as anything I have ever read in my life."

Grutman wanted the jury to feel what Jerry Falwell felt, so he played the scene slowly, exploring Falwell's first exposure to the ad in painstaking detail.

"Would you tell His Honor and the members of this jury what your personal reaction was when you read this ad in Exhibit One over for the first time?"

"I think I have never been as angry as I was at that moment. My first impression was that Campari had purchased an ad in the magazine, because I had seen a similar ad in decent magazines earlier, and my first thought was to get on the phone to Campari. Our in-house attorney and I talked it over. My anger became a more rational and deep hurt. I somehow felt that in all of my life I had never believed that human beings could do something like this. I really felt like weeping. I am not a deeply emotional person; I don't show it. I think I felt like weeping."

"How long did this sense of anger last?"

"To this present moment."

"You said a moment ago that you had seen Campari ads in decent magazines. Had you ever seen an ad that had a text like this?"

"I was raised up—as I said, my father was an agnostic; I didn't own a Bible. I had gone into two years of college before I became a Christian and purchased a Bible. I think I had heard—both my brothers were in the Navy. I think I have heard about everything you could hear, that human mouths could speak. I played football, captain of the football team. I can't imagine at any of our wildest events ever hearing language like this or seeing or feeling the garbage nature of this kind of production."

"You say that it almost brought you to tears. In your whole life, Mr. Falwell, had you ever had a personal experience of such intensity that could compare with the feeling that you had when you saw this ad?"

"Never had. Since I have been a Christian, I don't think I have ever intentionally hurt anybody. I am sure I have hurt people, but not with intent. I certainly have never physically attacked anyone in my life. I really think that, at the moment, if Larry Flynt had been nearby I might have physically reacted."

"But, of course, you didn't?"

"I did not and I have not and I would not."

This testimony by Falwell was intriguing. Although the intensity of Falwell's distress certainly rang true, his distress did not appear to have come so much from the content of the ad *as such,* as from his sudden confrontation with such great evil. He was less appalled at the satire of his having had sex with his mother than with the perverseness of the mind capable of publishing such malicious filth. Falwell had finally met the devil face-to-face, and the confrontation was so distressful that Falwell sued him. (One might imagine a sort of theological *People's Court,* in which Judge Wapner's announcer righteously admonishes: "If Satan does something wrong to you, you don't have to stand for it. You take him to court!")

"When you saw this publication, Mr. Falwell, did you think that it was funny?" asked Grutman.

"Not in the least."

"Did you think that any of the things that I have shown to you were funny?"

"Not in the least."

"Did you think that the average person seeing these things would find them funny or hilarious?"

"I did not."

"Mr. Falwell, as a man active in public life and who has taken positions about subjects which may be considered controversial, have you been criticized or opposed in your ideas by various publications?"

"Daily, almost."

"Have you ever had caricatures drawn of you by cartoonists?"

"Again, almost daily."

"Have you ever felt badly about criticism that you read about yourself or responsible caricatures?"

"I rather enjoy most of it."

"But with respect to the materials that I have shown to you in this case, what is your reaction or response to it in terms of your feelings?"

"It is the most hurtful, damaging, despicable, low-type personal attack that I can imagine one human being can inflict upon another."

Chapter 16

W as Falwell hypocritical in coming down so hard on *Hustler*'s satire? It is not as if Falwell himself has never inflicted any distress. Falwell argues, however, that unlike Flynt, he has never lost sight of the basic proprieties of civilized discourse. Which is not to say that Falwell has never been caught in his own reckless gaffes. In a Moral Majority rally in Alaska, he claimed that at a meeting at the White House with President Jimmy Carter, Falwell and other evangelists had pointedly asked Carter why he had "known, practicing homosexuals" on his staff. Falwell alleged that Carter replied that it was because he considered himself "president of all the American people." When the White House got wind of the story, angry presidential aides released a transcript of the meeting, proving that no such exchange had ever taken place. Falwell recanted. "I shouldn't have said it," he said. "Obviously it was a reckless statement."

Falwell's pitches, at times, have come dangerously close to selling indulgences. One mailing that went out over his name states: "Maybe your financial situation seems impossible. Put Jesus first in your stewardship and allow Him to bless you financially." Falwell denied knowledge of the letter, but it went out under his watch.

Some of Falwell's biggest miscalculations have been close to home, in Virginia. A liberal Virginia state senator and long-time Falwell rival, Joseph F. Fitzpatrick, introduced a resolution in the state senate that encouraged schools to distribute copies of Thomas Jefferson's famous Virginia statutes on religious freedom. Falwell

JERRY FALWELL V. LARRY FLYNT 119

took the resolution as a rebuke and sent a letter to every state senator condemning the resolution. But in Virginia, not even Jerry Falwell can tangle with the memory of Thomas Jefferson. Whether or not a majority of modern Virginians would vote to pass a ringing proclamation of separation of church and state as an original proposition is beside the point. Falwell was slapped back by unanimous vote.

In all of these battles, however, Falwell claims he never experienced anything so dirty and personal as Flynt's attack. Flynt had struck a low blow; his bizarre attack is well beyond the bounds of the sort of vigorous, but always civilized, discourse Falwell is used to.

Falwell, for example, had engaged in a spirited exchange on the Phil Donahue show in a debate over disarmament with Reverend William Sloane Coffin, the liberal former Yale chaplain, who is remembered for his resistance, with Dr. Benjamin Spock and others, to the war in Vietnam. Both men were cordial to one another, but deadly serious in their views. Falwell argued for an arms build-up, saying, "If I trusted my neighbors, I would not lock my door at night. But I do lock my door at night, and I don't trust the Russians." Coffin responded that, while he did not trust Russian behavior toward dissidents or an open society, he trusted them to "realize we have a moral responsibility to avoid global suicide." Coffin then attacked Falwell where it hurts, saying in a rising voice, "If you want to talk about being moral, I would suggest to you that *abortion* is the issue, the abortion of the entire human race." Falwell responded with his own impassioned plea for a strong defense, actually winning over a majority of the studio audience—an audience normally not disposed to favor Falwell's views. Never, however, did Falwell degrade the debate with a personal attack on Coffin.

Falwell has excellent instincts regarding the use of the media. He does not worry excessively about the attacks he receives from the press because he is convinced that these attacks don't play well in Peoria. Television is the difference. "Someone in the print media can make what you say sound the way he wants it to sound," Falwell explains. "This is not possible on *Face the Nation, Meet the Press,* or with Phil Donahue or Tom Snyder, where we have been able to eyeball the people."

Falwell's talent at charming and disarming his enemies was displayed during a tour of Ivy League campuses. Yale President A. Bartlett Giamatti first invited Falwell to speak in the fall of 1982, and Falwell later delivered addresses at Harvard and Dartmouth. The crowds were openly hostile, with some at Harvard chanting "Hitler, Falwell, go to hell" and "Racist, fascist pig." Falwell maintained his aplomb and good humor. He chastised one questioner for accusing the Moral Majority of book-burning, answering that the Moral Majority has never advocated that any book be banned and pointing out the double standard of falsely accusing him of book-burning while trying to keep his ideas off campus.

Perhaps nothing makes the point so well as Falwell's relationship with his ideological nemesis, Senator Edward Kennedy. Kennedy came to Lynchburg at Falwell's invitation to speak to five thousand students at Liberty Baptist College. Falwell and Kennedy disagree on matters of substance, but they got along well. Kennedy dined at Falwell's home and attended a reception later. As Cal Thomas, a spokesman for the Moral Majority, quipped, "Sadat went to Jerusalem, and now Kennedy has come to Lynchburg."

At the trial Grutman asked Falwell to contrast Flynt's attack on him with the civilized debates he has had with William Sloane Coffin or Ted Kennedy.

"Have you ever debated with Ted Kennedy?"

"Well, I have had Ted Kennedy as a speaker at Liberty Baptist College, and I will be debating him February 5th in Washington at the Congressional Prayer Breakfast."

"Would you regard Ted Kennedy as a person who shares or is opposed to many of the principles and ideas that you hold?"

"I can think of two or three things he and I agree on."

"But that is all."

"That would be approximately."

"If you had to talk about somebody that you might think of as a philosophical enemy, would Ted Kennedy be one of them?"

"Without a question, he would lead the list, and I think he would say the same about me."

"Have you ever personally attacked Ted Kennedy?"

"We are very good friends. I think probably I would say that he has attacked me, and I think he would say that I have attacked him philosophically."

"Has Ted Kennedy ever attacked you concerning your personal family life?"

"Never once, and never have I attacked his family or him in any personal way."

Indeed, not only has Falwell always been civilized toward his ideological enemies, he has also always been civilized toward those whom he so loves to hate: the pornography pushers of the world. If

Jerry Falwell fights smut-peddlers with every breath in his body, he claims it is still nothing personal.

"Mr. Falwell," asked Grutman, "in opposing pornography as a philosophical idea, have either you or the Moral Majority ever personally picked on the intimate personal life of any person who was himself in your judgment a pornographer?"

"Never at any time. I don't know anything about the personal lives of the people I consider to be the porn kings."

"Let's take a man by the name of Larry Flynt; I ask you, Mr. Falwell, at any time from 1979 until the present or from 1956, when you first entered the ministry, have you ever personally attacked the private, personal, intimate life of Larry Flynt?"

"I have never at any time attacked his personal life. I have known nothing of his personal life; I have never met him. We have never crossed paths."

"In opposing pornography, however, have you opposed that concept?"

"I think that anyone that follows my messages would hear me occasionally refer to the names of Hugh Hefner, Bob Guccione, Larry Flynt, and others that I refer to as porn kings and whose right to perform and do their business under the law, I agree, is unimpeachable, but whose profession I consider to be abhorrent."

"I show you, Mr. Falwell, and I will hold this up in front of the jury; this is Exhibit Three in evidence, the re-publication of your picture in that Campari ad was placed in the magazine next to a feature called 'Asshole of the Month,' a man named Al Goldstein. Do you know who Al Goldstein is?"

"Yes, he is one of those porn kings that I constantly preach about."

"Do you know the publication that he produces?"

"Its name is *Screw Magazine.*"

"Now, this feature 'Asshole of the Month,' had you ever been given that title, to your knowledge, in any prior publication of *Hustler Magazine*?"

"Yes, I have."

"On page twenty, the same ad that was published in the November issue appears again. Did you learn that this re-publication of the ad on which you were suing in this lawsuit had again been inserted into the pages of *Hustler Magazine*?"

"I did."

"When you learned of that, Mr. Falwell, what was your reaction or response or feeling?"

"It was a re-opening of an already very deep wound of personal anguish and hurt and suffering, such as nothing in my adult life I ever recall before."

"Did you you feel debilitated by it?"

"I did, indeed."

"Now, you have mentioned what your reaction was within the first days after first seeing the November 1983 issue. Had those feelings that you have earlier described to us gone away between October or November of 1983 and February or March of '84?"

"They had not."

"To what extent did they continue to affect you in your daily living, thinking, and feeling?"

"I have never been to a psychiatrist or a psychologist in my life for personal help. I am not sure but what I feel that, as a Christian and a minister—I am not sure it would not be wrong for me to do it. I just have a personal feeling that, as a Christian, I should be able to take my personal burdens to the Lord. I did not cut my schedule back; I did not stop anything I was doing, but I can tell you it has created the most difficult year of performance, physically, mentally, emotionally, in all of my life. Those who work near me can tell you that my ability to concentrate and focus on the job at hand has been greatly, greatly damaged."

Grutman then attempted to establish the reputational damage Falwell had suffered. He turned first to the damaging impact of alcoholism on the part of a minister: "Do you do any work involving ministers who are supposed to be teetotalers but who are, in fact, alcoholics?"

"I work on a regular basis as a pastor of pastors. We have an alcoholic institution. A pastor just gave his testimony two Sunday nights ago in my pulpit who lost his pulpit, lost his family, because of excessive drinking. We took him into our ministry free. We ministered to him and led him back to the Lord. We are now trying to reinstate him with his family and with his ministry.

"We have worked with hundreds through the years. Pastors, like all others, are human beings. That is why I don't like to use 'Reverend' or 'Doctor.' I think I am just a Christian. I think I am just Mister Falwell. I object to being elevated above others, because pastors, like all other Christians, are human beings who often do fall."

"And the one that you referred to was a man with an alcoholic problem in the real world; is that right, yes or no?"

"An alcoholic in the real world."

The statements in the *Hustler* ad on drinking, however, were not truly at the heart of the case. For Falwell, it is sex, not alcohol, that gives the ad its true sting. With eerie prescience, Falwell remarked in 1980 that "There are only two things a preacher just can't afford to be accused of. One of them is sexual impropriety, the other is messing with church funds." Falwell was worried that the *Hustler* ad would be taken seriously, if not by people who knew him intimately, than by those people he considered to be in "the real world."

"I decided immediately with the filing of the lawsuit," Falwell explained, "after much soul-searching and a meeting with my own staff and counsel, to go public, because while most of the supporters of our ministry would not read that magazine—at least, I hope that is the case—they all live out in the real world. They work in plants and offices, factories; they live in communities where people do read it and who meet them at the office and say, 'I heard about your pastor who had sex with his mother or who is drinking before he preaches.' "

"In connection with the work that you do and are trying to do," asked Grutman, "can you tell us to what extent you think your image or your reputation is involved?"

"Well, I am sure there isn't anyone here who doesn't know that the reputation of a pastor is his most precious holding. We sometimes use the word 'testimony.' The secular world probably would refer to it as one's reputation. Whenever that is blemished or in any way tarnished, he has little left."

"Mr. Falwell, in your dealing with ministers, as a pastor of pastors, in the real world, have you ever known of ministers who have fallen from the correct way of social and moral life, vis-à-vis their sexual lives? Have you ever known such people?" asked Grutman.

"There are four hundred thousand pastors in this country, and we work with them weekly, who have fallen morally."

"So, in your own experience there are pastors who preach sexual morality and yet who have themselves, to your knowledge, in fact not adhered to those principles?"

"I doubt there is a person in the courtroom who doesn't know the name of a pastor who has so fallen, and, unfortunately, the church too often expels, steps on, rejects persons when they fall. We have tried to help pick them up."

Chapter 17

To place Jerry Falwell's testimony in its proper cultural and historical perspective, it is worth considering just how *respectable* this quintessential American religious fundamentalist has become. How does one account for the enormous influence that fundamentalists like Falwell or Pat Robertson are able to exert on modern American life?

In the twentieth century the first great burst of fundamentalist political activity was personified by William Jennings Bryan.[1] A central plank in Bryan's fundamentalist political-religious platform was vigorous opposition to the teaching of Charles Darwin's theory of evolution in the public schools. Bryan fought the climactic battle over evolution against Clarence Darrow in the famous *Scopes* trial in Dayton, Tennessee. The *Scopes* trial is an intriguing backdrop for *Falwell v. Flynt.* The cause of fundamentalism was dealt a crippling blow by the reaction to the trial, a blow so close to being mortal that fundamentalist crusaders waited decades before emerging once again in the arenas of politics and litigation. The *Scopes* case is also a fascinating foil for *Falwell v. Flynt,* for the "second time around" it was the fundamentalist who appeared rational and controlled and the opponent who played the buffoon.

Tennessee passed a statute in 1925 that made it unlawful for any public school teacher "to teach any theory that denies the story of the divine creation of man as taught in the Bible, and to teach instead that man has descended from a lower order of animals." When

Tennessee Governor Austin Peay signed the bill into law (Peay privately thought the bill absurd, but would not become a political martyr by vetoing it), Bryan joyously wired Peay: "The Christian parents of the state owe you a debt of gratitude for saving their children from the poisonous influence of an unproven hypothesis." Bryan profusely proclaimed that "The state is now leading the Nation in the defense of Bible Christianity. Other states North and South will follow the example of Tennessee."

Liberals around the nation were afraid that Bryan was quite right in his prediction: The Tennessee statute very well could be the model for a sweeping national tide of legislatively imposed fundamentalist thought. And so the opposition forces mobilized in what was one of the first great public-interest group trials in American history. We are so accustomed to interest-group lobbying and litigation today—to lawsuits and lobby efforts financed by the NAACP, Common Cause, the ACLU, People for the American Way, the National Conservative Political Action Committee, or the Moral Majority—that we forget that the phenomenon is relatively new in American history. The *Scopes* case is an early example of litigation in which the named players, John Thomas Scopes and the State of Tennessee, were not the actual driving forces.

Motivated by the fear that other states would soon follow Tennessee's example, the American Civil Liberties Union resolved to make the case a *cause célèbre*. America's premier defense lawyer, Clarence Darrow, did not just happen onto the scene in Dayton, Tennessee, to defend an obscure twenty-four-year-old science teacher. The ACLU made a deliberate decision to force the "Monkey Bill" to a judicial test. The ACLU spread the word through Tennessee newspapers that it was ready to guarantee legal and financial support to any teacher who came forward to test the anti-evolution law. John Scopes stepped forward, wiring the ACLU that "the stage was set and that, if they could defray the expenses of production, the play could open at once." The ACLU had hoped to secure the services of the famous Wall Street lawyers John W. Davis and Charles Evans Hughes to defend Scopes, but both men declined. Clarence Darrow was anxious to take the case, and the ACLU and Scopes agreed to him as counsel.

Nor was it some coincidence of history that brought William Jennings Bryan to the stage as Darrow's protagonist. The ACLU's counterpart in the case was the World Christian Fundamentals Association, which voted to hire Bryan as a pinch-hitting attorney for the State of Tennessee. Bryan was delighted and agreed to act "for your great religious organizations and without compensation assist in the enforcement of the Tennessee law, provided, of course, it is agreeable to the Law Department of the State." Tennessee was only too eager to procure Bryan's help as the prosecutor against Scopes. The case was thus not so much "Tennessee v. Scopes" or "William Jennings Bryan v. Clarence Darrow" as it was "World Christian Fundamentals Association v. American Civil Liberties Union."

The drama of the *Scopes* trial is now an American legend. Dayton, Tennessee, was clearly Bryan territory. Reporting on the events for the *Baltimore Sun* and *The New York Times,* H. L. Mencken wrote that "an Episcopalian down here in the Coca-Cola belt is regarded as an atheist." The closest thing Scopes could get to a balanced jury was the inclusion of four Methodists; Mencken reported that "It is the four Methodists on the jury who are expected to hold out for Scopes's Christian burial after he is hanged."

Bryan won the trial, but he and his dogma lost in the court of public opinion, and the national humiliation suffered by Bryan in Tennessee so seared the fundamentalist psyche that it was decades before preachers such as Falwell and Pat Robertson dared to resurrect Bryan's brazen mixing of political and religious pulpit-thumping. Clarence Darrow brought the fundamentalist house down with one of the most famous cross-examinations in legal history. It is fascinating to look back at Darrow's cross-examination of William Jennings Bryan and compare it to the trial examination of Jerry Falwell.[2] There simply *is* no comparison. Darrow, for example, asked about Adam and Eve:

"Mr. Bryan, do you believe that the first woman was Eve?"
"Yes," said Bryan.
"Do you believe she was literally made out of Adam's rib?"
"I do."
"Did you ever discover where Cain got his wife?"
"No, sir; I leave the agnostics to hunt for her."
"The Bible says he got one, doesn't it? Were there other people on the earth at that time?"
"I cannot say."
"You cannot say? Did that ever enter into your consideration?"
"Never bothered me."

Darrow asked about Jonah and the whale. Bryan insisted that he took the whale story literally, for Bryan believed "in a God who can make a whale and can make a man, and make both do what He pleases."

"You don't know whether it was the ordinary mine-run fish, or made for that purpose?" asked Darrow.

"You may guess," answered Bryan, "an evolutionist guess."

"You are not prepared to say whether that fish was made especially to swallow a man or not?"

"The Bible doesn't say, so I'm not prepared to say," responded Bryan, with an attitude typical of his responses throughout the questioning. It was a miracle, explained Bryan, and one miracle was just as easy to believe as another. "A miracle is a thing performed beyond what man performs," he said. "When you get beyond what man can do, you get within the realm of miracles, and it is just as easy to believe in the miracle of Jonah as any other miracle in the Bible."

Darrow asked about Joshua and the sun. How could the sun stand still, when the earth moves around the sun?

It was merely the language of the day, explained Bryan, and, if anything stopped, it must have been the earth.

"Now, Mr. Bryan, have you ever pondered what would have happened to the earth if it had stood still?"

"No," replied Bryan. "The God I believe in could have taken care of that, Mr. Darrow."

"Don't you know it would have been converted into a molten mass of matter?"

"You testify to that when you get on the stand," Bryan rejoined. Bryan challenged Darrow to turn to the Bible for answers. "I will believe just what the Bible says. Read the Bible, and I will answer."

"All right, I will do that," said Darrow. " 'And I will put enmity between thee and the woman and between thy seed and her seed; it shall bruise thy head and thou shalt bruise his heel. Unto the woman he said, I will greatly multiply thy sorrow and thy conception; in sorrow thou shalt bring forth children; and thy desire shall be to thy husband, and he shall rule over thee.' That is right, is it?"

"I accept it as it is."

" 'And God said to the serpent, Because thou hast done this, thou art cursed above all cattle and above every beast of the field; upon thy belly shalt thou go and dust shalt thou eat all the days of thy life.' Do you think that is why the serpent is compelled to crawl upon its belly?" asked Darrow.

"I believe that," replied Bryan.

"Have you any idea how the snake went before that time?"

"No, sir."

"Do you know whether he walked on his tail or not?"

"No, sir, I have no way to know."

Bryan's answers began to draw derisive laughter, at least from the out-of-town spectators present, and even Bryan seemed to sense that things were beginning to go badly. He tried to cut the damage short, in one of the most famous colloquies of the trial:

"Your Honor," said Bryan, "I think I can shorten this testimony. The only purpose Mr. Darrow has is to slur at the Bible, but I will answer his questions . . . and I have no objection in the world. I want the world to know that this man, who does not believe in God, is trying to use a court in Tennessee—"

"I object to that," said Darrow.

"—to slur at it, and, while it will require time, I am willing to take it."

"I object to your statement," protested Darrow again. "I am examining you on your fool ideas that no intelligent Christian on earth believes."

Darrow incessantly hammered Bryan on this same theme, seeking a victory of the skeptical, open-minded, rationalist side of the American mind over the gullible, close-minded impulses of blind faith. Darrow's cross-examination of Bryan has haunted the fundamentalist cause. William Jennings Bryan may have claimed divine revelation on the age of the earth and Oral Roberts may have claimed that God had engaged in strong-arm loan-shark tactics by threatening to strike him dead if he failed to raise six million dollars by the end of the month, but many Americans have taken to heart the essential wisdom that if you talk to God you are praying—if God talks to you, you are schizophrenic.

In the aftermath of the *Scopes* debacle Evangelicals at first tended to stay true to the political isolationism of the early colonial Baptists. Perhaps because many Evangelicals were in the South and were associated with southern racism, anti-Catholicism, and anti-Semitism, mainstream national political leaders were, in turn, wary of getting too close to Evangelical preachers.

Reverend Billy Graham is the principal exception, but Graham's political involvement is different in kind from what came from the Jerry Falwells and Pat Robertsons of the 1970s and '80s.[3] While Graham can spin a web of conspiracy among Satan, Communists, and atheists with the best red-baiters in the country, his political program is a relatively diffused attack on such evils, a modest extension of the standard religious sermon. Graham's message lacks the focused political intensity of the platforms of Falwell and Robertson. Graham is perceived as relatively moderate because his role in the

political arena is essentially ceremonial. Graham concentrates primarily on external threats, and so is not internally divisive. Indeed,
he had the grace and generosity to shun the anti-Catholic prejudices
of many of his fellow Evangelicals during the presidential campaign
of John Kennedy. Graham ritually hobnobbed with presidents as
diverse as Dwight Eisenhower, Lyndon Johnson, and Richard
Nixon, but for the most part, the association was *only* ritual. He is
a convenient flesh-and-blood symbol for the sort of obligatory and
watered-down invocation of God that presidents find so useful.
Graham is the Baptist preacher leading us in bowing our heads for
a few moments of prayer in the southern state university football
game of national life: "Oh, Heavenly Father, we pray that you bless
us and guide us on this beautiful fall afternoon, and give us the
strength to go out there and whip those Commies!"

Graham's ceremonial entry into political life was as far as most
conservative Christian preachers cared to go for most of this century.
The old-time television evangelists like Rex Humbard or Oral Roberts continued to stay away from political and social issues. Jerry
Falwell's early career, in fact, tracked this political reticence. In a
well-known 1965 sermon, "Ministers and Marchers," Falwell quite
eloquently puts the case for rendering unto Caesar the things that are
Caesar's, and to God the things that are God's:

> While we are told to "render unto Caesar the things that are Cae-
> sar's," in the true interpretation we have very few ties on this earth.
> We pay our taxes, cast our votes as a responsibility of citizenship, obey
> the laws of the land, and other things demanded of us by the society
> in which we live. But at the same time, we are cognizant that our only
> purpose on this earth is to know Christ and to make him known.
> Believing the Bible as I do, I would find it impossible to stop preaching
> the pure saving gospel of Jesus Christ, and begin doing anything
> else—including fighting Communism, or participating in civil-
> rights reforms.[4]

That Falwell mentions "civil-rights reforms" as an area where
preachers do not belong might be cynically seen as an apology for
the obstructionist racism of much of his southern constituency in the
early 1960s and as a veiled jibe at priests, ministers, and rabbis from
the North who came to Georgia, Alabama, or Mississippi to participate in marches, sit-ins, and freedom rides. But that interpretation
of Falwell's 1965 sermon is unfair, for he also eschews fighting

communism from the pulpit, a fight his constituents would heartily embrace. Falwell's 1965 call for the separation of church and state is, rather, bound up in his vision of what the fundamentals of fundamentalism really were at the time—a deep, spiritual, direct, immediate, *internal* relationship with the Word of the Gospels. Falwell preached:

> As far as the relationship of the church to the world, it can be expressed as simply as the three words which Paul gave to Timothy— "Preach the Word." We have a message of redeeming grace through a crucified and risen Lord. This message is designed to go right to the heart of man and there meet his deep spiritual need. Nowhere are we commissioned to reform the externals. We are not told to wage war against bootleggers, liquor stores, gamblers, murderers, prostitutes, racketeers, prejudiced persons or institutions or any other existing evil as such. Our ministry is not reformation, but transformation. The gospel does not clean up the outside, but rather regenerates the inside.[5]

This powerful internal vision changed, however, and was replaced by an even more powerful external vision. The second coming of Jerry Falwell began to crystallize just as the countercultural energies generated by the civil rights movement and Vietnam had spent their force. By 1976 Falwell was organizing "I love America" rallies on the steps of state capitols all over the country.

The perspective of several years remove has made it clear that the immediate cultural perception that the Moral Majority exploded onto the American scene in the early 1980s and dramatically altered the prevailing political calculus is inaccurate.[6] Just as inaccurate, however, are the backlash perceptions that dismissed the entire phenomenon as superficial media hype. The American press tends to discover every significant American social change only after the fact. The press didn't see disenchantment with Vietnam coming, it didn't see Richard Nixon coming, it didn't see Jimmy Carter coming, it didn't see Ronald Reagan coming, and it didn't see the new Christian Right and Jerry Falwell coming. This, in itself, is no great indictment. Most American journalists are neither philosophers nor historians; they report the news, under fierce deadline pressure, as it develops. The best journalists do manage to place events in a larger perspective, linking the present to the past, and also attempt to triangulate from the past and present into projections for the future. But in that effort they have not been significantly more prescient than any other reasonably well-informed group of Americans.

If the inability of the press to predict the future is not a valid ground for criticism, however, the tendency of the press grossly to overreact once the future is suddenly thrust on it is. The press is too often guilty of a cyclical boom-and-bust mentality in which it is initially caught by surprise by new events and, as if to compensate, exaggerates the significance of those events, later only to deflate the initial story with a new exposé that the original events were over-rated. In this final bust stage, the press usually ascribes its inflated first reports of the story to the hype of the actors in the events—it is seldom self-critical enough to acknowledge its own complicity, either in being duped or in consciously or unconsciously exaggerating matters to make them more newsworthy. These wild media mood swings skew our ability to assimilate and make sense of developing events and, at times, artificially alter the nature of those events. In truth, such events normally do not come totally out of the blue, are not as dramatic as initially portrayed, and do not evaporate as quickly as they are made to appear. In Gary Hart's first 1984 run for the presidency, for example, he went from unknown to front-runner to phoney also-ran in the space of three weeks. In reality, he was never as obscure, never as strong, and never as out-of-it as he was pictured.

This is exactly the pattern that characterizes media coverage of Falwell and the Moral Majority. Falwell first claimed that the Moral Majority had four million members, at a time at which the organization was still in its start-up phase and had scarcely any members at all. Falwell claimed to have between twenty-five and fifty million viewers of his *Old Time Gospel Hour,* when the actual ratings were in the range of only one and one-half million. The press, however, overwhelmed by the newly discovered clout of the Christian Right, gullibly swallowed these inflated claims, creating more power for the fundamentalists than they ever had and helping them fulfill their prophecies. *Newsweek* estimated Falwell's television audience at eighteen million viewers. *The Washington Star* called Falwell the "second most watched TV personality in the country, surpassed only by Johnny Carson." *The New York Times* credited Falwell with having suddenly "created something very similar to a political party." Tina Rosenberg of National Public Radio put the whole business in more sober perspective by analyzing the press coverage in terms of the dynamics of all involved. "Falwell wants attention, liberals want an ogre, the press wants a good story," Rosenberg observed. "Whenever all parties want the same thing, they tend to get it whether they deserve it or not."[7]

The hard-core Christian Right, those card-carrying contributors to the Moral Majority, *Old Time Gospel Hour, PTL Club,* or Pat Robertson's presidential campaign, may still be a relatively small percentage of the American populace. But this core is surrounded by a halo of much wider circumference—Americans who do not watch Jerry Falwell preach on television or contribute to his ministry but who do share most of his views on moral and social issues and who are influenced in their intensity by his intensity.

Falwell's contributors, therefore, may still tend to be predominately southern, white, and less-educated, but it is not his list of contributors that matters. Falwell's importance in the culture is more subtle; he is part of the mood swing that characterizes the Reagan years, a swing in which the moderate right and center became increasingly receptive to the policies of the hard-core Right. This is Falwell's extended constituency, a part of America in which his television-cool manners play well. This constituency finds the perspiring, screaming, faith-healing of the revival tent much too distasteful (never let them see you sweat). But Falwell or Pat Robertson are controlled, well-dressed, graying with dignity, proper chairmen of the spiritual board. The physical appearance and political and social values of the lives of Falwell and Robertson are now, indeed, indistinguishable from a wide segment of right and center America. The "fundies" are no longer an extremist sideshow; they have entered the mainstream; they are material and media successes. When Jerry Falwell appears on *Donahue* (he is one of Donohue's most frequent guests), he does not appear as a cultural freak but as a social equal of Donahue, fit to do serious battle, just as Pat Robertson was taken seriously as a bona fide candidate for the Republican presidential nomination.

Falwell and the fundamentalists have come a long, long way from the debacle of the *Scopes* trial. Falwell was not about to let Larry Flynt knock him down.

Chapter 18

The jury had seen Jerry Falwell's testimony. It was now time for the jurors to balance Falwell's performance against Larry Flynt's. The outcome of the case turned primarily on the jury's assessment of these two principals. All else was secondary. Judge Turk had already ruled on the eve of the trial that the jury could be shown the videotape of Flynt's deposition in North Carolina. Grutman first presented to the jury an edited version of the deposition. Isaacman and Carson, believing that the edited tape was even more damaging than viewing the entire deposition in context, decided to rerun for the jury the whole deposition, uncut and uncensored.

The jury saw more than a videotape of Flynt, however. Flynt came to Roanoke for a live encore performance. When he arrived in Roanoke for his part in the trial, he seemed dramatically changed, much more in touch with reality than he had been during the Butner, North Carolina, deposition.

In talking to the press in Roanoke during the trial, Flynt got to the heart of matters as he saw them. "This is a libel case, not an obscenity case," he maintained. "I know I'm in the minority. I know I'm not everybody's cup of tea. But I have a significant readership." Flynt also got directly to his perception of the difference between himself and Falwell. "I'm going to be myself," Flynt said, referring to how he planned to behave when he took the stand. "That's one thing people can say about me that they can't say about Jerry Falwell. I'm me, and he should admit that he's a politician and not a preacher." Flynt also attacked Falwell's claim that his reputation had been damaged. "Why, if I damaged his reputation so bad, did Ronald Reagan ask him to deliver the benediction at the Republican National Convention?" Flynt asked. "How can he sit there with a straight face and say I damaged him?"

At the trial in Roanoke, Flynt was completely transformed. Gone was the bearded, angry man strapped to a hotel gurney that the jury had seen in the videotape deposition. Flynt rolled into the courtroom in a wheelchair, neatly groomed, wearing a three-piece suit. Flynt was, however, still Flynt—even his wheelchair had the custom Flynt touch—gold-plated, with seat, back, and arms of crimson velvet, and tires an elegant oyster gray. Flynt was calm and relaxed as he once again engaged in a battle of wits with his old nemesis, Grutman. During cross-examination Grutman tried to goad Flynt into losing his temper, but Flynt kept his cool, actually needling Grutman several times by calling him "Norman." Grutman remarked during a recess that "He did that on purpose. He knows I don't like to be called by my first name."

Flynt's trial performance began on friendly territory, with direct examination by his own attorney, Isaacman. Flynt's live testimony was, to say the least, crucial to the case. His television deposition had been ruinous. If that was the only Larry Flynt the jury ever saw, Flynt was a dead man. Flynt's only hope for resurrection was his live performance, and no one—not even Flynt—held up much hope that even that would help. To the extent that Flynt had any chance at all, he had somehow credibly to disown the Butner deposition. Flynt tried to engage in a damage-control exercise by dismissing the significance of the videotape deposition. "I feel fine today," Flynt said on the stand, "but at the time of the deposition I was in terrible pain. I had a terrible bedsore . . . and I'd been in solitary confinement for several months, handcuffed to my bed most of the time."

Isaacman did a skillful job of presenting Flynt as a person who had shed the manic bitterness of his deposition but who still believed firmly in his First Amendment right to publish outrageous satires of public figures. Since Isaacman knew that Grutman would hammer in on the stark contrast between Flynt's wild behavior during the deposition and his restrained lucidity at the trial, Isaacman chose to try to defuse the impact of the cross-examination by meeting the question of Flynt's behavior at trial head-on. Better for the jury to hear the explanation first during direct examination, so as not to leave the impression that Flynt was trying to pull the wool over their eyes.

Isaacman asked Flynt how he felt at the time of his Butner deposition.

"Something triggers something in me," said Flynt, "I really don't know what this is. I think, if people have certain mental and psychological problems, they're usually not aware of them. As I told you earlier, I sought treatment, you know. I feel, you know, that I'm fine today. But my doctor said that I was in a manic phase at the time . . . that I was suffering from manic depression. And my doctor explained to me, you know, that stress can trigger things. My company had been placed in a conservatorship. I've already explained my physical condition, and in walks this attorney who had, in the past, got two forty-million-dollar judgments against me, both of them thrown out on appeal, because they were frivolous lawsuits—"

Grutman interrupted, "Now, Your Honor, this—"

"And I see another one coming at me—" finished Flynt.

"Your Honor," complained Grutman, "How he feels is not the question—"

But Judge Turk cut him off. "We've played the tape in its entirety," said the Judge, "and I'm going to let him tell us how he feels."

"Your Honor," pleaded Grutman, "may I have equivalent latitude on cross-examination?"

Judge Turk assured Grutman that he would have his turn at Flynt without undue restrictions.

"You were saying," continued Isaacman, "in walks this attorney—you recognized Mr. Grutman, is that right?"

"Yes, I recognized Mr. Grutman. But what I'm trying to establish is my frame of mind, you know: I had been shot, prosecuted, imprisoned, fined, you know, for my ideas, my beliefs on the First Amendment. I realize that I'm not in the majority, that I'm in the minority, but minority rights, I feel, are important. So, when someone files a lawsuit against you, you know, that has no merit and you know that it's going to be extremely expensive, things like this put you in a depressed state of mind."

Why, asked Isaacman, was Flynt so depressed?

"I was very upset, you know; you know, I felt that everything had been taken away from me, because all of my assets had been placed in conservatorship, you know. You know, I felt that my attorneys were working against me. I was extremely, you know, paranoid. Because if you're not using a telephone, you know, you don't have a TV or a radio, and all this is going on in your life, you know, to think of one specific thing that caused me to go off the deep end, I can't. But I think you have, you know, you have to look, you know, at all the circumstances. But, you know, my doctor could probably better address the issue."

Isaacman asked about Flynt's attitude toward Flynt's regular corporate counsel, David Kahn, at the time of the deposition.

"I was very upset with David, because I felt he had been part, you know, of the conspiracy to take over my company. But, you know, I now realize since I have sought treatment, you know, that the conservatorship was necessary."

"What was your attitude toward Jimmy Flynt?"

"Well, he's—"

"First of all, who is Jimmy Flynt?"

"He's my brother, and I was very upset with him, for the same reasons, for the same reasons."

"All right. What relationship did he have to the conservatorship?"

"Ah, he was the conservator."

"Now, what was your attitude towards Mr. Jimmy Flynt?"

"I was furious."

"And what was your attitude toward me at that time?"

"I had written you a couple letters to come and see me, and you couldn't find time. So, I was very upset with you, because I felt that you were also involved with David Kahn and my brother. I mean, at the time I didn't—even though I look back on it, I did not realize that I was in a manic phase at that time. I just don't remember, you know, what was said. The only thing I remember is my feelings."

"And what's your attitude toward Jimmy Flynt today?"

"Same—we get along fine."

The most important elements of Flynt's testimony were his answers on the underlying merits of the case. Why had the ad been published? What did it mean?

"Now, how do you determine the people or the subjects that you want to parody in the magazines?" asked Isaacman.

"There is no way of really determining it. We have a readership that we have to respond to, and they're really only interested in public figures and people that are in the news. And, you know, what might be funny or parody or satire to somebody, you know, is not to another person. It depends often, you know, on what your ideologies, you know, values are."

"Do you have an idea of who your average reader is?"

"Yes. Our average reader is twenty-eight years old, eighty percent of our readership is male, twenty percent female. They tend to be well-educated and in a high-income bracket," claimed Flynt.

Isaacman next tried to diminish the significance of the ad parody by drawing attention to other parodies done by *Hustler* featuring product advertising slogans. One of the ad parodies involves John DeLorean and Coca-Cola, with the punchline "Things go better with Coke."

"Can you tell us what the idea in the Coke parody ad is?" asked Isaacman.

"When John DeLorean was getting all of the publicity, we took part of a Coca-Cola ad, but at the same time made it look like it was cocaine instead of Coca-Cola, where there was a razor blade that you were cutting it with, and I believe it said, you know, 'Things go better with Coke.' So it was sort of a parodox, you know. You could take it either way."

Isaacman asked next about a parody involving the Marlboro man.

"Well, this is about Marlboro cigarettes," explained Flynt. "The idea was to have a Marlboro man in the hay with his horse, you know, having a cigarette, you know, after sex, you know, just sort of a preposterous situation."

After setting the stage with the other product parodies, Isaacman turned to the Falwell Campari satire. He put the $64,000 question to Flynt: What was intended to be conveyed by the ad?

"Well," Flynt began, "we wanted to poke fun at Campari for their advertisements, because the innuendoes that they had in their ads made you sort of confused as to if the person was talking about their first time as far as a sexual encounter or whether they were talking about their first time as far as drinking Campari. Of course, another thing that you had to do is to have a person, you know, that is the complete opposite of what you would expect. If someone such as me might have been in there, I don't know how people would have interpreted it. But if somebody like Reverend Falwell is in there, it is very obvious that he wouldn't do any of these things; that they are not true; that it's not to be taken seriously. But where the irony and the humor is found in this, while it might not be funny to certain people and they may not see the satire in there, they have to consider how different people around the country perceived Falwell to be in terms of his political activities, his beliefs, how he wants people to perceive him as, you know, he would like to be loved, have recognition, acceptance by the people. There's nothing wrong with this, but when it happens, you know, ego comes into play. The best example I can say is when somebody asks me why Reverend Falwell, the only thing I can point out is why did Walter Mondale, during the debates in Louisville, ask 'Do you want Reverend Falwell to be involved in selecting the next Supreme Court?' Now, that was strictly to make a political point, but that means that he, more than any other evangelist, is involved in the mainstream of politics. And there is a great deal of people in this country, especially the ones that read *Hustler* magazine, that feel that there should be a separation between church and state. So, when something like this appears, it will give people a chuckle. They know that it was not intended to defame the Reverend Falwell, his mother, or any members of his family, because no one could take it seriously. When we published this in 1983, had this been a serious article, the national media would have reported on it."

Isaacman next turned to the issue of whether Flynt really wanted to damage Falwell's reputation by printing the satire.

Flynt explained, "If I wanted to hurt Reverend Falwell, we would do a serious article on the inside and make it an investigative exposé and talk about his jet airplane or maybe Swiss bank accounts. I mean, I don't know if such accounts exist, but, I mean, if you want to really, you know, hurt someone like that, you put down things that are believable. You don't put down things that are totally unbelievable."

Was the ad, Isaacman wanted to know, something to be treated seriously?

"Well, you know, as far as making it with his mother, I mean, that's so outrageous, I mean, that no one can find that believable," said Flynt. "The irreverence and the whole iconoclastic appeal about your mom, 'Isn't that a bit odd?' 'I don't think so. Looks don't mean that much to me in a woman.' I mean, if this stuff was true, it would be extremely inflammatory and offensive, but the fact that you know it's not true, you know, I can't comprehend how anyone could take it seriously. I mean, someone may not like it, but that's not what we're here for today, is whether somebody likes it or not, but whether it's in violation of the law."

"What effect, if any, did you intend for the ad parody to have on Jerry Falwell?" asked Isaacman.

"We were responding to our own readership; we didn't intend for it to have any effect on him. And the fact that he's, you know, responded they way he has, you know, is just as, you know, unbelievable as the ad is."

Isaacman then moved to an extremely delicate line of questioning: what to make of the myriad other blasts against Falwell that had appeared in *Hustler* over the years. This long train of abuses would be heavily emphasized by Grutman. Somehow, Isaacman had to try to blunt its impact. He chose the strategy of creating the sense that *Hustler* attacked Falwell so much that no one in his or her right mind could fail to see the Campari ad as anything other than dinner as usual—*Hustler* blowing off steam at the man it so loves to hate. Isaacman thus asked Flynt about cartoons suggesting that Falwell milked poor people for money they actually needed for their own basic subsistence.

Such commentary by *Hustler* is "not necessarily in good taste," conceded Flynt, "but there's, you know, there's a tremendous amount of people that feel that people who can't, cannot afford to give, should not be asked to give. This, this seems to be a basic contention with the letters, and, you know, and the ideas that we get, you know, about not only Reverend Falwell, but other evangelists."

"Why has Mr. Falwell been picked to be a subject of some of the parodies of your magazine?" asked Isaacman.

"I hope the jury understands me when I say, you know, that Reverend Falwell is good copy. That means, in terms of getting a response to the readership, his name triggers strong feelings from both sides, just as was observed in the recent election. I mean, right, wrong, or indifferent, it really doesn't matter. I don't have any, you know, personal animosity towards, towards Reverend Falwell. I put him, you know, like all politicians and all evangelists, basically in the same category. *Hustler* satirizes and parodies, and our basic editorial content is built around politics, sex, and religion. Those three categories. That is what makes up our entire editorial focus."

"Can you describe the 'Asshole of the Month' column?"

"That's an award that we give every month to various people."

"How do people qualify for that award?"

"Again, it, it just depends on who they are, how well known they are, what the circumstances are."

"Give us some idea, as to, really, what kinds of people would qualify for that award."

"Anyone who, who is in the limelight, that may not necessarily share, you know, our readers' views, or my personal views, or the editor's personal views. Anybody that appears to be hypocritical, you know, or inconsistent, you know, in their philosophy."

"Name some of the people who have been selected, and tell us, if you can, why those people qualified."

"I've been in there myself. I mean, that column, in a way, is not much more serious, you know, than the rest of the magazine. Mr. Grutman has been in there one month, as an example. Everyone from, you know, the President of the United States, to Pat Boone."

Isaacman asked a few final clarifying questions and then ended his examination. Flynt had given a good performance; he had explained away his Butner deposition as best he could and had been relatively articulate and reasonable in driving home his most important points: that the ad satire was so outrageous that it could not possibly be taken seriously by anyone and that it was a commentary on Flynt's perception of Falwell's hypocrisy and, as such, should be absolutely protected under the First Amendment.

Chapter 19

T he time again came for Flynt to face his arch-rival, Norman Roy Grutman. As Grutman rose to commence his cross-examination, he was faced with the fact that the jury had just seen a relatively sympathetic performance. The Flynt in front of them in a wheelchair was no ogre.

Flynt was showing perfect respect for the court proceedings. Gone were all the "fuck you's" and "assholes" of his prior deposition. Maybe he simply *was* out of his mind before; maybe the deposition *should* be discounted. Grutman wanted to turn the momentum around instantly; he went straight for the jugular with his very first question. Commenting on Flynt's subdued courtroom demeanor, Grutman badgered Flynt, "I notice in your examination today, that in answering the questions put to you by your counsel, there was not a single obscenity, not a single vile word uttered by you. Is the Larry Flynt that we are seeing here in court today the real Larry Flynt, or is the real Larry Flynt the one we saw on the television screen in your June 15 deposition?"

"I'm under treatment," Flynt responded calmly, "but I'm more myself today than I was then. And the reason why I didn't use any obscenities is I see no need to offend this jury here."

Grutman's initial strategy in attempting to discredit Flynt was to remind the jury of just how vile and profane Flynt was capable of being. Who was the real Larry Flynt? Grutman wanted to remind the jury that however polite he now seemed, Flynt had in fact

screamed out in a different court—the United States Supreme Court—
that the justices were "motherfuckers, with one token cunt."

"Mr. Flynt, could you tell His Honor and the members of the
jury, did you use that language in the Supreme Court of the United
States on November 8, 1983? Yes or no?"

"Yes, I did."

"And that kind of language, Mr. Flynt, is the kind of language
which you ordinarily use, don't you?"

"No."

"You don't use profanity?"

"No, I really don't."

"You don't use obscenities?"

"No, I don't."

"Fine. Mr. Flynt, do you read the Scriptures?"

"Sometimes."

"Are you familiar with that quote in the Scriptures which says,
'By their fruits, so shall ye know them?' " It was a rhetorical question, and Grutman needed no answer.

He next explored with Flynt his editorial policy at *Hustler*. "Mr.
Flynt, I'll stand alongside of you, and you can read with me. Above
your signature as editor and publisher in the June 1976 issue of
Hustler, before you were ever shot or imprisoned, the following
language appeared: 'How will this latest restriction of our individual
rights affect *Hustler* and its "no bull-shit" reporting policy? It won't.
We'll continue to report matters as we see them, in the same forthright, down-to-earth manner. Whether a person is a private citizen
or a public figure, if he's an asshole, a shithead, or a scumbag, that's
just the way you'll see him in *Hustler.*' Period. And in the last
sentence of the last paragraph: 'There will be no compromises.'
Signed, 'Larry Flynt, Editor and Publisher.' "

"What's your question, Mr. Grutman?" asked Flynt.

"Now that I show that to you, Mr. Flynt, would you agree that
that was published to the world above your signature in 1976 under
the 'Publisher's Statement' of your magazine?"

"Yes."

"And whether you think someone is an asshole, a shithead, or a
scumbag, you're going to say so in your magazine? Right?"

"Mr. Grutman—"

"Just 'yes' or 'no.' "

"I think everyone is an asshole. And if something cannot be
defined, it's not libelous. And you're talking about an editorial opinion. It may be in bad taste, but am I being persecuted because of my

tastes today, or am I being sued because of a libel action?" Flynt demanded.

Grutman pounded away. "Mr. Flynt, have you ever said, 'Free expression is absolute'?"

"Yes, I believe free expression is absolute, as long as no one is hurt."

"And 'absolute' means that you can say whatever you want?"

"Yes. I feel you have a right to say whatever you want to."

"No matter how somebody's feelings may be affected?"

"Ah, again, you're talking about areas of taste. What I'm trying to say is, I don't think a person should be imprisoned for what they say! You know, if you don't like what they're saying on television, turn them off."

"Mr. Flynt, you weren't imprisoned by Judge Robert Takasugi and Judge Manuel Real for what you wrote, were you? You're not suggesting that, are you?" Grutman was referring to the obscene outbursts by Flynt which had led to Flynt's contempt of court sentences.

"Norman, you're trying to make it sound that I was okay last fall. I was not okay. I had problems."

"Mr. Flynt—"

"—You know, from the early fall last year, you know, throughout my time in prison. And anyone who knows me knows that I do not conduct myself that way in public."

"Mr. Flynt, do you say you were imprisoned because of what you had published, or was it because of contempt of court?"

"It was for contempt of court, technically, but I still feel it had to do with a variety of things involving free expression."

Isaacman tried to interject, but Judge Turk was way ahead of him. "Ladies and gentlemen of the jury," said the Judge, "the fact that he may or may have not have been in prison—doesn't have anything to do with this case. Do all of you understand that? This doesn't have anything to do with whether or not a person has been in prison."

Isaacman and Grutman then went back and forth for a time arguing objections, each constantly cutting the other off. Judge Turk finally broke in, asking Flynt if he had fully finished his answer. Flynt responded by mocking both lawyers. "I'm a little confused. We'll just proceed."

The courtroom burst into laughter. "Just tell him to ask the next question then," said Judge Turk.

"Mr. Flynt," asked Grutman, "on June the 15th, 1984, in a

three-and-one-half hour deposition, which His Honor and the members of the jury have seen a part of yesterday and the conclusion this morning . . . among other things, you said: 'I'm not crazy.' "

"But, Mr. Grutman, you can have, you can have—"

"Your Honor, I didn't ask—" Grutman tried to cut Flynt off.

"—a mental illness or psychological problems without being crazy," finished Flynt.

"He's entitled to give an—" started in Judge Turk.

"I mean, just because someone's emotionally upset doesn't necessarily mean they're crazy," interrupted Flynt.

"And did you say in that deposition, if you recall, Mr. Flynt, 'I know that I'm under oath'?" asked Grutman.

"I don't recall."

"Do you deny having said it?"

"I don't—"

"He said he doesn't recall," snapped Judge Turk.

"All right," continued Grutman, "Do you recollect, Mr. Flynt, having said in that deposition, 'I'm not crazy. I'm under oath, and I know the penalty for perjury'?"

"I don't recall that."

"Are you suggesting to His Honor and the members of this jury, that at the time that you gave that deposition that we've seen, that you were not competent?"

"I definitely was not competent, because the only thing that I remember was—is my feelings on that particular day. I do not remember what I said."

Isaacman objected strenuously to this whole line of questioning. A "side-bar" conference among the lawyers and Judge Turk took place, outside the presence of the jury. Grutman complained that Isaacman was trying to harrass him with objections. "I would like to observe," he said to Judge Turk, "that during the course of Mr. Flynt's direct examination, a number of my objections were overruled, enhances were permitted that I thought were certainly very expansive, and—"

"I told you I would—I'm going to give you an opportunity to extensively cross-examine," said Turk.

"Fine," said Grutman. "Well, I would like to do that, Your Honor, but I think it is a calculated tactic of my adversaries to interrupt and temper the continuity of my examination so as to dissipate its effectiveness, and to interrupt its—"

Before he could finish, Isaacman was all over him, and the two lawyers debated for several minutes over whether it was legitimate for Grutman to question Flynt on issues relevant to Flynt's sanity at the time of the deposition. Isaacman tried to convince Judge Turk that the question of Flynt's competence during his deposition at Butner was a technical, legal question and a matter for experts, such as psychiatrists, and that it was improper to question Flynt about it in front of the jury. Judge Turk, however, sided with Grutman, applying the "I'll trust in the good common sense of the jury" approach that characterized his handling of the whole trial. By this time, the jury had, after all, seen the whole videotape deposition. The question of which Larry Flynt was the real Larry Flynt was a critical matter for the jury to consider. Turk decided therefore that the lawyers on both sides should be given wide latitude in questioning Flynt on his mental state at the time. Turk indicated that he would allow Grutman considerable freedom in questioning Flynt about his mental state and character. But Turk also made it clear that he would pull in the reins if Grutman got carried away. On this last point, however, there appeared to be a difference between what Judge Turk said and what Grutman heard. For Grutman took the Judge's ruling as a license to rough up Flynt any way he could.

"Mr. Flynt," said Grutman, "Did you say to Judge Henry Worker, United States District Court Judge for the Southern District of New York, quote: 'In retrospect, I wish I would have filed a petition for bankruptcy and let you wipe your ass with the order to execute on the judgment. Dumb assholes like you should be removed from the bench for abusing the process of our justice system!' Is that your letter to Judge Worker, Mr. Flynt?"

"Yes, it is—"

"I offer it into evidence."

"You were representing the plaintiff in that case, Mr. Grutman, and it was overturned on appeal," Flynt impishly pointed out.

Grutman turned to ask Flynt about another case in which the two of them had tangled. "This morning, when you mentioned several things to the jury, and talked about certain cases, was one of the cases that you referred to this jury the case in which I took your deposition and to which I've just drawn your attention?"

"You're talking about the *Penthouse* case in Columbus, Ohio, is that—"

"No, I'm talking about the Keeton case, the Guccione case in Columbus, Ohio."

"You mean Kathy Keeton, Mr. Guccione's girlfriend, whom you represented?"

"That's correct. Against you, individually. Remember that case?"

"Yes."

"All right. Now, do you remember in that case—"

"Your Honor," objected Isaacman, "may I just enter an objection at this point? It's not impeachment, number one, because he asked him whether he uses profanity. That's present tense. He didn't ask him in 1979, 'Did you use profanity?' And, number two, it's collateral evidence."

"Well," said Judge Turk, "I think we've just about spent enough time on this point—"

"I have one more question, Your Honor."

"All right," said Judge Turk.

But Grutman's "one last question" turned out to be an extended line of questions, including some of the most explosive in the trial.

"In 1975," he asked, "before you were shot, you weren't in pain, were you?"

"No."

"You weren't on drugs, were you?"

"No."

"In 1975, did you give an interview in which you said, 'I like to lay beneath a glass coffee table—' "

Isaacman knew what was coming and leaped up to try to cut off Grutman's question. "Your Honor, I—"

But Grutman shouted over him, "and watch my girl shit—"

"I would beg Your Honor, please," pleaded Isaacman.

"I have this under oath, and—"

"Not—"

"—His Honor says this goes to credibility."

"We can't both—both sides cannot talk at the same time," said an exasperated Judge Turk. Turk was clearly used to greater gentility from the Virginia lawyers who regularly appeared before him. It was time to cut Grutman off. "I think we have gone just about far enough as to whether or not he uses profanity," Turk ruled. "I'll let him ask that question, and then let's move—"

"Last question," interrupted Grutman.

"—on to something else," finished Turk.

Isaacman realized he had just won the ruling from the Judge but that Grutman was going to bull forward anyway with his "last question." "Your Honor, could the Court look at what he's going to read? He's going—"

"These are his words under oath, and I'll finish," said Grutman.

"Can he read what happened ten years ago?" protested Isaacman. "I mean—"

"Well, the jury would understand that it happened some time ago. All right. All right. Go ahead." Judge Turk had, in effect, just reversed himself, caving in to Grutman's obstinance. When in doubt, trust the jury. Anything to stop the lawyers from bickering.

"Did you say—" Grutman started.

"Is the court—" shouted Isaacman simultaneously.

"Did you say—"

"Is it going—"

"Overrule the—" tried Judge Turk.

"Overruled!" boomed Grutman, helping the Judge along.

"—objection, all right," finished the Judge.

Isaacman was defeated. "Thank you, Your Honor," he said.

"Let's go," said Turk.

Grutman needed no encouragement. He dropped his bombshell. "Did you say," he asked Flynt, "and 'I like to lay beneath the glass coffee table, and watch my girl shit. It's not the turd coming out or the way that it plops down on the glass that turns me on, but the opening and the closing of the asshole. That's the reason turds are tapered on the end, so the asshole doesn't slam shut. I also have this fantasy about fucking ten-year-old paper boys in the ass, and just when they're going to come, I want to reach around with a sharp razor and slit their throats.' Did you say that in an interview that was published in *Screw* magazine, that was published in 1975? Yes or no?"

"The whole thing was a bizarre joke and had no more seriousness to it than the Jerry Falwell parody," answered Flynt. But after that question, no answer could save the day. Grutman had managed to bring before the jury the kinds of things that Larry Flynt considered funny in all their gory glory.

Grutman again reached into his trick bag and tried to surprise Flynt with questions concerning Flynt's conduct only the day before, when he first arrived in Roanoke. "Mr. Flynt, did you arrive in Roanoke, Virginia, the day before yesterday?"

"Objection," said Isaacman. "It's irrelevant to this case, Your Honor."

"Well, I'll let him tell when he arrived," said the Judge.

"When did you get here?"

"Night before last."

"And yesterday, during the day, were you interviewed by various members of the media?"

"Yes, I was."

"And did you give an interview to each of the television stations in this town?"

"I don't recall."

"I doubt that he would know how many television stations are in this town," pointed out Judge Turk.

"All right. If Mr. Keith Humphrey is in this courtroom, I ask him to please stand," said Grutman, dramatically. A man stood up in the seating area.

"Are you Keith Humphrey, sir?" asked Grutman.

"Yes, I am," replied the standing man.

"Mr. Flynt, have you ever seen that man before?" asked Grutman.

"Yes, I have," said Flynt.

"You recognize him as an interviewer for one of the media?"

"Yes, I do."

"Did you have a conversation with him yesterday about the Falwell ad? Did you, Mr. Flynt?"

"Yes, I did."

"Do you remember what you said to him?"

"No, I don't. If you have a specific question, I may recall."

"Yes, I do. Do you have a recollection of saying to Mr. Keith Humphrey yesterday, 'I would like to confront Falwell in court and ask him whether he ever fucked his mother.' Did you say that yesterday to Keith Humphrey in words or substance?"

"No, that is not what I said."

"What did you say?"

"The question came up about how my attorneys were handling the case. I said I thought they should have handled it in a much more direct manner with Mr. Falwell. I said I would have. I said, just to show the absurdity of it, I would ask him if he had ever had sex with his mother. I did not use the word 'fuck' that you used."

"You didn't use that word?"

"No, I didn't. It wasn't necessary at that particular time."

"Now, before we recessed for lunch we were talking about a competency hearing. Do you remember that?"

"Yes."

"And you remember that while you were still in prison, you attended a competency hearing that was held before Magistrate Jean Dwyer on June the 26th, 1984?"

"Yes."

"That was at a time nine days after you had the deposition which I took of you at Butner, wasn't it?"

"That's true."

"Do you remember telling Magistrate Dwyer, 'I don't mind being in prison, but I don't want my hands cuffed, because I can't masturbate when I got the handcuffs on'? Remember saying that at the competency hearing?"

"No, I do not recall that."

"If I show you a transcript of it, will it refresh your recollection?"

"I don't know."

"Your Honor," complained Isaacman, "This is irrelevant."

"Yeah, I don't think this has anything to do with this," agreed Judge Turk. "I think we're going a little too far. All right, let's proceed."

But nothing, it seems, neither rain nor snow nor sleet nor ruling of court, could deter the faithful Grutman from asking his appointed question. He proceeded as if Judge Turk had just ruled in his favor, not against him.

"In the competency hearing—do you remember it, Mr. Flynt, on June the 24th?"

Flynt said he remembered.

"And in the course of that competency hearing, do you remember, sir, that you were maintaining to Magisrate Dwyer that you were competent? Do you remember doing that?"

Isaacman tried again. "Your Honor—"

Judge Turk didn't need to hear Isaacman through. He took a compromise course. Turning to the jury, he instructed, "Ladies and gentlemen of the jury, let me say to you in connection with this— I have permitted to be shown here a deposition that was taken of Mr. Flynt in June of 1984. It's the court's understanding that there was a hearing held before a federal magistrate some nine or ten days later. The purpose of that hearing was to determine whether or not, at that time, Mr. Flynt was competent to stand trial, to participate in the defense of the case. Now, that doesn't have anything at all to do with this, the merits of this case, one way or the other. I'm letting it in for the purpose of aiding you in determining the weight or what not to be given the deposition of June the 15th. Do all of you understand that? It doesn't have anything to do with the merits of this claim. But I'm letting it in for the purpose of assisting you in evaluating or giving what credence, if any, you want to give to the deposition that was taken in June, nine days before the competency hearing. All right."

The Judge had stepped in more assertively and reestablished the ground rules. The battle could continue.

"You used in your testimony the term 'parody' a number of times. Do you recall that?" asked Grutman.

"Yes," Flynt replied.

"And I gather that you say that this ad, which is Plaintiff's Exhibit One in this case, is a parody. Right?"

"Yes."

"In order to parody something, Mr. Flynt, you have to know what it is that you're parodying. Am I right?"

"True."

"You called me your 'personal nightmare.' Did you say that this morning?"

"I think so, yes."

"You do remember that I was at Butner on June 15th, 1984, don't you?"

"Yes," replied Flynt. How could he forget?

"And you knew that I was there to take your deposition in this case, did you not?"

"Yes."

"And do you remember the way in which I comported myself during the course of that deposition, which I took of you on that day that year?"

"I remember you as being somewhat more aggressive than you are today. I don't know if that's proper or not," challenged Flynt.

"Well, the jury has heard how I was. Beside being aggressive, what else was I, Mr. Flynt?" Grutman was trying to set a trap.

Flynt simply said nothing.

"Say it nicely, now," Grutman coaxed. The courtroom exploded in laughter.

Isaacman objected, "Your Honor, I'm going to object to these comments of Mr. Grutman. If he has a question—" But not even Isaacman could make his objection without cracking up, and the courtroom was filled with laughter again.

Judge Turk tried to settle things down. "Let's don't suggest the answers to him," he chided Grutman.

"Fine. What else was I besides aggressive?" asked Grutman.

"What do you want me to say, Mr. Grutman?" asked Flynt. "You trying to bait me?"

"Oh, I—"

"I mean, do you want me to call you an asshole in front of the jury? If it'll make you feel better, I will."

"No, no, Mr. Flynt," denied Grutman. "I want to know what you remember I was on June 15th."

"Ah," said Flynt. Now he understood. "You were one of the most truculent individuals I've ever met. And, you know, I have already told you about that deposition—"

"Well, I want you to tell me a little bit more about what you remember about it, and how you were acting at that deposition. Did the way in which you conducted yourself at that deposition have—anything to do with me?"

"Mr. Grutman, people don't like to admit it when they have a mental problem. I didn't want to admit it to myself. I was sick when I was in North Carolina. You knew it. You came down there and took advantage of me, and you're sitting here in this courtroom, or standing here, trying to turn this thing around, and make it sound like I was okay. I wasn't okay! You know I wasn't okay."

"Mr. Flynt, during the course of that deposition, had you ever said you were parodying me?"

"You're a parody of yourself, Mr. Grutman." Again, the courtroom filled with laughter.

"I asked you if you ever said that in the course of that deposition you were parodying me."

"I don't remember."

"Let me see if I can refresh your recollection. Last night, Mr. Flynt, did you speak to various television interviewers?"

"Yes, I did."

"All right, I'm going to ask, if you would, to have someone turn your wheelchair around so that you can look at the television monitor, and see if—"

"We have objections to any extrinsic evidence being offered at this time, Your Honor," said Isaacman.

Judge Turk overruled the objection. He allowed Grutman to use the news footage from the prior evening's television coverage of the trial to cross-examine Flynt. The jury was told to watch the television monitors. This was a remarkable tactic by Grutman. A key witness in a trial was now being cross-examined with the use of a

videotape of comments made by that witness about the trial on
television the night before! This was a startling intrusion of technology into customary ways of doing things in a trial. The instant replay
in NFL football games pales in comparison. Grutman called for the
TV technician to roll the tape. The jury saw the following colloquy
between Flynt and the TV reporter:

"Because they're making the case a situation of Good versus Evil.
The Preacher versus the Pornographer," said Flynt. "And the jury
is going to have a lot of peer pressure on them, to rule in Falwell's
favor."

The reporter then explained, "He was at the Marriott Hotel in
Roanoke, giving a deposition that will be used in another trial. He
looked relaxed and comfortable as he spoke with reporters. Flynt
said he does not plan any outbursts in Roanoke federal court Thurs-
day. He also stated that he does not have any proof that Jerry Falwell
committed incest with his mother."

Flynt then appeared again on the screen. "None of that is true.
I mean, my deposition was just a parody of the way this attorney was
behaving," he explained.

The videotape ended. Grutman then asked, "Mr. Flynt, now that
we've played the television clip which has just been shown, do you
deny having said what appears to have been uttered by you, as it was
just shown on that video monitor?"

"Yes. It's very difficult to take you seriously," said Flynt.

"Do you deny having said last night to the television interviewer
that your conduct on June 15th, 1984, was a parody of my behavior?
Do you deny having said—"

"No."

"—what you just heard?"

"No. I just said it, you know, and, ah, it's true. You may have
been the very person that helped trigger a lot of my behavior in
Butner."

"By definition, Mr. Flynt, in order to parody something, you
have to know what you're parodying, don't you?"

"Yes. I think each individual responds to how they're being
treated. You know, I think if someone, you know, if someone has a
problem, you know, you're going to affect their behavior, or you're
going to affect someone in a normal condition, you're going to affect
their behavior in the terms of the way you behave."

"Mr. Flynt—"

"Yeah, I mean, you're a very offensive and rude individual, Mr.
Grutman."

Flynt was giving as well as he was taking. Grutman *does* have a rude streak, after all, but there was no profit for Grutman in giving the jury excuses to build up any sympathies for Flynt.

Grutman turned to the final theme of his assault on Flynt, the climactic artillery barrage. What Flynt was really trying to do, Grutman tried to convince the jury, was to attack not just Reverend Falwell, but all clerics, all religion, all scripture, and perhaps even God Himself.

"Are you saying by that answer that you gave this morning," asked Grutman, "that no one would believe about a high or exalted political or religious person anything other than that they are what they profess to be?"

"Ah, people largely, you know, believe what they read and what they see in the media. But *Hustler* is a magazine that has a particular market, it has a particular flavor to it, and none of our readers, you know, would have ever taken that ad seriously, and nobody that didn't read the magazine would—"

"Mr. Flynt," interrupted Grutman, "for example, are you aware that it has been suggested in a publication recently that the late Cardinal Spellman was a homosexual? Have you heard about that?"

"No, I don't recall."

"Well, if such a thing appeared in a publication, are you suggesting that because he was a cleric of such imminence, no one could possibly believe that?"

"If it appeared in *Time* magazine, you're going to believe it. If it appeared in *Hustler* as part of a parody or a cartoon, they're going to treat it for what it is. I mean, people have to have some common sense."

"Were you, by this ad in your magazine, hoping to reveal Reverend Falwell as a hypocrite?"

"To a certain degree. Not—not in a sense, that he doesn't necessarily mean or believe what he's doing, but, you know, he's as much a politician as he is a preacher, and he wants admiration and love and recognition, and support. And, it's very obvious. So, to see him wrapping himself in—you know, in the flag and Bible both adds, you know, somewhat of a, you know, humorous paradox to his behavior. And I'm not the only one that perceives Mr. Falwell in this light."

"Mr. Flynt, I asked you not how other people perceived him. I asked whether you thought the publication of this ad in your magazine would reveal Reverend Falwell as a hypocrite. Would you answer that 'yes' or 'no'?"

Without waiting, Grutman continued. "Mr. Flynt, in the year

1984, do you remember having an interview for a magazine called *Vanity Fair?*"[1]

"What date was that?"

"Sometime in 1984."

"Sometime in 1984?"

"Yes. Do you remember in February of 1984, do you remember an interview appeared of you in *Vanity Fair* magazine?"

"Okay. I knew there was an interview. And that was during the time that I was having my problems."

"But you know that that interview appeared, do you not?"

"Yes."

"Do you remember in that interview to the reporter of *Vanity Fair* magazine, saying of the Bible, 'This is the biggest piece of shit ever written'?"

Flynt explained that, while he could not recall making the statement, he could not deny saying it.

"Very well," said Grutman, happy with that answer. "And do you remember in that interview with the reporter from *Vanity Fair* magazine saying, 'Parody has become so real that we're going to stop doing parody'?"

Again, Flynt couldn't recall. The answer was good enough for Grutman. The jury could see the point: The man they had before them did not truly distinguish between parody, satire, and reality. Parody and satire were just useful weapons in Larry Flynt's arsenal of perverted hate. Larry Flynt's gospel was to say whatever he wanted, to whomever he wanted, whenever he wanted. The man before them, Grutman was telling them, didn't care. Larry Flynt would list "Jesus H. Christ" as the publisher of *Hustler*; he would call Reverend Jerry Falwell a motherfucker; he would describe the Bible as a piece of shit.

Chapter 20

T he evidence was all in, and the lawyers for each side had delivered their closing arguments. Flynt's defensive position remained what it always had been: The ad was a joke, and it was ridiculous to predicate an award of damages on a matter so patently frivolous. Grutman's closing argument for Falwell was also true to form. Grutman painstakingly reviewed the evidence the jurors had seen, parading before them horror after horror. Grutman's passionate summation reached its oratorical climax as he reminded the jury of the cultural and philosophical conflicts that the case would force them to resolve. It was Grutman at his best.

"Certainly the eyes of the country are on Roanoke," he passionately exhorted. "And you are going to make a statement. And that statement that you are going to make from this courthouse is going to spread throughout the length and breadth of this land. The nation is watching. The nation wants to know where the Constitution stands. Which way, America? Are you going to give vindication to these synthetic arguments by the defendants? Are you going to let loose chaos and anarchy? Are you going to turn America into the *Planet of the Apes*?"

As the time approached for the jury deliberations to begin, it was clear that Falwell and Grutman had the momentum. There was not much left that Isaacman or Carson could do. Abraham Lincoln, once faced with similarly dismal trial prospects, told a story of a case in which a young boy was convicted for the murder of his parents. His parents were wealthy, and he murdered them for their money. At sentencing, the judge asked the defense attorney if there was any reason why the sentence of death should not be passed upon him. The boy's lawyer promptly replied, "I hope that Your Honor will see it fit to have mercy on a poor orphan." Flynt's case was not much stronger than Lincoln's.

Judge Turk gave the jury its final instructions, carefully explaining the complex rules of law governing the case. He did not allow the jury to consider the claim that the Campari ad constituted an appropriation of Falwell's name and likeness "for purposes of trade" without his permission. Turk ruled that the use of Falwell's name and photograph was not for "purposes of trade," since he was not really selling Campari Liqueur. Turk then turned to the two counts that he would permit the jury to consider—libel and intentional infliction of emotional distress.

On the libel count Turk explained to the jury that the first question he wanted them to answer was could the ad "reasonably be understood as describing actual facts about plaintiff or actual events in which plaintiff participated?" Turk then explained that the jury could consider the full range of circumstances surrounding the ad in reaching its conclusion.

Turk told the jury that if the answer to question one was "yes," they should go on to consider the second question: Did the defendants publish the ad with "actual malice"? Judge Turk meticulously reviewed with the jury the meaning of the term "actual malice," emphasizing that it does not mean ill will or hatred, but rather "knowledge of falsity or reckless disregard for the truth." Turk then turned to his instructions on the count of intentional infliction of emotional distress. The jury must first decide, he instructed, that the defendants acted intentionally to inflict emotional distress on Falwell. If the jury found that the defendants did act intentionally to inflict distress, he explained, they must then decide whether the ad offended generally accepted standards of decency.

Judge Turk had done the best job possible in maintaining a reasonable semblance of order and decorum in the trial and an admirable job of explaining fairly and neutrally the complicated legal rules in the case to the jury.

How would the jury respond? Was it a foregone conclusion that all Jerry Falwell now had to do was waltz up to the teller window and collect his winnings? Neither Grutman nor Isaacman nor Judge Turk really knew how the Roanoke jury of eight women and four men would decide the case. For, as all seasoned veterans of the American legal system understand, juries work in mysterious ways.

The American lore about jury behavior is rich and sharply divided. One school of thought is that juries for the most part want to do justice. They take their role seriously. According to Judge Herbert Stern, an accomplished federal judge in New Jersey:

> It isn't the velvet tongue, in my opinion, that makes a man a good trial lawyer. Those days are gone forever. I don't think juries want that. Juries want to do the right thing. They want to come to the right decision. The trick is not to persuade them that you are eloquent, but that you are right. If you convey the impression in a courtroom of being too facile of tongue, or even too brilliant—but not right—you may look good, but you will go home with an empty basket. The one quality above all other that the trial lawyer needs is sincerity.

The great Clarence Darrow, on the other hand, was of the pop sociology school. Darrow's methodology for picking a jury still has its adherents, though some of the details may have changed. "Never take a German; they are bull-headed," counseled Darrow. "Rarely take a Swede; they are stubborn. Always take an Irishman or a Jew; they are the easiest to move to emotional sympathy. Old men are generally more charitable and kindly disposed than young men; they have seen more of the world and understand it."[1]

Perhaps no one ever captured the mysterious forces that move juries better than Supreme Court Justice Hugo Black, who loved to tell a story from his days as an Alabama trial lawyer.[2] A sharecropper was charged with the crime of stealing the mule of his landlord, Black would explain. The landlord was rich and arrogant, without many friends among the common folk. The evidence against the sharecropper, however, was overwhelming. The judge gave the instructions to the jury, laying down the law with meticulous care. In five minutes the jury returned.

"Have you reached a verdict, Mr. Foreman?" asked the judge.

"We have, Your Honor."

"Then hand it to the clerk."

The clerk put on his glasses, took the paper, unfolded it, and read, "We, the jury, find the defendant not guilty, provided that he returns the mule."

The judge was beside himself and brought his gavel down sharply on the bench, saying, "There is no such verdict in the law. The defendant is either guilty or not guilty." The judge painstakingly repeated his legal instructions and told the jury to retire and come back with a lawful verdict.

Once more, the jury returned in only five minutes. "Have you reached a verdict?" asked the judge.

"We have, Your Honor."

"Then hand it to the clerk."

The clerk put on his glasses, unfolded the paper, cleared his throat, and read: "We, the jury, find the defendant not guilty. And he can keep the mule."

Flynt's lawyers must have feared that much the same psychology might prevail among the jurors in Roanoke. There was great internal pressure on the jury to work its own instinctive brand of "juster justice" on Larry Flynt, something along the lines of "We find that *Hustler* told a dirty joke that no one in his right mind could take seriously. And Flynt should pay Falwell one million dollars."

These fears, it turned out, were not completely unfounded. The jury deliberated in the matter of *Falwell v. Flynt and Hustler Magazine* and returned to the courtroom with its verdict. Could anyone have understood the Campari ad as factual? The jury answered "No." Score a major victory for Larry Flynt. Did Flynt and *Hustler* publish with intent to cause Falwell emotional distress? The jury answered "Yes." Jerry Falwell had just tied the score. Now, for the tiebreaker: Did the ad offend generally accepted standards of decency? The jury answered "Yes." Jerry Falwell had won. What damages did the jury find would compensate Falwell for his injury and deter future such conduct by Flynt and *Hustler*? One hundred thousand dollars in compensatory damages and one hundred thousand in punitive damages.

An American jury had drawn the line. The verdict makes perfect sense in light of the law the jury had been told to apply. The jury had reached the only plausible conclusion on the libel claim. No reasonable person *could* possibly have found the Campari ad to be a serious assertion of facts. The jury had also reached perfectly forthright conclusions on the emotional distress count. Flynt and *Hustler* probably did want to inflict distress on Falwell. How could such an ad *not* inflict distress, and how could anyone doubt that Flynt hated Falwell and all he stood for? The jury's verdict is completely defensible. And, as to the question of whether the ad offended generally accepted standards of decency, again the jury's judgment cannot be faulted. The ad is outrageous, mean-spirited, and vulgar.

Anyone can see that. The jury's verdict makes perfect sense.

If one disagrees with the outcome of the trial, therefore, one cannot blame the jury. For the jury had delivered an absolutely straightforward and fair-minded set of answers to the questions put to it. If one disagrees with the outcome, one's disagreement is not with the jury's application of the law but with the law itself.

The jury's award had thrust the intentional infliction of emotional distress count to the forefront of the litigation. Does the First Amendment permit a jury to award damages merely for emotional distress, when the jury has explicitly found that the speech at issue is not libelous?

Chapter 21

W hen a final decision is rendered in a federal district court, the losing side has the right to appeal that decision to a federal court of appeals. There are several regional courts of appeal in the United States, each with jurisdiction over a number of states, grouped together in "circuits." Thus a losing party in federal district court in Chicago, Illinois, would appeal his or her case to the United States Court of Appeals for the Seventh Circuit, which hears appeals from the midwest states of Illinois, Indiana, and Wisconsin. A losing party from a federal district court in New York would appeal to the Second Circuit, while a losing party from California would appeal to the Ninth Circuit, and so on. A losing party in the federal district court in Roanoke, Virginia, must appeal to the United States Court of Appeals for the Fourth Circuit, which covers the states of Virginia, West Virginia, Maryland, North Carolina, and South Carolina. The Fourth Circuit's headquarters are in Richmond.

In order more efficiently to manage the heavy caseload of a federal court of appeals, every appellate judge does not sit on every case. Instead, the members of the court hear cases in panels of three judges each. The panels are randomly constituted and are constantly realigned. Grutman and Isaacman thus knew that the appeal in *Falwell v. Flynt* could be heard by any three of the judges on the Fourth Circuit. When a decision of a three-judge panel is rendered, the losing side may request that the case be reheard by the entire complement of judges on the circuit court, a procedure known as "rehearing *en banc.*" Such a rehearing *en banc* is discretionary. The court does not have to grant the request and will do so only if a majority of all the judges agree. Such permission is extremely rare—only a miniscule number of *en banc* cases are heard in any given year. As a practical matter, therefore, it is the decision of the three-judge panel that is critical, and the composition of that panel is purely the luck of the draw.

The three Fourth Circuit judges drawn to hear the case *Falwell v. Flynt* were Kenneth K. Hall, of Charleston, West Virginia, Robert F. Chapman, of Columbia, South Carolina, and John D. Butzner, Jr., of Richmond, Virginia.

Although Falwell had won $200,000 in the federal district court, he had not prevailed on all of his claims. He was a winner on the emotional distress count, but he had lost before the jury on libel, and he had lost before Judge Turk on his appropriation-of-likeness theory. Technically, therefore, both Falwell and Flynt had the right to appeal parts of the decision in the lower court. Flynt and *Hustler,* of course, appealed the $200,000 emotional distress award. Falwell appealed Judge Turk's decision on the appropriation claim.

In an extremely intriguing strategic decision, however, Grutman decided that he would *not* appeal the jury's adverse determination on the libel count, though he later stated that he was not sure he had made the correct tactical decision in not appealing this issue. If he had taken that issue up to the appellate court, then the entire case would have been on appeal. As it stood, however, only two-thirds of it, the emotional distress and appropriation counts, remained alive in the Fourth Circuit.

There were understandable reasons for not appealing the libel count. First, it is always difficult to get an appellate court to reverse a jury verdict because the American legal tradition treats a jury's decision with reverence. It is much easier to get the court to reverse a lower judge's ruling than the ruling of a jury. Since the elimination of the appropriation claim had been solely Judge Turk's doing, that seemed easier pickings than the libel count. Second, the jury's decision on the libel count makes a great deal of sense. If the jury's rationale was that no one could have taken the ad as factual and thus it could not have been truly libelous, that rationale is certainly well within the type of common-sense discretion juries are routinely called upon to exercise. Since the jury had, in effect, accepted part of *Hustler*'s "it's a joke" defense, perhaps it was best not to emphasize that defense before the Fourth Circuit. From Grutman's perspective, perhaps sleeping dogs should be left to lie; the less said about the libel count, the better.

Grutman is a brilliant and accomplished tactician, however, and he knew that this tactic had its down-side risks. *Hustler* could now try to exploit the failure to appeal the libel claim, arguing that the jury's decision on that issue should topple Falwell's case on all three of his counts. If the ad is "just a joke" for libel purposes, they would argue, it is just a joke for all other purposes in the suit.

Having made the finding that the ad is not factual, *Hustler* argued, the jury should not have been permitted to turn around and still award damages for intentional infliction of emotional distress. *Hustler* asserted that any time a libel claim and a claim for infliction of emotional distress are joined in the same lawsuit and the libel claim fails, the intentional infliction of emotional distress claim should also fail. Several interlocking arguments by *Hustler* support this assertion.

First, if plaintiffs are permitted to recover for emotional distress in situations in which no libel has been established, then the tort of emotional distress will effectively swallow up the whole law of libel. Why would any plaintiff go to the trouble of proving that the offending statement is factually false, and thus libelous, when the tort of emotional distress is available without any need to demonstrate falsity? Over hundreds of years the law of libel had evolved into a delicate balance between the defendant's interest in freedom of speech and the plaintiff's interest in a good reputation. The requirement that the allegations against the defendant be factually false is critical to that balance.

Never had the law of libel permitted recovery for the hurt feelings caused by insults, epithets, and verbal abuse alone. A well-entrenched line of cases had established that no cause of action for libel could be maintained for such things as calling the plaintiff a "son-of-a-bitch," an "asshole," a "cocksucker," a "bastard," or a "motherfucker." There is a world of difference, these cases hold, between a libel and an insult. A libel is a lie, and the law punishes lies. An insult is a mere expression of anger and vulgarity, and the law does not punish anger or vulgarity alone. Lying and swearing may both be sins, but only lying is illegal.

When the insulter says to the insultee, "you are a son-of-a-bitch," the message is not "you are the offspring of a female dog." The phrase "son-of-a-bitch" has no literal meaning at all—it exists purely to express raw emotion. (Johnny Carson, for example, loves to play on this sort of word game by using the word "bitch" in its literal sense, to describe a female dog, savoring the frustration of the NBC censors, who are forced to let the word go through unbleeped.)

Since there is no real misstatement of fact communicated in epithets like "son-of-a-bitch," "asshole," or "motherfucker," such insults are not libelous. They are devoid of factual content, conveying emotion, not information. The law of libel historically has been unwilling to extend its coverage to such insults, for two reasons. First, the libel suit is regarded as the remedy for diminished reputations, not for mere hurt feelings. Conventional libel theory holds that an insult does not lower the reputation of the victim but rather the reputation of the accuser. When Flynt calls someone an asshole, it is Flynt, not the butt of his insult, who suffers diminished esteem.

Another reason the law of libel does not recognize insults as actionable is more practical: Insults are the stuff of everyday life, too common to be worthy of legal remedy. If that government is best that governs least, the law cannot provide a remedy for every wrong. Some harms are just too trivial and evanescent to merit the attention of a courtroom. Not even Judge Wapner on *People's Court* hears "he-called-me-an-asshole" claims. The law should not encourage the collective thinning of the American skin. A certain toughening of the hide is called for in a robust and open culture. The law would be an oppressive pressure-cooker if it attempted to place the lid on every angry vulgarity through which people blow off steam.

What the jury was permitted to do, *Hustler* argued, was to render this whole line of precedent irrelevant. Its award of $200,000 was essentially a penalty for mere verbal abuse. Admittedly, what *Hustler* had said about Falwell is at once a bit less and a bit more than the typical street insult "You are a motherfucker." But the immunity granted to swearing has never been conditioned on the pedestrian caliber of the insult. Creative vulgarity is covered, too.

The second argument made by *Hustler* to support its appeal—that recovery for infliction for emotional distress should be denied whenever a libel claim in the same lawsuit fails—involves a relatively mechanical interpretation of the actual malice standard from *New York Times Co. v. Sullivan*. The *Times* holding had been extended, of course, to libel suits brought by public figures such as Falwell. *Hustler* argued that the First Amendment protection of the *Times* holding could not be circumvented through the clever expedient of changing the theory of recovery from libel to intentional infliction of emotional distress. The First Amendment is not that sneaky. If the

Times actual malice standard applies to Falwell's libel claim, then
it must also apply to Falwell's emotional distress claim.

If this logic is correct, *Hustler* maintained, then the jury's verdict
on the emotional distress count had to be reversed. *Hustler* and Flynt
could not possibly be guilty of "actual malice"—knowing or reckless
disregard for falsity—because there is *no falsity* in the Campari ad.
The jury's verdict that the ad is not factual necessarily means that
no actual malice existed. If the ad contains nothing that is either true
or false, if even to speak of it as "true" or "false" is nonsense, then
certainly Flynt and *Hustler* had not printed the ad with knowledge
of or reckless disregard for its falsity. The jury's decision that the ad
is not factual, indeed, makes it clear that the whole satire is simply
Hustler's "opinion" concerning Falwell, and it cannot be held liable
for mere opinion.

For Falwell's part, the Fourth Circuit was invited by Grutman
and Jeffrey Daichman first to affirm the jury's award of $200,000 on
the emotional distress count and second to reverse Judge Turk's
decision on the appropriation of likeness theory. The emotional distress theory, Grutman and Daichman urged, should be analyzed
independently of the libel count and allowed to stand on its own
merits. On the appropriation issue, Falwell's attorneys argued that
it should make no difference that the ad is a parody and not the real
thing. Falwell's face and name had in fact been used without his
permission in connection with a product, and that is all the law
requires.

Chapter 22

T he decision of the three-judge panel of the United States Court
of Appeals for the Fourth Circuit in *Falwell v. Flynt* was announced on August 5, 1986. The decision was unanimous; Judge
Robert Chapman authored the opinion.[1]

The court agreed completely with Judge Turk's decision throw-
ing out the appropriation of name or likeness claim. The purpose of
the law, the court reasoned, is to protect persons from the theft of
their publicity value in endorsing commercial products, a purpose
completely inapplicable to the use of Falwell's name and likeness in
the Campari ad parody.

The court's analysis of Flynt's appeal of the $200,000 emotional
distress award is similarly seductive in its simplicity. The constitutional rules established in *New York Times Co. v. Sullivan* and its
progeny, the court reasoned, may not be avoided through the artful
pleading of alternate tort theories: "It is not the theory of liability
advanced but the status of the plaintiff, as a public figure or official
and the gravamen of a tortious publication, which gives rise to the
First Amendment protection prescribed by *New York Times.*"

So far, things sounded very good for *Hustler.* The court appeared
sensitive to the potential problems of the tort of infliction of emotional distress serving as an end-run around all of the First Amendment safeguards created by the *Times* decision. This promising start
for *Hustler* was followed, however, by a more problematic insight.
To state that the defendants should receive the same quantum of

protection required by *The New York Times* decision does not mean, the court reasoned, that the actual malice standard of the *Times* case—knowing or reckless disregard for falsity—should be literally applied in the emotional distress context. Isaacman and Carson had argued for *Hustler* that the *Times* test must be literally applied to the emotional distress count and that, since the jury found that the ad is not factual, it surely could not be knowingly or recklessly false. The court, however, did not buy this argument. It saw the problem as a bit more subtle. The *Times* standard, the court pointed out, focuses on knowing or reckless *falsity*. The emotional distress tort, by contrast, has nothing to do with truth or falsity. The *New York Times* decision, the court argued, does not change any of the elements of the tort of defamation but merely raises the level of fault to actual malice. The *Times* decision, the court claimed, leaves the essential nature of the tort of defamation unchanged. So too, the court reasoned, the First Amendment should not be employed to alter the essential elements of the emotional distress tort, but rather should merely require a minimum threshold of fault equivalent to that which would be required in the defamation context. The court reasoned that because the cause of action for intentional infliction of emotional distress under Virginia law contains a requirement of "intentional or reckless" misconduct, it already has "built-in" a level of fault equivalent to that required in the defamation context by *New York Times*.[2] The court then held that the record supported the conclusion that *Hustler* and Flynt acted intentionally or recklessly to inflict emotional distress on Reverend Falwell in publishing the ad parody.

Significantly, out of the entire trial record, the court selected only a few short passages to quote in support of its reasoning. The first is from a colloquy between Grutman and Flynt during Flynt's deposition:

"Did you want to upset Reverend Falwell?"

"Yes."

"Do you recognize that, in having published what you did in this ad, you were attempting to convey to the people who read it that Reverend Falwell was just as you characterized him, a liar?"

"He's a glutton."

"How about a liar?"

"Yeah. He's a liar, too."

"How about a hypocrite?"

"Yeah."

"That's what you wanted to convey?"

"Yeah."

"And didn't it occur to you that, if it wasn't true, you were attacking a man in his profession?"

"Yes."

"Did you appreciate, at the time that you wrote 'okay' or approved this publication, that for Reverend Falwell to function in his livelihood, and in his commitment and career, he has to have an integrity that people believe in?"

"Yeah."

"And wasn't one of your objectives to destroy that integrity, or harm it, if you could?"

"To assassinate it."

It is a fair inference from this dialogue, the court held, that Larry Flynt acted intentionally to inflict severe distress upon Jerry Falwell.

The other passage from the trial quoted by the court supports the finding that Falwell had suffered severe emotional distress. The court singled out Falwell's testimony concerning his reaction to the ad:

"I think I have never been as angry as I was at that moment," Falwell had testified. "My anger became a more rational and deep hurt. I somehow felt that, in all my life, I had never believed that human beings could do something like this. I really felt like weeping. I am not a deeply emotional person; I don't show it. I think I felt like weeping."

"How long did this sense of anger last?"

"To this present moment."

"You say that it almost brought you to tears. In your whole life, Mr. Falwell, had you ever had a personal experience of such intensity that could compare with the feeling that you had when you saw this ad?

"Never had. Since I have been a Christian, I don't think I have ever intentionally hurt anybody. I am sure I have hurt people, but not with intent. I certainly have never physically attacked anyone in my life. I really think that, at that moment, if Larry Flynt had been nearby, I might have physically reacted."

The court finally turned to *Hustler*'s objection that the Campari ad is opinion and thus protected by the First Amendment. The fact/opinion distinction, the court maintained, is only relevant to the law of defamation; it has no role to play in the tort of infliction of emotional distress. Defamation, the court emphasized, is grounded in proof of falsity, and, since opinions cannot be either true or false but only good or bad, there can be no defamation through opinion. Infliction of emotional distress, however, has nothing to do with falsity. Therefore, the fact that the statement is neither true nor false but rather mere opinion is immaterial since it is the intent to cause distress, not the intent to spread a falsehood, that triggers liability. *Hustler* could thus scream bloody murder over the fact that the ad is opinion, but from the court's perspective that argument remained irrelevant.

The Fourth Circuit's opinion was a great victory for Falwell and a stunning defeat for Flynt and *Hustler*. Moreover, the opinion hit the media world like a bombshell. For the first time in a major case a respected court had held that liability could be predicated on mere intent to induce severe distress, even though the published material is neither libelous nor an invasion of privacy. Perhaps most frightening of all to the press was the disturbing realization that the Court of Appeals' decision is a very neat and tidy piece of judicial craftsmanship. The first time it is played through, the logic seems sound. The court had certainly *appeared* to show fidelity to the "knowing or reckless" standard of *New York Times*. No one really doubted that Flynt intended to inflict distress on Falwell—it would be impossible to publish such an ad parody and not intend to inflict distress. How could the seemingly tight logic of the court's opinion be attacked?

Chapter 23

As media lawyers around the country, including Isaacman and Carson for *Hustler,* began to replay the court's opinion in "super slo-mo," a few potential chinks in the armor started to appear. As the Fourth Circuit itself recognized, it is not enough to lift the terms "intentional" or "reckless" out of the *New York Times* case, plug them into the elements of the emotional distress tort, and assume they mean the same thing. The court, however, may have dissipated its good instincts on this point, lapsing into the very mechanical trap it sought to avoid. For, arguably, the court failed to perceive that moving from one tort context to another changes not only the elements of the tort but also the balance of First Amendment interests. The attempt to puzzle out how the court's argument might be refuted involved a good deal of quite ethereal debate.

To some First Amendment experts around the nation, the principal difficulty posed by the case was the natural tendency of lawyers to use the same terms of fault in a wide range of different contexts. Terms describing levels of fault, however, have no meaning in the abstract. The terms "intentional," "reckless," or "negligent" are always relational: They make sense only as descriptions of the relationship between an actor's conduct and specific risks. For most American lawyers the most famous explication of the term "negligence" appears in an opinion by the great Judge Benjamin Cardozo, in a landmark case studied by all American first-year law students, *Palsgraf v. Long Island Railroad Co.* [1] Cardozo emphasized that there is no such thing as "negligence in the air" and that it is impossible even to think of negligence except in relational terms. The same is true for "intentional" or "reckless" conduct.

When the Supreme Court made part of the law of defamation in *New York Times Co. v. Sullivan* constitutional,[2] it established a relational connection between the publisher's conduct and a specific risk: the risk of publication of a defamatory false statement of fact. It is logically impossible simply to lift the *New York Times* formulation out of the context of defamation and apply it literally to the tort of infliction of emotional distress because the relationship between the publisher's conduct and the risks encompassed by the emotional distress tort is different in kind from the relationship between the conduct and risk at stake in defamation. The term "actual malice," as used in *New York Times,* is nonsensical when applied mechanically to the emotional distress claim in Falwell's suit. One cannot speak meaningfully about the publisher's subjective doubt as to truth or falsity when neither the initial decision-making process of the publisher nor the subsequent injury to the plaintiff has anything to do with the truth or falsity of the communication or with its capacity to inflict reputational damage.

The terms "intentional" and "reckless" are meaningful in *Falwell v. Flynt* only in their relation to a very different risk: the risk that the publisher's conduct would cause severe emotional distress. It was only confusing to ask, how should the standard of *New York Times Co. v. Sullivan* apply to this case? For the "standard" in the *Times* decision was crafted for a different relationship between an actor's conduct and risks of social harm. The proper question is, how should the First Amendment be applied to restrict a state's decision to impose penalties for this sort of conduct in relation to this sort of risk? When conceived in these terms, the First Amendment issue posed is both profound and stark: Can compensatory and punitive damages be awarded to a public figure in a tort suit when a publisher acts intentionally or recklessly *only* in relation to the risk that his publication will inflict severe emotional distress on another?

This abstract philosophical analysis did not, of course, magically unlock the key to the case. It did not suddenly make everything self-evident, producing some talismanic flash of insight in which all concerned instantly saw that Larry Flynt should win. What it did do, however, was clear away some of the distracting underbrush so that the real conflicts could be more thoughtfully considered. The *New York Times* decision is sacred to the press, sacred to the whole First

Amendment tradition, but it does not answer every question—and it could not by itself solve the Falwell case. The natural instinct of everyone to focus on the *Times* case as the starting point for analysis may have done more harm than good, for fitting the *Times* formulation into *Falwell v. Flynt* created an insoluble conundrum; it was forcing a square peg into a round hole. From *Hustler*'s perspective the key to overturning the Fourth Circuit's opinion might thus be to do the one thing that ran counter to the instincts of all good media lawyers—relax the tenacious vise-hold on the *Times* standard as the be-all and end-all of press litigation and look to other elements of the First Amendment tradition for principles that would protect Larry Flynt's and *Hustler*'s actions.

As the litigation battle thus advanced, the theater of war was dramatically expanded. This was no longer just a libel suit fought on a single front but a suit implicating multiple battles over multiple First Amendment frontiers.

Hustler's first avenue of recourse was to seek to have the Fourth Circuit panel's opinion reheard *en banc* by the entire membership of the court. *Hustler* and Flynt filed the proper "petition for rehearing *en banc*." The petition for rehearing was circulated to every member of the Fourth Circuit Court of Appeals, including one of its youngest members, Judge J. Harvie Wilkinson, III, of Richmond, Virginia. Wilkinson was appointed to the Court of Appeals in 1984. He has a background in journalism and had been the editor of a newspaper, the *Norfolk-Virginian Pilot,* for three years. He is a graduate of Yale and the University of Virginia Law School. After law school, he served as a law clerk for Supreme Court Justice Lewis Powell, a fellow Virginian. Wilkinson came to respect deeply Powell's jurisprudence, and Powell's views clearly have an influence on Wilkinson's own judicial attitudes. Wilkinson is a scholar; he taught as a professor at the University of Virginia Law School and is the author of several books, including a study of Harry S. Byrd and Virginia politics and *From Brown to Bakke,* a study of Supreme Court civil rights decisions.

Unlike many of his colleagues on the bench, Wilkinson was not persuaded that the jury award against Larry Flynt should stand. It was not that Wilkinson had any use for *Hustler*'s hatchet job on Falwell; he thought the Campari ad was base and unworthy of the great tradition of American satire. But Wilkinson was convinced that, no matter how vulgar the *Hustler* satire is, it is still satire and still fully protected by the First Amendment.

Wilkinson crafted a thorough and stirring opinion explaining why the jury's award should be reversed.[3] Wilkinson's opinion concentrates on the nature and function of satire: "Satire is particularly relevant to political debate because it tears down facades, deflates stuffed shirts, and unmasks hypocrisy. By cutting through the constraints imposed by pomp and ceremony, it is a form of irreverence as welcome as fresh air." While *Hustler*'s foul ad may not be as "welcome as fresh air," to penalize it would intolerably threaten other forms of satiric speech. Wilkinson thus argues that, while "*Hustler*'s base parody is unworthy" of "any tradition," the precedent in the Falwell suit "may one day come to stifle finer forms of this genre."

Wilkinson notes that attacking members of the clergy is a well-established strain of the satiric tradition. Garry Trudeau's *Doonesbury* has satirized all points on the religious spectrum, from Pat Robertson's direct line to divine inspiration to the sanctuary movement of liberation theologians. *Doonesbury*'s instinct for debunking religious leaders and public moralists has a history that goes back a long way. Molière parodied the French lay clergy; H. L. Mencken chided novelists for failing to penetrate the facades of American evangelists, and Sinclair Lewis, moved by Mencken's suggestions, wrote *Elmer Gantry,* a blistering indictment of the gullible public's willingness to support demagogues and the hypocrisy of the Protestant clergy. America's first great political cartoonist, William Charles, was actually forced to leave Scotland in 1806 because of a cartoon called "A Fallen Pillar of the King," which shows a clergyman bouncing a bare-breasted young woman on his knee while exclaiming ecstatically, "Oh, Lord, what good things dost thou provide for us men!"

Satiric attacks have always been a staple in American political life. George Washington was once depicted on a donkey, led by his aide, David Humphreys. The caption reads: "The glorious time has come to pass when David shall conduct an ass." Thomas Jefferson, a constant victim of vicious rumors concerning sexual adventures, is depicted in one cartoon as a lecherous beast waiting in his shirttails outside his wife's bedroom and in another as the keeper of a slave harem who auctions his own mulatto offspring into slavery. Cartoonists portrayed President Grover Cleveland as the father of an illegitimate child (which he was), showed James Garfield as an unwed mother in a dress, and Ulysses S. Grant as an incestuous drunk.

For the first time since *Falwell v. Flynt* began, a judge had seen the universe from Larry Flynt's perspective. Wilkinson's opinion raised some haunting doubts about the jury award. That speech is satiric should not, standing alone, either enhance or diminish the protection to which the speech is otherwise entitled. Labeling speech "satire" or "parody" does not immunize that speech from all legal restraint. If the satirist impermissibly steals from a copyrighted work, for example, he may be subjected legitimately to the penalties of the copyright act. If the satirist crosses the line into the legally obscene or the commercially fraudulent, the speech may be regulated.

At the same time satiric speech is in no sense a second-class First Amendment citizen. Whatever level of First Amendment protection the speech would otherwise enjoy is not diminished by the fact that it is spiced with humor. More importantly, the satirist's First Amendment protection is not lessened because the speech is cruel, crude, mean-spirited, unfair, or viciously biting.[4] In the defamation context, it has long been axiomatic that common law malice—hatred, spite, or ill will—is not enough to satisfy the "knowing or reckless" actual malice test of *New York Times*. The hatred with which speech is published does not effect its value in the marketplace of ideas. American life is replete with examples of speech protected by the core of the First Amendment, dripping with venom.

Satire is often effective, in fact, precisely because it is shocking to mainstream cultural sensibilities. The satirist's very purpose is often to be "outrageous" and "indecent," to incite anger, revulsion, and controversy. Through wicked, callous, vulgar, and taboo attacks, the bite of satire is often what supplies its potency; it works when it hurts.

One unavoidable consequence of the emotive power of satire is that it may often carry more capacity to inflict pain than other genres of speech. It is a fact of American life that an attack on a public figure in a context such as Garry Trudeau's comic strip *Doonesbury* may have more impact than scores of detached analytic essays by commentators on op-ed pages. But it has never been part of our First Amendment jurisprudence to penalize speech because it is effective.

The satire run by *Hustler* is, Wilkinson concedes, crude—he describes it as "base" and "unworthy of the grand American tradition of public satire." If it is "unworthy," however, it is only unworthy of praise as particularly humorous, clever, or tasteful. It is certainly not "unworthy" of the First Amendment. The famous statement in *New York Times Co. v. Sullivan* describing a "profound national commitment" to the principle that debate on public issues should be "uninhibited, robust, and wide-open" is not a mere slogan. The words "uninhibited" and "wide-open" gather their force when they are extended to protect speech at the fringes, speech that is indecorous and irreverent.

In order to persuade his colleagues to reverse the jury award for Falwell, Judge Wilkinson first needed to get a majority of them to vote to rehear the case *en banc.*

The votes of the other judges filtered in. As expected, the judges on the original panel voted not to reopen the case. They were joined by Judges Donald Russell, H. Emory Widener, Jr., Francis D. Murnaghan, Jr., and William W. Wilkins, Jr. Only Judges Harrison L. Winter, James Dickson Phillips, James M. Sprouse, and Sam J. Ervin, III, voted with Wilkinson. Larry Flynt and *Hustler* had lost again, by a vote of six to five.

On November 4, 1986, the court formally announced that the petition for rehearing was denied. Wilkinson's efforts were not, however, wasted. He dissented from the denial of rehearing *en banc* and took the very rare step of publishing his written opinion explaining why the full court should rehear the case. (While judges frequently write dissenting opinions from decisions on the merits, it is quite unusual for a judge to write a dissenting opinion from a mere vote not to rehear a previously decided case.) Wilkinson's views thus became part of the formal record in the case, as Alan Isaacman and David Carson pondered their last available hope, a petition for a review of the case in the United States Supreme Court.

Chapter 24

The United States Supreme Court reviews only a minuscule fraction of the cases decided by lower American courts each year. The famous lawyer's battlecry "I'll fight this case all the way to the Supreme Court!" is a piece of fiction; no lawyer can guarantee that the Supreme Court will accept a case for review—indeed, the odds are overwhelmingly against any given case ever reaching the high court. Every year the Supreme Court gets many thousands of petitions for review, but it accepts only a few hundred for resolution, and the number of cases that get a "full dress" treatment in any year is usually less than 150.[1]

This selectivity is not the product of arrogant elitism but rather a matter of practical mathematics. The function of the Court is to resolve the most pressing and difficult federal legal questions confronting American courts at the time. The thoughtful consideration of such cases and the writing of opinions attempting to articulate rationally the principles on which the results are reached are difficult and time-consuming processes. The justices of the Supreme Court, along with their law clerks and staffs, are among the hardest-working federal employees in the nation.[2]

Even to refer to a justice of the Supreme Court as a mere "federal employee," of course, has a ring of blasphemy. Abraham Lincoln once called law the "political religion" of American life. Our first great secular prophet, Thomas Paine, declared that "In America, law is king." Lincoln and Paine are correct: In America law *is* king, and Supreme Court justices are our secular high priests.

Cases reach the Supreme Court in three ways. Occasionally, the Supreme Court hears a case without its having to come up through a lower court. The case is filed directly in the Supreme Court at its very inception. Such cases are known as "original jurisdiction" suits and under the Constitution are limited to a very narrow range of disputes, including lawsuits between one state and another (such as California suing Arizona over the right to water from the Colorado River) or suits involving foreign diplomats. Most Supreme Court cases arise from lower courts and are known as "appellate jurisdiction" cases. The Court's appellate jurisdiction is divided into two types of cases: those in which review exists as a matter of right and those in which the decision to review is discretionary. "Appeals" are cases in which the losing party in the court below has an automatic right to have the result reviewed by the Supreme Court. Appeals in which the Supreme Court is required to entertain the case are actually quite rare, and in many cases in which technically there may be a right to have the Court hear the case, the Court deals with the appeal "summarily" (without any elaborate briefing or argument and with no opinion by the Court issued), so that as a practical matter even appeals are discretionary. The bulk of the Court's work comes through "petitions for *certiorari.*" *Certiorari* petitions involve cases in which no appeal exists as a right, and the Court is completely free to decide whether to accept or deny review of the case.

In deciding whether to grant certiorari review of a lower-court decision, the Supreme Court follows the so-called "rule of four," in which four justices must vote in favor of granting review for a case to be accepted by the Court. The rule of four is an intriguing institutional tradition. Four is the perfect number, striking a sensitive balance between principle and pragmatism. The fact that the votes of only four members (one less than a majority) are needed tends to prevent decisions of whether to take a case from degenerating into raw power politics. It is important that a minority of justices may require the Court to take a case they deem significant. In any decision-making body, power lies as much in who controls the agenda as in who has the most influence on its merits.

Many important issues that come before the Court are simply too close to call on their merits in advance. No one can be sure what the final outcome will be when the case is thrashed out. If someone has a monopoly over what will be placed on the table to be considered at all, that procedural leverage translates into extraordinary power over substantive results. If the chief justice, for example, decided the

Court's docket, he or she could alone effectively control the direction of the Court. If five members of the Court controlled the docket, on the other hand, the voting decision on what cases to take would inevitably become almost indistinguishable from votes on the merits of the case once taken—the very decision to take a case would have already engaged the justices in a sneak-preview sort of struggle over the merits. The rule of four acts to alleviate much of the stress over the decision to review. There is less incentive to play hardball over the decision when less than a majority may dictate results. The justices have the freedom to be motivated by principle in voting to grant review of cases that they may think are truly pressing in shaping the future course of the law. On the other hand, the rule of four is a sufficiently high number of votes to insure that few frivolous or insignificant cases will ever be taken by the Court.

In *Jerry Falwell v. Larry Flynt and Hustler Magazine* Alan Isaacman and David Carson filed a petition for *certiorari*, asking the Supreme Court to exercise its discretion to review the case. Norman Roy Grutman and Jeffrey Daichman filed a response with the Court, asking it to deny review and leave undisturbed their victory in the Fourth Circuit.

In addition to the briefs filed by the actual parties to a lawsuit, the Supreme Court permits parties not directly connected to a case to file briefs as outside advisors to the Court. Such briefs are known as *amicus curiae* (for "friend of the Court") briefs. Such briefs are typically written by lobby groups, trade associations, governmental entities, corporations, or private persons whose interests will be affected by the outcome of the litigation. To write an *amicus curiae* brief, the interested party must either petition the Court for permission or obtain the consent of the actual litigants. When a large number of interested outside parties join in filing *amicus curiae* briefs, the justices are sent a powerful signal that the decision they are pondering could impact on interests far wider than the parties immediately before the Court.

When the Fourth Circuit Court of Appeals' decision affirming the jury award became final with its denial of rehearing *en banc*, media organizations around the country began to contemplate petitioning to intervene as *amici curiae* to try to convince the Supreme Court first to accept the case for review and then to reverse the Fourth Circuit.

Most major media organizations, however, felt a certain degree of conflict over whether to intervene. This was *Hustler* in trouble, not *The New York Times* or *CBS News.* Would it be unseemly for the "respectable press" to rally to *Hustler*'s aid? Perhaps it would be better for mainstream media outlets to distance themselves from the likes of *Hustler* and simply dismiss the verdict in favor of Falwell as an aberrational decision that could only affect outrageous fringe publications. The mainstream press could, in effect, attempt to place a "spin" on the Falwell decision, creating a popular wisdom that the case should not serve as precedent for more conventional press activity.

But this fleeting fear of guilt by association with *Hustler* did not last long. Across the country press groups and First Amendment lawyers quickly perceived *Falwell v. Flynt* as too important a case to risk standing by on the sidelines. If allowed to stand, the Fourth Circuit's opinion could unravel major elements of the First Amendment jurisprudence that had evolved in the last thirty years to protect freedom of speech and of the press.

One of the first courageous entries into the fray by a major media power came from Falwell's home state of Virginia. John Stewart Bryan, III, the publisher of the *Richmond Times-Dispatch* and *The Richmond News Leader,* instructed his Richmond attorney, Alexander Wellford, to work on a brief urging the Supreme Court to overturn the Fourth Circuit. Wellford and his younger partner, David C. Kohler, both well known as top-flight press attorneys, wrote a brief (working along with other First Amendment experts) that was ultimately supported by a number of other media organizations, including the New York Times Company, the Free Lance-Star Company of Fredericksburg, Virginia, the Times Mirror Company, the Virginia Press Association, the American Newspaper Publishers Association, and the Magazine Publishers Association. (Rodney A. Smolla, author of this book, assisted in the writing of this brief.)

At the same time that the Richmond Newspapers group was preparing its brief, a brief favoring *Hustler* was also being prepared by the Reporters Committee for Freedom of the Press. A host of other news and entertainment organizations soon pitched in with *amicus curiae* briefs of their own. Home Box Office, Inc., for example, hired a prominent Seattle media attorney, P. Cameron DeVore, to write a brief explaining to the Court how many of the movies and comedy specials run by HBO could be endangered by lawsuits similar to the suit brought by Falwell against Flynt and *Hustler.* Other briefs were filed by the Law and Humanities Institute, the Volunteer Lawyers for the Arts, and the American Civil Liberties Union Foundation.

The most interesting *amicus curiae* brief was written by Roslyn A. Mazer and George Kaufmann, of the Washington, D.C. law firm, Dickstein, Shapiro and Morin. Mazer, widely regarded as one of the bright young stars among media lawyers, wrote a brief with her senior partner, Kaufmann, on behalf of the Association of American Editorial Cartoonists, the Authors League of America, and the political satirist Mark Russell.

Mazer and Kaufmann's brief set out to give the Supreme Court a better sense of historical perspective on rough, satiric attacks by using the brief to present a nutshell history of editorial cartoons and political satire. In England and America public figures have always been subject to vitriolic attacks from essayists and cartoonists. The most effective part of the brief is an appendix containing samples of such satiric attacks, drawn from a wide range of American and English sources. If a picture is worth a thousand words, this brief is worth a thousand legal arguments; the justices could see just how mean-spirited cartoonists' sketches and essayists' pens have been over the ages. The message of the appendix is unmistakable: Perhaps what *Hustler* did really was not that extreme, at least for a well-known figure like Falwell.

The Mazer and Kaufmann brief includes a song by Mark Russell, called "Mr. Meese is Coming to Town." (The opening lines: "Oh, you'd better be nice, not cranky and rude,/ And don't ask for things like shelter and food./ Mr. Meese is coming to town.") The brief also quotes the poetic commentary on satire of Alexander Pope in his *Epistle to Dr. Arbuthnot*—lines that seem written for *Falwell v. Flynt*:

Let *Sporus* tremble—A. "What? that Thing of silk,
"*Sporus,* that mere white Curd of Ass's milk?
"Satire or Sense, alas! can *Sporus* feel?
"Who breaks a Butterfly upon a Wheel?"
P. Yet let me flap this Bug with gilded wings,
This painted Child of Dirt that stinks and stings;
Whose Buzz the Witty and the Fair annoys,
Yet Wit ne'er tastes, and Beauty ne'er enjoys,
So well-bred Spaniels civilly delight
In mumbling of the Game they dare not bite.
Eternal Smiles his Emptiness betray,
As shallow streams run dimpling all the way.
Whether in florid Impotence he speaks,
And, as the Prompter breathes, the Puppet squeaks;
Or at the Ear of *Eve,* familiar Toad,

Half Froth, half Venom, spits himself abroad,
In puns, or Politicks, or Tales, or Lyes,
Or Spite, or Smut, or Rhymes, or Blasphemies.
His Wit all see-saw between *that* and *this,*
Now high, now low, now Master up, now Miss,
And he himself one vile Antithesis.
Amphibious Thing! that acting either Part,
The trifling Head, or the corrupted Heart!
Fop at the Toilet, Flatt'rer at the Board,
Now trips a Lady, and now struts a Lord.
Eve's Tempter thus the Rabbins have exprest,
A Cherub's face, a Reptile all the rest;
Beauty that shocks you, Parts that none will trust,
Wit that can creep, and Pride that licks the dust.[3]

The justices of the Supreme Court got the message. This was much more than a dispute over a dirty little joke. On March 20, 1987, the Supreme Court of the United States announced that it was granting the petition for a writ of *certiorari* to review the Fourth Circuit's decision in *Jerry Falwell v. Larry Flynt.*

Chapter 25

*F*alwell v. *Flynt* had been characterized by raw and violent confrontations. Flynt's deposition in Butner, North Carolina, the attempt by Isaacman and Carson to disqualify Grutman, and Grutman's searing cross examination of Flynt in Roanoke are not the stuff of routine litigation. This crazy litigation history now gave way, however, to a wide-ranging philosophical and legal discourse over the function and purpose of the First Amendment. Very few cases have ever implicated so many different themes of the First Amendment tradition.

In writing in support of *Hustler* and Flynt, the various lawyers who filed *amicus curiae* briefs were faced with a number of diplomatic and strategic perplexities. Since many mainstream media groups were anxious to defend Flynt in principle but not in person, echoing the tone of the dissenting opinion by Fourth Circuit Judge J. Harvie Wilkinson, there was a tendency among the media organizations to disassociate themselves from *Hustler* while steadfastly defending its right to print the Falwell satire. Diplomacy aside, the allegiance with *Hustler* posed a classic strategic debate over how best to defend wild and crazy forms of speech. There is a temptation to try to denigrate the plaintiff or the prosecution for grossly exaggerating the harm caused by such speech. Censorship is often attacked by making the censor appear ridiculous. The law should not trifle with the trivial, suppressing speech that carries no plausible potency for real damage. Under this tactic, Falwell's suit should be dismissed as a witch-hunt.

This type of First Amendment defense, as attractive as it is, is also perilous. It tends to concede too much by appearing to accept as an underlying premise the notion that innocuous speech is more deserving of constitutional protection than noxious speech. Impotent expression is safe; potent expression is suspect. This threatens, of course, to give away the store. *Hustler* would be protected only to the extent that *Hustler* doesn't really matter. For those media outlets that think they *do* matter, this argument can do more harm than good. It hardly benefits Garry Trudeau to support the principle that *Doonesbury* is sheltered by the First Amendment only as long as everyone treats it as just a comic strip, devoid of serious impact on the real world. And from the perspective of Larry Flynt, why should he be forced to suppress the real guts of his message in order to be granted the First Amendment's saving grace? To try to whitewash the Campari ad would be to try to make Flynt somebody other than Flynt. It would not be believable. Why argue that the Campari ad is protected because it causes no real harm when nobody believes that it did not cause *some* harm, at least to Jerry Falwell's psyche? Thus the boomerang potential of the "no harm, no foul" argument.

Alan Isaacman and David Carson, as well as the various *amici curiae* briefs, tended to steer a middle course on this point. A certain amount of token argument was served up to discount the harmful potential of the Campari parody. But, when pressed, all of the defense interests argued that it really didn't matter—even if the ad was highly effective in causing emotional disturbance, it should still be completely protected.

For Falwell's part, Norman Roy Grutman cast his arguments before the Supreme Court in terms of what might be called the "back side" of the First Amendment tradition.[1] The history of the First Amendment is *not* that all speech in all contexts is fully protected but rather that government has a great deal of power to curtail speech in order to protect other vital social interests.

In wrestling with *Falwell v. Flynt,* the Supreme Court was thus forced by the lawyers on both sides to confront a long series of conflicts. Should there be an uninhibited marketplace of ideas or should the marketplace be inhibited by granting government latitude to regulate that market in the service of elevating the level of public discourse? Is all speech created equal, or are different types of speech of different value, thereby creating a hierarchy of First Amendment protection in which legal protection increases with the importance of the speech? Is all speech speech, or is some speech so taboo that it forfeits its title, to be cast away as completely outside the protection of the First Amendment? And what is the relation between the First Amendment's guarantee of freedom of speech, its injunction against the establishment of religion, and its guarantee of the free exercise of religion? Can government penalize speech for being blasphemous and sacrilegious so as to permit persons freely to exercise their religious beliefs without harassment or persecution? Or is the very notion of penalizing blasphemy or sacrilege an impermissible establishment of religion?

Chapter 26

The "back side" of the First Amendment tradition contains a number of examples of speech deemed beneath the protection of the Constitution. Jerry Falwell could gather great sustenance from these examples in attempting to fashion a theory of the First Amendment that would justify the jury's award in his favor.

One of the most important Supreme Court decisions from Falwell's perspective is a case entitled *Chaplinsky v. New Hampshire,*[1] decided in 1942. *Chaplinsky* has long been one of the most controversial decisions in the Court's history. Depending on whom you ask, *Chaplinsky* is either a triumph for truth, justice, and the American way or a stunning victory for the dark side of the force.

Mr. Chaplinsky, a Jehovah's Witness, was distributing religious literature on the streets of Rochester, New Hampshire, on a busy Saturday afternoon. A number of passersby complained to the City Marshal, named Bowering, that Chaplinsky was denouncing all religion as a "racket." What happened next was a matter of dispute. According to Bowering's version of events, Bowering told the citizens that what Chaplinsky was doing was lawful. Bowering also warned Chaplinsky, however, that the crowd was getting restless. Some time later, a disturbance ensued, caused by persons reacting negatively to Chaplinsky's message, and the traffic officer on the scene started escorting Chaplinsky toward the police station but did not place him under arrest. While on their way to the station, they met up with Bowering, who had been informed of the disturbance and was hurrying toward the scene. Bowering repeated his warning to Chaplinsky about the natives growing restless, at which point Chaplinsky said to Bowering, "You are a goddamned racketeer" and "a damned fascist, and the whole government of Rochester are fascists or agents of fascists."

Chaplinsky's story was a bit different. He claimed that when he met Bowering, he asked him to arrest those responsible for the disturbance. In reply, Bowering cursed Chaplinsky and told him to come along. At this point, Chaplinsky admits, he did use the language he was accused of using, except he never said "goddamned," just "damned."

Chaplinsky was convicted of violating a New Hampshire law providing that "No person shall address any offensive, derisive, or annoying word to any other person who is lawfully in any street or public place, nor call him by any offensive or derisive name, nor make any noise or exclamation in his presence and hearing with intent to deride, offend, or annoy him, or to prevent him from pursuing his lawful business or occupation."

The Supreme Court unanimously affirmed the conviction. The opinion states that certain "well-defined and limited" classes of speech "have never been thought to raise any constitutional problem." In language that obviously bears strongly on the analysis of *Falwell v. Flynt,* the Court elaborates that these classes of speech "include the lewd and obscene, the profane, the libelous, and the insulting or 'fighting' words—those which by their very utterance inflict injury or tend to incite an immediate breach of the peace." In effect, the Court in *Chaplinsky* wrote these classes of speech out of the First Amendment, as if they were not speech at all. "Such utterances," according to the Court, "are no essential part of any exposition of ideas, are of such slight social value as a step to truth that any benefit that may be derived from them is clearly outweighed by the social interest in order and morality." Quoting a prior decision, the Court states that "Resort to epithets or personal abuse is not in any proper sense communication of information or opinion safeguarded by the Constitution." Under this analysis the Court had no difficulty affirming Chaplinsky's conviction, asserting that "Argument is unnecessary to demonstrate that the appellations 'damned racketeer' and 'damned fascist' are likely to provoke the average person to retaliation, and thereby cause a breach of the peace." Effectively, the Court's analysis boils down to the judgment that in Rochester, New Hampshire, in 1942, "Dem's fighten' words!"

The *Chaplinsky* decision clearly lent substantial force to Jerry Falwell's suit against Flynt and *Hustler. Hustler*'s Campari ad seemed a perfect nominee for inclusion among the string of evil speech types identified in *Chaplinsky*: "The lewd and obscene, the profane, the libelous, and the insulting or 'fighting' words." And more importantly, *Chaplinsky* stands for two propositions central to Falwell's whole lawsuit: first, that some speech is simply "no essential part of any exposition of ideas" and second, that when speech is of such "slight social value," it is constitutionally permissible to regard its protection as outweighed by "the social interest in order and morality."

Chaplinsky is what Falwell's suit is all about—the case fits perfectly into Falwell's worldview: *Hustler*'s ad is pure trash, of little or no social value, and Falwell's tort suit is an expression of the need to preserve order and morality.

Falwell's difficulty, however, was that it was not at all clear how successfully the *Chaplinsky* decision had weathered the forty-six years since it was decided. Many scholars and judges had taken a second look at *Chaplinsky* and questioned whether it was either theoretically or factually sound.[2] Mr. Chaplinsky had been engaged in the lawful exercise of his freedom of speech and freedom of religion rights at the time the trouble started. The violence was not his fault but the fault of those reacting against him. If his religious proselytizing was lawful, why weren't those actually causing the disorder arrested or made to dispense? And were Chaplinsky's words really "fighting words" at all, when uttered to Marshal Bowering after Chaplinsky had been removed from the scene and was with Bowering and the other police officer? This was not a referee calling a technical foul on an abusive coach on the sideline but a public official being called a "damned fascist" by a person angry at the police for arresting him and not the other troublemakers. And what of the claim that Bowering had started swearing first? Finally, to Chaplinsky this whole series of events certainly may have seemed to be the government strong-arming an unpopular speaker. Maybe calling the whole government of Rochester "fascist" was a bit strong, but was it fair to say this was "no essential part of any exposition of ideas"? Chaplinsky obviously had pretty intense ideas about Rochester government. Was he convicted merely for not expressing those ideas nicely? Was the Court saying that the words "damned" and "fascist" and "racketeer" were not *essential* to any ideas he had?

Perhaps it was out of some lingering subconscious institutional guilt over *Chaplinsky* or some mystical corrective turn in the legal karma wheel that future Chaplinskies invariably succeeded in the Supreme Court over the next forty years, to the point where the one sure bet in modern First Amendment jurisprudence became: Jehovah's Witnesses always win.[3]

A second important case that strongly supported Falwell's claim is *Beauharnais v. Illinois,*[4] decided in 1952. *Beauharnais* is a criminal libel case, involving an Illinois statute that criminalized any publication that portrayed "depravity, criminality, unchastity, or lack of virtue of a class of citizens, of any race, color, creed or religion," which exposed them "to contempt, derision, or obloquy or which is productive of breach of the peace or riots." A racist Chicago organization called the White Circle League of America distributed leaflets calling on the mayor and city council of Chicago "to halt the further encroachment, harassment, and invasion of white people, their property, neighborhoods, and persons, by the Negro." The leaflet called on "one million self-respecting people to unite" and proclaimed that "If persuasion and the need to prevent the white race from becoming mongrelized by the Negro will not unite us, then the aggressions . . . rapes, robberies, knives, guns, and marijuana of the Negro, surely will."

The defendant Beauharnais was president of the White Circle League, and, in his defense to the Illinois criminal prosecution, he asked that the jury be instructed that he could not be found guilty unless the leaflets were "likely to produce a clear and present danger of a serious substantive evil that rises far above public inconvenience, annoyance, or unrest." This instruction was refused, Beauharnais was convicted, and the United States Supreme Court affirmed.

Beauharnais has never been overruled, though its continued validity has been sharply questioned. The case came against the backdrop of the world's realization of how Nazis in Germany had used group libel as a method for rationalizing mass murder. The case also came years before *New York Times v. Sullivan* first engrafted constitutional restraints on libel. If *Beauharnais* is still good law, it lends impressive support to Falwell's claim. The only social harms caused by the speech in *Beauharnais* were the distress the leaflets must surely have inflicted on black citizens in Chicago and the racial intolerance the leaflets may have whipped up in the hearts and minds of some Chicago whites. Despite the label "criminal libel," the speech was not libelous in the accepted sense of that term, for it contained no reputation-injuring false statements of fact. The leaflets were pure hysterical diatribe, expressions of racist opinion calculated to create hate. No clear and present danger to any more palpable social interest was established—the repugnance of the message alone was deemed by the Supreme Court as sufficient to support the conviction. Reverend Falwell's case, indeed, was even stronger than *Beauharnais*. In his suit the emotional distress was focused on a single individual, and the intent to inflict distress was supported by actual record evidence. In *Beauharnais* the diffused distress was suffered, one must simply assume, by the entire black population of Chicago. Conventional legal doctrine for tortious libel has always disqualified such generalized racial or religious group references as too large to support liability. Furthermore, the elements of emotional distress that Falwell had to establish actually gave more protection to the defendant than anything provided in the Illinois criminal statute.

Chapter 27

Not all the precedents in Jerry Falwell's favor were decades old. The "back side" of the First Amendment had decisions of quite recent vintage, particularly in the areas of obscenity and regulation of indecent speech on radio and television.

In *Chaplinsky* the Court lists the "obscene" as one of the categories of speech outside the First Amendment. Over the years the problem of obscenity has proven to be among the most intractable speech problems faced by the Supreme Court.[1] One of the first obscenity cases to reach the Court arose from Edmund Wilson's novel, *Memoirs of Hecate County.* Wilson was one of America's great men of letters; F. Scott Fitzgerald called him "my artistic conscience." Wilson's novel includes some racy sex scenes, and it drew a complaint from an Orwellian-sounding organization, the New York Society for the Suppression of Vice. In a trial that included such evidence as the testimony of Lionel Trilling, who attested to the importance of the sexual passages to the literary merit of the novel, the book was declared obscene under New York's obscenity statute. The decision was upheld by the New York appellate courts. When the case reached the Supreme Court in 1948, Justice Frankfurter did not participate. The other eight justices split four-to-four, resulting in an affirmance of the conviction.

But in a significant decision in 1949, a Philadelphia judge, Curtis Bok, refused to find William Faulkner's *Sanctuary* and *The Wild Palms,* James T. Farrell's *Studs Lonigan* trilogy, and Erskine Caldwell's *God's Little Acre* obscene under Pennsylvania's obscenity statute.

Eight years after Judge Bok's decision the Supreme Court's modern approach to obscenity had its genesis in the 1957 case, *Roth v. United States.*[2] Justice William Brennan wrote the opinion of the Court. The obscenity of the material before the Court could not be disputed, he asserted. The only issue was whether obscenity is protected by the First Amendment. Relying on the statements made by the Court previously in *Chaplinsky* and *Beauharnais,* Brennan's opinion notes that it had always been assumed that obscenity is not protected. While "All ideas having even the slightest redeeming social importance—unorthodox ideas, controversial ideas, even ideas hateful to the prevailing climate of opinion—have the full protection" of the First Amendment, obscenity is "utterly without redeeming social importance." Justice Brennan's opinion declares flatly that "obscenity is not within the area of constitutionally protected speech or press."

Roth includes a dissent by Justices Douglas and Black. Douglas and Black reject the notion that obscenity as a class of speech is beyond the protection of the First Amendment: "To allow the State to step in and punish mere speech or publication that the judge or jury thinks has an undesirable impact on thought, but that is not shown to be a part of unlawful action, is drastically to curtail the First Amendment."

The difficult legacy left by *Roth* has been, first, to explain what is meant by "obscene" and, second, to explain why obscene speech is not protected. The Court's definition of obscenity evolved over the years, through a series of cases,[3] the most important of which was a 1973 decision entitled *Miller v. California.*[4] Three criteria have emerged: (1) the material must, applying community standards, appeal to the prurient interest of the average person; (2) the material must depict or describe sexual conduct in a patently offensive way; and (3) the work, taken as a whole, must lack serious artistic, literary, political or scientific value.

Jerry Falwell could not argue that the *Hustler* Campari ad falls literally within this definition. But he could make very effective use of the rationales behind the regulation of obscenity to justify regulation of the kind of speech contained in the *Hustler* ad.

While it is arguable that the depiction of Falwell as having sex with his mother in an outhouse is patently offensive and devoid of serious redeeming social value, the ad does not seem to appeal to "prurient interest." For that reason alone, the ad is not legally obscene under the *Miller v. California* standard. Speech appealing to prurient interest is speech in which the goal is sexual stimulation; in its classic form prurient speech is essentially an aid to masturbation. Under this view the problem with obscenity is that it is more physical than mental: It's not really speech—it's arousal.[5] In its first attempt to define the term "prurient interest," the Supreme Court thus relied on a dictionary definition describing it as: "itching; longing; of persons, having itching, morbid, or lascivious longings; of desire, curiosity or propensity, lewd, drawing from the etymological meaning of 'prurient' from the Latin *pruriens,* meaning literally 'itch.' " Under the Supreme Court's definition, if the only message in the speech is sexual arousal, if there is no other fancy window-dressing to give the message a veneer of serious literary, artistic, political, or scientific value, then the message may be censored.

But why isn't sexual arousal itself a thought, a message that is redeemed in the pleasure, however cheap or evanescent, it gives the speaker and listener, the writer and reader, the poser and voyeur? Most pornographic speech is an aid to fantasizing about sex, an aid that may provoke reactions that are intellectual, emotional, or physical. Isn't the banning of obscenity essentially a social declaration that those fantasies are impure and improper? And if that is what is really going on, doesn't the banning of obscenity put the government in the role of acting as the "thought police"?[6]

One response to these questions is that the government should police some thought. Why should individuals be permitted to publish material that invites others to engage in thoughts that the community believes are immoral and that the community suspects will lead to antisocial behavior? Contrary to the shallow cliché "you can't legislate morality," law has always been based largely on moral judgments. Laws against incest, adultery, prostitution, and fornication are direct regulations against sexual behavior, grounded in collective community judgments about morality. Indeed, in a landmark 1986 decision, *Bowers v. Hardwick,*[7] the Supreme Court upheld the constitutionality of a Georgia statute criminalizing homosexual sodomy. A number of justices in *Bowers* expressed the view that Georgia could not constitutionally criminalize oral or anal sex between a consenting adult man and a consenting adult woman. Georgia could, however, make the same physical act illegal between two consenting adult males. If engaging in oral sex is within a constitutionally protected sphere of privacy for heterosexuals, why not for homosexuals?

The constitutional difference in the minds of these justices had to be in their perception of the strength of the state interest in the regulation of morality. Homosexuality is historically a moral taboo, and that moral judgment, whether rational or not, could be imposed by a majority on a minority.

If government may regulate adult consensual sexual behavior on the basis of moral judgments concerning that behavior, may it also regulate sexual speech on the basis of moral judgments concerning that speech? The line of Supreme Court cases supporting the prosecution of obscenity give this question at least a qualified "yes." These cases are grounded at least partially in the assumption that books, magazines, and films aimed only at sexual arousal do not communicate actual thoughts but rather communicate something more animalistic and visceral, something more akin to action, which the state may legitimately regulate. A picture that is aimed only at turning you on is not communication, because the sexual turn-on is not an activity of the cognitive side of the brain but rather an activity of the lesser brain functions, brain functions beneath the concern of the First Amendment. If the only reaction to a triple-"X"-rated movie is physical, if it is restricted to "itching" or quickened pulse rates, then the state may ban the photographs because they do not communicate thoughts but are mere surrogates for sex. Lust is not an idea.

Usually the attempt is made to take this approach one step further by arguing that these lustful impulses may lead to overt deviant behavior. Under this view, which forms a prominent part of Attorney General Edwin Meese's controversial 1986 Report on Pornography,[8] such speech does not merely reflect sexual promiscuity, it encourages, and, yes, it *causes* promiscuity.

This argument has been recently augmented with a new boost of respectability from feminists. The feminist critique of obscenity sees it as an incessant message that women are proper objects for exploitation, dominance, and violence. The improbable alliance of fundamentalists and feminists on obscenity is forged by the clear conviction that obscene speech encourages men both to cheat and beat on women.

The application of the rule that obscene speech is not protected by the First Amendment has not been easy. Supreme Court justices have been put to the unseemly exercise of viewing sex movies in the film room of the Supreme Court basement so that they can judge them for prurience, offensiveness, and redeeming value. (The one "redeeming value" of this ritual is that it often gave Justice Thurgood Marshall a chance to use his earthy sense of humor to loosen up his fellow justices. One such case involved a showing of *Vixen,* a soft-core porn film. The sexual plot involves a trip to Cuba, and in the last thirteen minutes the narrator talks about the comparative merits of Western and Communist culture. "Ah," said Marshall, "the redeeming social value!" On another occasion, Marshall turned to Justice Harry Blackmun and cracked, "Well, Harry, I didn't learn anything, how about you?" Blackmun blushed heavily and then joined the other justices and law clerks in wild laughter.)[9]

More significantly, the American experience with prosecution of the obscene is that the judicial system is not always sensitive to claims of redeeming social value. Americans know sexual arousal when they see it, and if given the power, they will often persecute it. James Joyce's *Ulysses* at many points is very sexually arousing, and for decades *Ulysses* was banned in the United States. If today you pick up a Random House or Vintage Books edition of *Ulysses* from your bookshelf or library, you will see printed in the foreword the opinion of federal Judge John Woolsey lifting the ban on the book, as indelible testimony to the place where the presumption that government may choose between good and bad speech will inevitably lead. There is an air of promiscuity to *Leaves of Grass,* and in our history that poem was banned. *Tropic of Cancer* is sexually graphic and blunt; it was censored. *Lady Chatterly's Lover* is a tribute to sensuality and was in its time officially pronounced obscene.

It is perhaps telling that two of the Supreme Court's most respected modern intellectuals, Justice John Marshall Harlan and Justice Potter Stewart, have been frustrated in grappling with obscenity. Dissatisfied with the Court's attempt to define obscenity as if it were as distinct, recognizable, and classifiable as poison ivy, Harlan wrote that since obscenity standards "do not readily lend themselves to generalized definitions, the constitutional problem in the last analysis becomes one of particularized judgments which appellate courts must make for themselves." Likewise, in a famous statement in *Jacobellis v. Ohio*[10] Justice Potter Stewart expressed similar exasperation with trying to define obscenity. "I shall not today attempt further to define the kinds of material I understand to be embraced within that shorthand description; and perhaps I could never succeed in intelligibly doing so," he said. "But I know it when I see it, and the motion picture involved in this case is not that." Justice Stewart's statement "I know it when I see it" became one of the most celebrated judicial quips in First Amendment history. The statement is funny, refreshingly candid, and seems to ring true—most people *do* know obscenity when they see it, whether they can define it in fancy legal language or not. Stewart's statement has a certain earthy pith.

Pith, however, is no substitute for analysis. While the second half of Stewart's discussion—"I know it when I see it"—became the famous line, what is really most important is the first half of his analysis: "I can't define it."

For it has long been understood that speech cannot be penalized on the basis of a standard as subjective and mutable as "I know bad speech when I hear bad speech." The speaker must be told in *advance* exactly what can and cannot be said, and the boundary must be precisely drawn. While Stewart's statement became a popular punch line for those who favored prosecution of obscenity and quoted as an example of the good common sense of at least one Supreme Court justice—a justice who wisely realized obscenity *does* exist and *can* be identified—in truth, Stewart's statement is testimony to the utter arbitrariness of prosecuting obscenity. In a free society, if it can't be defined, it shouldn't be prosecuted.

If the courts have struggled to define obscenity, how could Jerry Falwell convince the Supreme Court that it should add to those struggles by including within the categories of taboo speech such material as the *Hustler* ad? No one is sexually aroused by the thought of Falwell in the outhouse with his mother—the image is nauseous and disgusting but hardly arousing. On the other hand, the *Hustler* ad seems to partake of many of the qualities that are cited to justify barring obscenity. It surely offends community moral sensibilities, and it arguably lacks any serious redeeming social value. Perhaps Falwell could convince the Supreme Court to include *Hustler*'s ad within another of the categories mentioned in *Chaplinsky,* the profane.

Chapter 28

J erry Falwell's effort to include the profane as among the categories of speech deserving little or no First Amendment protection drew support from the one area of American experience in
which profane speech has traditionally been subject to legal penalty:
the regulation of radio and television.

The Supreme Court had dealt with profanity on the airwaves in
a 1978 decision entitled *FCC v. Pacifica Foundation.* [1] The case arose
from the radio broadcast of a twelve-minute comedy monologue by
George Carlin entitled "Filthy Words," which had been recorded
live before an audience in a California theater. Carlin's routine was
a hilarious play on language and cultural values. "A guy who used
to be in Washington who knew that his phone was tapped," cracked
Carlin, "used to answer, 'Fuck Hoover, yes, go ahead.' " Carlin
explained that he'd been thinking about the words you couldn't say
on the airwaves. "Bitch" you could say. "Bastard" you could say.
"Hell" and "damn" you could say. But certain words you could
never say. Carlin explained, "The original seven words were 'shit,'
'piss,' 'fuck,' 'cunt,' 'cocksucker,' 'motherfucker,' and 'tits.' " Those
are "the ones that will curve your spine, grow hair on your hands,
and maybe even bring us, God help us, peace without honor and a
bourbon."

This list is open to amendment, Carlin pointed out, and surely
critique. "And now the first thing we noticed was that the word
'fuck' was really repeated in there, because the word 'motherfucker'

is a compound word and it's another form of the word 'fuck.' You
want to be a purist, it doesn't really—it can't be on the list of basic
words." Carlin also pointed out that "cocksucker" is a compound
word and "neither half of that is really dirty." Each half is only a
"halfway dirty word."

Carlin's routine went on and on and on, ingeniously exploring the
linguistic nuances of the "seven dirty words." He gave a particularly
virtuoso performance on the word "shit," going through a veritable
thesaurus of "shit" expressions (i.e., "shit fit," "bull shit," "bat shit,"
"snake shit," "slicker-than-owl shit," "get your shit together," "shit
or get off the pot," "shit-load," "shit-pot," "shit-head," "shit-heel,"
"shit in your heart," "shit for brains," "shit face"—the list went on,
punctuated with constant raucous laughter from the studio audience.)

At about two o'clock in the afternoon on Tuesday, October 30,
1973, a New York radio station owned by the Pacifica Foundation
broadcasted the monologue. Pacifica is a nonprofit, "listener-owned"
radio network pitched to an avant-garde, politically left audience, a
sort of *Village Voice* of the airwaves. A *few weeks* after the broadcast
of Carlin's monologue, a man wrote a complaint letter to the Federal
Communications Commission. He claimed that he had been driving
with his young son when he heard the broadcast over the car radio.
The letter stated that, while he could perhaps understand the "record's being sold for private use, I certainly cannot understand the
broadcast of same over air that, supposedly, you control."

The FCC forwarded the complaint to Pacifica for comment.
Pacifica maintained that the monologue had been aired during a
program about contemporary society's attitude toward language and
that immediately before its broadcast listeners had been advised that
it included "sensitive language which might be regarded as offensive
to some." Pacifica compared George Carlin to Mark Twain and
Mort Sahl, other social satirists who examined the language of ordinary people. Carlin was not gratuitously mouthing obscenities but
"using words to satirize as harmless and essentially silly our attitudes
towards those words."

The FCC found the broadcast to be "patently offensive," though
not necessarily obscene, and declared that Pacifica's actions in broadcasting the monologue, at least during daytime hours when children
might be listening, violated a federal statute forbidding the use of
"any obscene, indecent, or profane language by means of radio communications." The Commission ruled that while it could have sanc-

tioned Pacifica for the broadcast, it would not do so in this case, but would rather place the matter in Pacifica's file, and, if further complaints were received concerning the station's performance, would consider further sanctions at that time. The FCC thus came down hard on Pacifica's conduct in theory but in practice gave it a mere administrative slap on the wrist.

Pacifica, however, considered any slap at all an abridgement of its First Amendment rights. It appealed the FCC's ruling all the way to the Supreme Court.

The Supreme Court affirmed the FCC's actions in a splintered decision involving four separate opinions. Justice John Paul Stevens wrote the principal opinion for the Court. Stevens held that the First Amendment did not bar the FCC from regulating indecent programming. While speech that is indecent, but not obscene, normally may not be circumscribed by the government in other media the Constitution would clearly not permit the government to ban George Carlin's monologue from distribution on records and tapes and in newspapers, magazines, books and movies or from live performances—the government *could* limit dissemination of the monologue over the airwaves. Broadcasting, the Court held, is special.

The Supreme Court has traditionally justified federal regulation of the airwaves under the so-called "scarcity" rationale. In a case involving the Red Lion Broadcasting Corporation,[2] the Supreme Court upheld the "fairness doctrine," a doctrine that requires balanced treatment of public issues on the grounds that the broadcast spectrum is "scarce," and thus licensees of the airwaves may be made to broadcast in the "public interest."

Scarcity is always a relative concept. It expresses a relationship between supply and demand. The demand side is a constantly shifting pattern of consumer preference; the supply side is also a constantly shifting pattern, a pattern determined both by the availability of investment capital and by the physical limitations of the particular electronic medium at issue. Whether scarcity exists on the airwaves thus depends on what you mean by "scarcity" and where you look for it. It is not the same for VHF, UHF, AM, FM, and cable; it is not the same in all markets.

Two things, however, are clear. The Supreme Court has declared that *economic* scarcity is simply not a constitutional basis for regulation of speech. The fact that economics dictate that very few cities in the nation can support more than one newspaper does not justify an equivalent to the fairness doctrine in the print context.[3] *Physical* scarcity, however, is a constitutional basis for regulation. The Supreme Court held in its *Red Lion* decision that the FCC could require equal time for opposing points of view. (The FCC in 1987 finally abolished the fairness doctrine, deciding that in practice its net effect was to encourage broadcasters to shy away from airing *any* controversial points of view so as to avoid equal time requirements.)

Whenever constitutional law is tied to physical reality, it is threatened with change as physical reality changes. And technology has altered and will continue to alter our relation to the physical electromagnetic world. There is little, if any, scarcity with cable. (We may be tempted to assume that technology must inexorably decrease scarcity, but while it constantly alleviates some scarcities, it creates others. There may be aspects of our physical universe yet to be discovered that will open up vistas of communication as unimaginable to us in 1988 as television was in 1798 or 1898, and those vistas may, like the early days of radio, be plagued by scarcity.)

If the existence of scarcity is an empirical matter that shifts with the physical world, however, the constitutional significance of scarcity is not the stuff of physical matter but of doctrinal matter. Even assuming the existence of scarcity, there are limits to how much scarcity will sustain exceptions to normal First Amendment principles. Scarcity may legitimately sustain the fairness doctrine because there is at least a logical link between the existence of scarcity and the requirement that licensees yield time to permit multiple voices to be heard.

But there is a world of difference between using scarcity to justify the fairness doctrine and using it to justify indecency rules. Indecency rules gather absolutely no analytic sustenance from scarcity because scarcity only justifies multiple voices—it does not justify control over what any individual voice says. Scarcity at most requires that the soapbox be shared—it cannot be used to set limits to what is said while a speaker has the soapbox. Indeed, the theoretical and empirical factors are exactly reversed: Indecency rules are theoretically unsound but empirically effective. The *in terrorem* effect of sweeping FCC rulings on indecency do make broadcasting more decent.

Precisely because scarcity is an intellectually bankrupt concept in relation to indecency, Justice Stevens chose *not* to emphasize scarcity in the George Carlin case. Instead, his analysis rests on two other attributes of broadcasting: its "pervasiveness" and its accessibility to children. Broadcasting has a pervasive influence on our lives,

Stevens argued, particularly on the lives of our children. If we are to teach our children well, then only radio appropriate for children can be aired during hours when children are likely to be listening.

There are, of course, a number of objections to the pervasiveness/protect-our-children rationale. First, pervasiveness is a vague and impressionistic term. Broadcasting may be a unique force in our cultural lives but not because it is uniquely pervasive. Magazines, books, newspapers, billboards, movies, records, compact disks, and video cassettes all bombard us, inside and outside our homes. We may lament that TV's are on too long in most of our houses—but so what? Is that a fact of constitutional significance? And does it even apply to most radio? The pervasiveness of broadcasting does not seem sufficiently different in kind from other media to merit sacrificing normal First Amendment principles.

The second objection is that it is too easy to turn the dial. Should the First Amendment be sacrificed because of the fleeting inconvenience of changing stations? Take George Carlin's "seven dirty words" routine. Even allowing for highly limited hand, eye, and ear coordination, most Americans should be able to switch stations in the interim between the first and second words. As John Madden would diagram it: You're drivin' in your car with your child, you turn on the radio—boom! It's tuned to a Pacifica station. Okay, you've got to listen for that first word. It's offensive! Zap! You turn the dial. Wack! You cover the kid's ears. You're listening to classical music.

The third objection is that, even if kids will furtively turn on indecent broadcasting when no adults are around, secretly viewing and watching it like so many dirty pictures, it is impermissible to reduce all adults to a child's level so that children can be protected. Parents must devise other methods to keep kids from seeing and hearing indecent broadcasts. In the wisdom of Nancy Reagan, "Just say no!"

The cogency of these objections is enough to raise the possibility that the FCC and Justice Stevens actually had a hidden agenda, perhaps so hidden it was subconscious. Pervasiveness and protection of children do not really tell the story. It is not the pervasiveness of broadcasting goading the FCC, but the pervasiveness of indecency. Much of American society—at least some members of the Supreme Court, most people in the recent Reagan administration, and a majority of the FCC—really do not believe in the side of our First Amendment tradition that holds that the indecent but nonobscene should be fully protected. To many *FCC v. Pacifica* should not represent a special broadcasting exception to the usual First Amendment rule—it should *be* the usual First Amendment rule. That expansion of *Pacifica* was precisely what Jerry Falwell hoped to persuade the Supreme Court to undertake.

Some passages of Justice Stevens' opinion in *Pacifica* seem to invoke a perspective on censorship not easily confined to broadcasting, a broader perspective that Falwell hoped to exploit. "It is true," Stevens concedes, "that the Commission's order may lead some broadcasters to censor themselves." This thought, however, did not worry Stevens much because he regarded the nature of the speech that would be censored as of very low social value: "At most, the Commission's definition of indecency will deter only the broadcasting of patently offensive references to excretory and sexual organs and activities." This type of speech, Stevens suggests, probably ought to be censored. "While some of these references may be protected," he states in the opinion, "they surely lie at the periphery of First Amendment."

Stevens insisted that the FCC had not come down on Carlin because of the political content of his monologue or because he was satirizing contemporary attitudes about "four-letter words." Instead, he reasons, the FCC was penalizing the use of these words for their intrinsic offensiveness: "These words offend for the same reasons that obscenity offends." Quoting from *Chaplinsky,* he argues that they form no essential part of any exposition of ideas, and whatever slight value they have is clearly outweighed by the social interest in order and morality. "A requirement that indecent language be avoided will have its primary effect on the form, rather than the content, of serious communication," claims Stevens. "There are few, if any, thoughts that cannot be expressed by the use of less offensive language."

Played back, it is possible to see that Justice Stevens basically dismissed Carlin's monologue as unworthy of the First Amendment because he did not consider it to be "serious communication." Stevens took on directly the view that the form of speech cannot be separated from its content. For Stevens, there is no imaginable content that cannot be expressed in nonoffensive form. Stevens indeed turned a famous line of Justice Harlan, that "one man's vulgarity is another's lyric," exactly upside down. He thus says in *Pacifica:* "one occasion's lyric is another's vulgarity." If Carlin has something serious to say, he can say it nicely. No thought that Carlin might have cannot be rephrased so as to avoid sexual and excretory language. There was no reason to bring "shit," "piss," "fuck," "cunt," "cock-sucker," "motherfucker," and "tits" into the picture.

Justice Stevens probably likes the *Bill Cosby Show,* but would have some trouble with Robin Williams, Eddie Murphy, or Richard Pryor. Justice Stevens probably didn't laugh much at the George Carlin monologue. Whether he laughed or not, he really didn't get Carlin's point. Stevens's argument that any thought Carlin has could be expressed just as easily with nice words is just plain wrong. There is no way that Carlin could have made people laugh uncontrollably over his long litany of "shit" expressions without using the word "shit" forty or fifty times. What was he supposed to say? "Feces?" "Poop?" "Number Two"? A gag based on "bull poop," "owl poop," "horse poop," "cow poop," "rat poop," and "bat poop" just doesn't make it. In arguing that Carlin didn't need to use words with shock value to express any serious thought he might have, Justice Stevens missed the point that the serious thought Carlin did have was an exploration of the curious reasons that these words have shock value. Carlin was using shock to be funny and to be intellectually provoca-tive. He couldn't shock without using the shock words. The shock was part of the thought. The shock was the thought.

Hustler and the various *amici curiae* participants supporting it had to try to convince the Supreme Court that, contrary to these themes in *Pacifica,* the First Amendment should be interpreted as not permitting the regulation of speech for its shock value alone.

Chapter 29

In attempting to determine the legitimacy of the theory that *Hustler*'s parody could be penalized as profane, the Supreme Court struggled with a theme that lies restlessly beneath the surface of *Falwell v. Flynt,* the problem of separation of church and state. While Falwell claimed that it was a proper function of law to regulate morality, Larry Flynt counterargued that it was precisely his disgust with Falwell's fusion of law, morality, and religion that formed the redeeming social value in his vulgar attack. What is the relation between the speech and religion clauses of the First Amendment? Can blasphemy and sacrilege be penalized?

In the context of the life and times of Jerry Falwell this question inevitably poses the difficult question of just how separate religion and politics in America are meant to be.

If it was a fateful radio broadcast tuned in by his mother in the winter of 1952 that triggered Jerry Falwell's religious conversion experience,[1] it was a more complicated series of social events in the 1970s that precipitated his political conversion experience. The formal founding of Falwell's Moral Majority came just as the first presidential term of Jimmy Carter was ending. Carter had to some degree co-opted the emerging political momentum of Evangelicals through his own repeated public invocations of religious faith. Once in office, however, Jimmy Carter was perceived by Evangelicals as Judas.[2] The Carter administration did not press for action on school prayer or abortion. It supported affirmative action and the Equal

Rights Amendment. Evangelical activists were not given federal jobs, and the Carter years were actually a period of gay liberation. About the only good any fundamentalists ever saw in Jimmy Carter was his vow to "whip Teddy Kennedy's ass." Ultimately, however, it was Ronald Reagan who did all the whipping. Indeed, Reagan and Falwell rose to prominence together as great communicators.

During the 1984 Reagan-Mondale presidential campaign, Falwell himself became a campaign issue. Falwell had made the impolitic boast that with Reagan "we will get at least two more appointments to the Supreme Court." Walter Mondale attempted to capitalize on that prediction with a television ad proclaiming that "Ronald Reagan and Rev. Jerry Falwell cordially invite you to their party on November 6." To participate, the ad continues, "Here's all you have to believe in. The secret war in Central America. All new Supreme Court Justices must rule abortion is a crime even in case of rape and incest. No Equal Rights Amendment. No mutually verifiable nuclear freeze." The ad is, to some degree, misleading; Falwell had actually been on record as favoring legalized abortions when rape or incest is involved or to save the life of the mother. Its general thrust, however, is accurate. Falwell certainly would like to have seen the Supreme Court reconstituted in his image. Falwell, for his part, took the Mondale attacks in stride, proclaiming with perfect aplomb that Mondale's barbs were actually helping his Moral Majority to grow. If Mondale were to praise him, after all, Falwell would have to be doing something awfully wrong. "If there was some way I could pay Mr. Mondale to mention us more often, I would," Falwell said. "I only hope that he keeps it up."

Mondale's efforts were, to say the least, ineffectual. Reagan had long since commandeered a majority of the electorate, managing to remake himself as a member of the "new Right," discarding the emphasis of the "old Right." The old Right, the Right of Barry Goldwater and the old Ronald Reagan, had stressed almost exclusively foreign policy and economic issues.[3] The new Right, the Right of Richard Viguerie and the new Jerry Falwell and the new Ronald Reagan, emphasized social issues, such as busing, abortion, school prayer, and pornography—issues that appealed to constituents largely definable in religious terms, born-again Christians and conservative Catholics.[4] One might even see Reagan's ascendancy as a shift in American religious politics, as the Republican party broadened its base from the high-church Protestant upper-middle class (who probably still care most about the issues of the old Right), to

Evangelicals and Catholics, part of the old Democratic coalition of big northern industrial cities and the solid South, for whom the new Right's agenda carried both the philosophy of the day and the electoral college.

Falwell's own political conversion experience was not disingenuous. In his 1980 book, *Listen, America!,*[5] Falwell renounces his old gospel of noninvolvement and calls forth his flock to a new agenda of religious and social reform. "I am seeking to rally together the people of this country who still believe in decency, the home, the family, morality, the free enterprise system, and all the great ideals that are the cornerstone of this nation," Falwell writes. "Against the growing tide of permissiveness and moral decay that is crushing our society, we must make a sacred commitment to God Almighty to turn this nation around immediately." In this new Falwellian vision the religious world can no longer remain aloof from the political world because in a fundamental sense religion *is* politics and politics is religion.

The point was succinctly stated by President Ronald Reagan at a "prayer breakfast" in Dallas in 1984: "The truth is, politics and morality are inseparable, and as morality's foundation is religion, religion and politics are necessarily related." Reagan was emphasizing a theme every bit as "American" as the First Amendment, a theme that has always been a powerful counter to the idea of separation of church and state.

There is nothing new in the contemporary surge of fundamentalist religious influence on American life. The First Great Awakening in the 1730s and 1740s, described by H. Reinhold Niebuhr as "our national conversion," began an almost cyclical American preoccupation with Evangelical conversion and revival. There is something about "that old time religion" that always sells in the American marketplace of ideas.[6]

Today the gospel is an element of mass culture spread through the medium of quasi-public utilities—the governmentally regulated broadcast spectrum and cable television franchises. There was once a time in America, however, when government regulated not merely the medium but the message. As Professor William Lee Miller, an expert on American religion from the University of Virginia, puts it, "Citizens of this now very liberated country may find it stunning and amusing that once upon a time some of the forbears thought of religion as a kind of public utility like the gas or water works, but they did." Taxes could be used to support the established church, because the established church supplied the secular state with the morality necessary for survival. Virginia's General Assessment bill in 1784 recited the equation: "The general diffusion of Christian knowledge hath a natural tendency to correct the morals of men, restrain their vices, and preserve the peace of society." These were virtually Ronald Reagan's very words, exactly two hundred years later.

South Carolina's version of establishment in 1778 went so far as to provide a precise legal definition of the "Christian Protestant religion" it was establishing, nicely reduced to five tenets:

1st   That there is one eternal God, and a future state of rewards and punishments.
2nd   That God is publicly to be worshipped.
3rd   That the Christian religion is the true religion.
4th   That the Holy Scriptures of the Old and New Testaments are of divine inspiration and are the rule of faith and practice.
5th   That it is lawful and the duty of every man, being thereunto called by those that govern, to bear witness to the truth.[7]

Depending on how the term is defined and when the sample is taken, over half the colonies had some form of established church, including New Hampshire, Connecticut, New Jersey, Georgia, North Carolina, South Carolina, and, with special reservations, Massachusetts. Massachusetts had established in its constitution the "Standing Order," the Congregational Church of Massachusetts. In 1780 a new Massachusetts constitution, heavily influenced by the efforts of John Adams, created a form of decentralized "multiple establishment." Each town was required to use its own tax money to hire "public Protestant teachers of piety, religion, and morality." The liberating element in this was that these preacher-teachers theoretically could be drawn from any Protestant church—Congregationalist, Anglican, Quaker, Baptist—though obviously no Catholics needed apply. (Several ethnic migrations later, in a climate of constitutionally disestablished religion, their turn came for political dominance in the state.) The provision in the new Massachusetts constitution, which retained the device of tax-supported religion, was supported by influential liberal or Unitarian elements in the state. (Even in 1780, it seems, liberals were important in Massachusetts, as if by some ironic form of political Calvinism it was predestined that Massachusetts would be the only state one day carried by George McGovern.)

To fundamentalists, indeed, the First Amendment's wall of separation between church and state had already come tumbling down like the walls of Jericho as American society began to embrace its own unique established church: the church of secular humanism. But for fundamentalists this was not the mode through which church and state should be combined. The cultural turmoil and permissiveness that began in the 1960s led Evangelicals in the 1970s to a general sense that the moral foundations of American society were crumbling.[8] Secular humanism, a pervasive quasi-religious set of values that conservatives see as dominated by amorality, evolution, and atheism, is the prime source of the moral decline. Not to enter the political arena would be to abdicate to that moral decline. Somehow the good moral instincts of Americans had to be tapped into and stirred to action. America's moral gyroscope was still there, somewhere, in that quiet law-abiding majority of men of good will, but it was being smothered by the magnetic tones of mass culture, which portrayed a licentious, narcissistic, selfish, and self-absorbed ethos of libertine materialism. If the majority was still moral, it was high time for it to rise up and assert itself.

Falwell's message of participation in the political arena is, from his perspective, clearly above reproach. It is, indeed, indistinguishable from the intense black-voter registration efforts of Reverend Jesse Jackson. After the regular Sunday morning church service in Lynchburg, Falwell would ask his whole congregation to stand. He would then instruct all the registered voters to sit down. Those still standing would be lectured on their duty to register and vote. Fundamentalist churches around the country followed this exercise, even setting up voting booths outside the church.

This sort of blatant politicizing of the Sunday church service, however, does not come without a heavy cost. Jerry Falwell's political conversion runs against the grain of that side of the American character that has always reacted with instinctive suspicion of any overt mixing of politics and religion.

Technically, of course, Falwell's actions raise absolutely no First Amendment problems. The First Amendment's majestic proclamation that "Congress shall make no law respecting an establishment of religion, or prohibiting the free exercise thereof" on its face appears to be a restraint only on *governmental* interference with the free exercise of or governmental establishment of religion. The words do not swing both ways: They do not purport to restrict efforts by religion to limit the "free exercise of" or to refrain from "respecting an establishment of" government. The First Amendment commands neutrality by government in relation to religion, not by religion in relation to government. Government may, of course, become captured by a religious group, enacting laws for religious rather than secular purposes. In such cases the courts strike down the governmental action involved for having run afoul of the establishment clause. The constitutional sin in such cases is the government's for giving into religious temptation. It is not the sin of religion for doing the tempting—the Constitution can't blame the church for trying.

Modern Supreme Court doctrines governing separation of church and state are sensitive to this difference. In a 1971 case involving programs by Rhode Island and Pennsylvania that provided various types of aid to parochial schools, the Supreme Court established a three-part test for assessing Establishment Clause issues.[9] The statute in question "must have a secular legislative purpose," its "principal or primary effect must be one that neither advances nor inhibits religion," and the statute must not foster "an excessive government entanglement with religion." This test works reasonably well when the alleged establishment of religion involves financial aid to religious enterprises. In financial aid cases the Supreme Court has applied this test with painstaking precision, often drawing extraordinarily sharp lines. Thus, the Court held that New York could not reimburse parochial schools for the costs of state-mandated testing of students, when those tests were "traditional teacher-prepared tests," because of the danger that the tests might be tainted by elements of religious instruction. New York could, however, reimburse parochial schools for the costs of administering state-mandated standardized tests and scoring services, since the inability of the religious school to control the test content avoided the danger of infiltration of religious elements and excessive church-state entanglement.[10]

When the alleged violation of the First Amendment involves some allegation of nonfinancial establishment of religion, however, matters become much more difficult. If a church is successful in getting the secular state to adopt laws in harmony with the value structure of the church, has the state impermissibly "established" religion? If the Moral Majority, for example, is able to convince a state legislature that its previous hospitality to homosexual lifestyle preferences was morally misguided and, after intense lobbying, persuades the legislature to crack down severely on homosexual conduct, has the First Amendment been violated? Or if, as in Falwell's

case against Flynt, antipathy for religion is part of what makes a
speaker's statements "outrageous" or "indecent," is the law impermissibly establishing respect for (and thus respecting an establishment of) religion?

In a magnificent book exploring the traditions of religious freedom in America, *The First Liberty: Religion and the American Republic,* [11] religious studies scholar William Lee Miller describes a
prototypical modern American battle over separation of church and
state. Moved by the proclamation of John 3:16 that "God so loved
the world, that he gave his only begotten Son, that whosoever believeth in him should not perish, but have everlasting life," a fundamentalist preacher posts the scriptural citation on the public water
fountain of the local municipal softball field, hoping to "combat
juvenile delinquency, fight communism, and maintain Godly softball." This foments an instantaneous attack from the ACLU, the
local Unitarian Church, and the liberal columnist at the state metropolitan newspaper, who collectively invoke "the First Amendment,
the Founding Fathers, and the principles that have made this country great" and who throw in for good measure "the bodies burned
in the Spanish Inquisition." The fundamentalist minister and those
who have joined his cause then counterattack, in their turn also
citing "the Founding Fathers," their "firm belief in God," the "principles that have made this country great—its institutions presupposing a Supreme Being—and mention angrily the dangerous inroads of
secular humanism." The mayor puts his head into the sand and
maintains total silence as soon as it is explained to him that it would
not do to have a menorah on the other side of the fountain. The
problem finally all gets dumped into the hands of a hapless judge
with one giant Excedrin headache, who must puzzle the matter out
as only lawyers do: "Are *taxes* used to pay for the water fountain?
Does any *state employee* turn on the water?"[12]

Within Falwell's own religious heritage two antagonistic strains
in the Calvinist tradition have always lived in tension. The Pilgrims
were Separatist, pietistic, and inward-looking; for them spiritual salvation would come from personal communion with God. The Puritans, in contrast, believed in a state church, a government itself
infused with the Holy Spirit. In his migration from Pilgrim to Puritan, Jerry Falwell can legitimately take his charge directly from
Calvin's writings: "I now commit to civil government the duty of
rightly establishing religion," Calvin says, "to present the true religion which is contained in God's law from being openly and with

public sacrilege violated and defiled with impunity." For Calvin the "appointed end" of civil government is "to cherish and protect the outward worship of God, to defend a sound doctrine of piety and position of the church," and "to adjust our life to the society of men to form our social behavior to civil righteousness."

Moral Majority reasoning thus has its roots in the Puritan insistence that "the wicked shall not bear rule" and that the state church of visible saints ruled by Puritan divines would determine who was wicked and who was not.

Against this tradition of religiously inspired social control, however, there is a countertradition equally venerable, a tradition of tolerance, freedom of conscience, and separation of church and state. The first great patron saint of this tradition of separation was Roger Williams, who came to Massachusetts Bay in 1631. While Williams resembled traditional Calvinist Puritans in most matters of religious doctrine, he separated from them on religious persecution and state-enforced religion. In his letter to the Town of Providence in 1655, Williams uses the parable of a ship to make his point:

> It hath fallen out sometimes that both Papists and Protestants, Jews and Turks, may be embarked in one ship; upon which supposal I affirm all the liberty of conscience that ever I pleaded for turns upon these two hinges; that none of the Papists, Protestants, Jews, or Turks be forced to come to the ship's prayers or worship, nor compelled from their own particular prayers or worship, if they practice any.[13]

Roger Williams was a passionate advocate of tolerance, whose writings are drenched in references to blood and the various methods by which the wrath of blood is spilled in the name of religious conscience: in the "bloody, irreligious, inhumane, oppressions under the mask or veil of the name of Christ"; in the "wrong and preposterous way of suppressing, parenting, and extinguishing such doctrine or practices by weapons of wrath and blood—whips, stock, imprisonment, banishment, death." Williams phrases his commitment to religious freedom with poetic violence, speaking of "spiritual rape," "soul yokes," "soul oppression," "rivers of civil blood," and "the blood of so many hundred thousands of slaughtered men, women, and children, by such uncivil and unchristian wars and combustions about Christian faith and religion."

Early Baptist preachers were often the most forceful and constant clerical advocates of freedom of religion in the emerging American nation. Baptists were once the upstarts in the American religious spectrum, decidedly not the religious establishment in law or social position. They had the most to lose from establishment and fought eloquently against it, creating an improbable alliance with Madison and Jefferson, perhaps the "secular humanists" of the day.

Jerry Falwell might very persuasively argue, however, that his ministry represents a synthesis of the two long-competing strains of Calvinism—that out of the thesis of state control of religion and the antithesis of religious liberty he has created a fusion of intense religious involvement in secular life within a framework of democratic tolerance. Falwell's Moral Majority is thus not inconsistent with Roger Williams's metaphor of the ship with "Papists, Protestants, Jews, and Turks," for the voyage of the Moral Majority was deliberately launched with Catholics, Jews, Protestants, and Mormons all on board. (Falwell would certainly argue that the absence of a token "Turk" or two is but a quibble.) For Falwell, the Moral Majority is not out to create a state religion but to prevent one—secular humanism. It is not the program of the Moral Majority to stack the Supreme Court with fundamentalists but with "moralists" of no particular denomination—a conservative Jewish Douglas Ginsburg with Robert Bork propensities would have done just fine. Falwell, indeed, might invite one to continue reading Roger Williams's famous letter to the Town of Providence, in which Williams makes it clear that religious tolerance does not imply moral anarchy:

> I further add that I never denied that, notwithstanding this liberty, the commander of this ship ought to command the ship's course, yea, and also command that justice, peace, and sobriety be kept and practiced, both among the seamen and all the passengers.[14]

On Roger Williams's ship of state the government must tolerate all faiths, but at the same time it may demand of all on the ship the observance of basic norms of good citizenship. All must pay their way and obey the ship's laws. If any on the ship should argue for mutiny *on religious grounds,* the captain may legitimately put down the rebellion and punish the mutineers:

> If any should preach or write that there ought to be no commanders or officers because all are equal in Christ, therefore no masters or officers, law or orders, corrections or punishments—I say, I never deny but in such cases, whatever is intended, the commander or

commanders may judge, resist, compel, and punish such transgressors according to their deserts and merits.[15]

Falwell's most forceful point, however, is that, while fundamentalists must tolerate the presence of Catholics, Jews, Episcopalians, or Mormons on the ship, fundamentalists are under no duty to refrain from trying to convert the others to the true faith and have a perfect right to try to influence the captain in his role as administrator of the ship's secular laws. "We're not religious fanatics who have in mind a Khomeini-type religious crusade to take over the government," says Falwell. "We support the separation of church and state. We want influence, not control." Falwell once stated that "I think America is great, but not because it is a Christian nation: It is *not* a Christian nation, it has never been a Christian nation, it is never going to be a Christian nation. It is not a Jewish nation. It is a nation *under God,* and a nation in which for two hundred years there has been absolute freedom to preach whatever religious conviction one might have, without ever impinging on the liberties and freedom of others." That liberty does not preclude, however, pressing vigorously for one's own moral agenda. Falwell can thus plausibly maintain that while Roger Williams may require that "Papists, Protestants, Jews, and Turks" all be given tolerant passage, the ship need not accommodate homosexuals, adulterers, pornographers, or abortionists.

It is against this legacy of profoundly different American impulses on what separation of church and state means that the Supreme Court considered whether it was legitimate to include the anti-religious insult in *Hustler*'s ad satire as part of the justification for treating it as so offensive that it forfeits its First Amendment protection.

The Court's consideration of the concepts of sacrilege and blasphemy in *Falwell v. Flynt* was not done on a completely clean slate. In other cultures of the world, it is clear, Larry Flynt's speech might be persecuted as sacrilegious or blasphemous. Thou shalt not attack the high priests. But in America there are Supreme Court precedents indicating that the high priests must fend for themselves; the secular state will not punish blasphemy or sacrilege. We place "In God We Trust" on our coinage, and the sessions of the United States Supreme Court begin with the invocation "God save the United States and this Honorable Court." But in fact, the statements "In God We Trust" and "God is dead" are both equally protected by our First Amendment tradition. The Constitution's guarantee of freedom of speech is not the exclusive—if even the primary—legal source of our cultural taboo against the official punishment of sacrilege and blasphemy. The prohibition against such punishment comes from the religion clauses themselves. To punish the sacrilegious is inevitably to prohibit the free exercise of one man's religion and to erect an establishment of another's.

The point is well made by the story of one Jesse Cantwell, a Jehovah's Witness. Cantwell stopped two Roman Catholic men on the street to push his religious wares, playing for them a phonograph record virulently attacking Catholicism. The two Catholic men were outraged and screamed at Cantwell to leave them alone, which he did. The confrontation did not end there, however. Cantwell was arrested and charged with breach of peace and soliciting without a license. Cantwell's conviction on both counts was overturned by the Supreme Court in the 1940 decision *Cantwell v. Connecticut*. The technical ground for the decision involves the failure of the breach of peace statute to be sufficiently narrowly drawn to define specifically the prohibited conduct. But in his opinion for the Court, Justice Roberts explains the perils of government intervention into religious disputes:

> In the realm of religious faith, and in that of political belief, sharp differences arise. In both fields, the tenets of one man may seem the rankest error to his neighbor. To persuade others to his own point of view, the pleader, as we know, at times, resorts to exaggeration, to vilification of men who have been, or are, prominent in church or state, and even to false statement. But the people of this nation have ordained in the light of history, that, in spite of the probability of excesses and abuses, these liberties are, in the long view, essential to enlightened opinion and right conduct on the part of the citizens of a democracy.[16]

The Supreme Court dealt even more directly with the concept of sacrilege in *Burstyn v. Wilson,* decided in 1952. An Italian movie called *The Miracle* was denied a license by New York on the ground that it contained sacrilegious material. The Supreme Court held that the term "sacrilege" was too amorphous to guide the censor and struck down the licensing law as impermissibly vague.

Sacred persons, places, and things may, it is clear, be protected just like any other persons, places, or things, by our routine criminal and tort laws covering such things as assault, battery, theft, or trespass. No one has a right to punch a priest, minister, or rabbi in the nose, to steal vestments or relics, or to burn, bomb, or deface a church or synagogue. There is no need to speak of sacrilege to punish such offenses.

The punishment of sacrilege or blasphemy, however, has historically been aimed at something quite different from common protection of people, places, and things. As Justice Frankfurter explains:

If "sacrilegious" bans more than the physical abuse of sacred persons, places, or things, if it permits censorship of religious opinions, which is the effect of the holding below, the term will include what may be found to be "blasphemous." England's experience with that treacherous word should give us pause, apart from our requirements for the separation of church and state. The crime of blasphemy in Seventeenth Century England was the crime of dissenting from whatever was the current religious dogma. King James I's "Book of Sports" was first required reading in the churches; later all copies were consigned to the flames. To attack the mass was once blasphemous; to perform it became so. At different times during that century, with the shifts in the attitude of government towards particular religious views, persons who doubted the doctrine of the Trinity (e.g., Unitarians, Universalists, etc.) or the divinity of Christ, observed the Sabbath on Saturday, denied the possibility of witchcraft, repudiated child baptism or urged methods of baptism other than sprinkling, were charged as blasphemers, or their books were burned or banned as blasphemous. Blasphemy was the chameleon phrase which meant the criticism of whatever the ruling authority of the moment established as orthodox religious doctrine.[17]

Frankfurter's eloquent words certainly hurt Falwell's cause, at least insofar as Flynt's attack on religion formed part of the outrage on which Falwell's recovery was based.

Flynt's attack was not just religious, however. It was also personal and premeditated, and Falwell could argue that, while under the establishment clause his status as a minister should not enhance his case, under the free exercise clause his religious status should not handicap him, either. The defense still had to meet Falwell's principal argument head-on: that this type of speech forms no essential part of the exposition of ideas, and, because it is vulgar, offensive, and distressing, it is undeserving of constitutional shelter.

Chapter 30

F or *Hustler* to overcome Falwell's arguments, it had to press vigorously a number of First Amendment theories that proceed from a philosophical tradition quite sharply opposed to Jerry Falwell's view of the First Amendment. One of these is the argument that the government should not be permitted to penalize speech for its emotionally disturbing qualities alone. To justify abridgement of speech, this argument goes, government must demonstrate a clear and present danger that the speech will cause some more palpable species of social harm.

This argument has suffered a checkered history.[1] In both England and the United States exactly the opposite has often been true: Speech has been subject to penalty on the mere suspicion of its bad tendencies, without any evidence of imminently pending harm. Historians continue to debate what the framers had in mind with the First Amendment. There is disagreement, for example, on the extent to which public opinion against prosecution for "seditious libel" had crystallized as of the adoption of the Bill of Rights. It is clear that many Americans, including James Madison, felt deeply that the American system should break sharply with the British tradition, a tradition that tended to fluctuate between tolerance for and persecution of dissent. Early "free speech" literature flourished in the middle of the seventeenth century. John Milton's great defense of freedom of speech, his *Areopagitica,* was published in 1644. During the rule of the inquisitorial Star Chamber in 1637, however, author

William Prynn was fined, pilloried, sentenced to life in prison, and had his ears cropped off for writing a book critical of the queen. The infamous case of John Twyn in 1663 is gory testimony to the sometimes bloody excesses of English prosecutions for sedition and treason. Twyn's book, *A Treatise on the Execution of Justice*, makes the argument that the king is accountable to the people and "that the people may take up arms against a king and his family and put the king to death if he refuses accountability." Twyn was convicted of treason on the sole basis of printing a "seditious, poisonous and scandalous book." Lest these dirty thoughts spread to others, the court imposed a sanction quite literally worse than mere death—a barbaric, torturous death:

> The judgment is that you be led back to the place from whence you came and from thence to be drawn upon an hurdle to the place of execution; and there you shall be hanged by the neck, and being alive, shall be cut down, and your privy-members shall be cut off, your entrails shall be taken out of your body, and you living, the same to be burnt before your eyes; your head to be cut off, your body to be divided into four quarters and your head and quarters to be disposed of at the pleasure of the King's Majesty. And the Lord have mercy upon your soul.[2]

Have a nice day! It was against this inconsistent backdrop of tolerance and barbaric punishment for dissent that the early American free speech tradition began to form.

Even the American free speech tradition, however, had a highly ambivalent start. One of the darkest episodes came shortly after the adoption of the Constitution, during the presidency of John Adams. The Federalist Congress and Adams, the last Federalist president, passed the Sedition Act of 1798, an act that criminalized speech merely because it was critical of the existing order. The act provided, in part:

> If any person shall write, print, utter or publish . . . any false scandalous and malicious writings against the government of the United States or either house of Congress of the United States or the President of the United States with intent to defame the said government, or either house of the said Congress, or the said President or to bring them or either of them into contempt, or disrepute; or to excite against them or either of any of them the hatred of the good people of the

United States . . . then such person being convicted shall be punished
by a fine not exceeding $2,000 and by imprisonment not exceeding two
years.[3]

The act was an Americanized version of the old English crime of
"seditious libel," or slander against the king. Most societies have at
some stage in their history employed some version of seditious libel.
Open societies constantly struggle with where to draw the line between dissent and sedition. Most closed societies have abandoned
that struggle, however, and instead employ seditious libel as a cornerstone in the edifice of state suppression. The crime of slander
against the state is the most vital weapon in the arsenal of despotic
government, the weapon that silences those who dare dissent.

The Sedition Act expired by its own terms after two years. At the
beginning of his term the new president, Thomas Jefferson, immediately pardoned everyone who had been convicted under the act.
(During a visit to Jefferson, the German scientist Baron Alexander
von Humboldt saw a newspaper in the President's study filled with
scurrilous abuse of him. "Why are these libels allowed?" he asked,
picking up the paper. "Why is not this libelous journal suppressed,
or its editor, at least, fined and imprisoned?" "Put that paper in your
pocket, Baron," said Jefferson, smiling, "and should you hear the
reality of our liberty, the freedom of the press questioned, show them
this paper, and tell them where you found it.")

James Madison, the primary author of the Bill of Rights, had
eloquently renounced the Sedition Act, rhetorically asking whether
but for freedom of speech, "Might not the United States have been
languishing at this day, under the infirmities of a sickly confederation? Might they not, possibly, be miserable colonies, groaning under
a foreign yoke?" Because of its short duration and the pardons
granted by Jefferson, no test of the Sedition Act ever reached the
Supreme Court.

The First Amendment's next great period of trial came during
the isolationist protests over World War I. Again, the Supreme
Court failed miserably to protect freedom of speech, as one protester
after another had his or her conviction affirmed by the Court. Perhaps the lowest ebb came with the Supreme Court's decision in 1919
affirming the conviction of Eugene Debs. Debs came to national
prominence as a labor leader in the 1890s, when he led a successful
strike for higher wages against the Great Northern Railroad in 1894
and drew sympathy and support from workers across the nation after

being sentenced to a six-month jail term for his role in the infamous Chicago Pullman strike. Debs was a warm, compassionate leader; he campaigned for William Jennings Bryan for president in 1896 and then went on to found the Socialist Party of America. Debs was the Socialist Party's candidate for the presidency four times between 1900 and 1920. His highest popular vote total was 915,000, which he received while in prison for having publicly criticized the prosecutions of others who had opposed America's entry into World War I.

On June 16, 1918, Debs spoke in Canton, Ohio, on the future of American socialism and the immorality of the United States' involvement in World War I. Debs said in the speech that he had just returned from a visit to three comrades who were paying the penalty for their devotion to the working class, having been convicted of aiding and abetting resistance to the draft. He stated that he "was proud of them." Speaking of the war, Debs said that "the master class has always declared the war and the subject class has always fought the battles, . . . the subject class has had nothing to gain and all to lose, including their lives," and "the working class, who furnish the corpses, have never yet had a voice in declaring war and have never yet had a voice in declaring peace." Debs exhorted, "You need to know that you are fit for something better than slavery and cannon fodder."

For this speech, Debs was brought to trial under the Espionage Act of 1917. He addressed the jury himself, and, while contending vigorously that his speech did not warrant the charges against him, he nonetheless courageously proclaimed, "I have been accused of obstructing the war. I admit it. Gentlemen, I abhor war. I would oppose the war if I stood alone." Debs was found guilty and sentenced to two concurrent ten-year terms of imprisonment.

When Debs's case reached the Supreme Court, Justice Holmes, writing for a unanimous Court, affirmed Debs's conviction without the slightest hint of reservation or remorse that Debs was being sent to jail for having expressed political opinions.[4] Justice Holmes's opinion states matter-of-factly that "one purpose of the speech, whether incidental or not does not matter, was to oppose not only war in general but this war," and that the opposition was so expressed "that its natural and intended effect would be to obstruct recruiting." Debs went to prison. He was released by presidential order in 1921, but his citizenship was never restored.

It was about this time that the "bad tendency" approach to the regulation of speech began to be challenged by some of America's best legal minds. The challenge began with an increasing emphasis on precision and specificity in governmental efforts to circumscribe speech. The requirement of precision in free-speech regulation was given its first brilliant articulation in 1917, by one of America's most penetrating jurists, Judge Learned Hand. The magazine *The Masses,* led by writer John Reed, had been prosecuted for its insurgent tendencies. (Reed wrote *Ten Days That Shook the World*; he is buried in Lenin Square in Moscow and was memorialized by Warren Beatty in the movie *Reds.*) In *Masses Publishing Co. v. Patten,* [5] Judge Hand quashed the prosecution, drawing a sharp distinction between an exact pinpointing of the element of the speech that violates the law and persecution for the "general ethos" of the speech. "The tradition of English-speaking freedom has depended, in no small part, upon the merely procedural requirement that the state point with exactness to just that conduct which violates the law," according to Hand. This "merely procedural" requirement is no less than elemental fair play in permitting the accused to mount a full and vigorous defense. For, as Hand notes, "It is difficult and often impossible to meet the charge that one's general ethos is treasonable."

This requirement of surgical precision in the regulation of speech is not instinctual. Indeed, it runs directly contrary to mankind's natural habit of mind, which is to stereotype others in terms of composite worldviews and then vow allegiance to or disgust for "everything they stand for." We label others "Reaganites," "knee-jerk liberals," "chauvinists," "feminists," "Communists," "long-hairs," "hippies," "yippies," and "yuppies," and then reflexively spout our preprogrammed prejudices accordingly. [6] These self-indulgent prejudices, however, are precisely what the government must rise above, never succumbing to the natural inclination to punish the likes of a Larry Flynt (a "sleaze peddler" or "porn king") merely for the unpopularity of what he represents rather than for what he actually does.

Easily the most important figure in giving impetus to the notion that speech should not be penalized for its bad tendencies was Justice Oliver Wendell Holmes. Following his anti-speech decision in the Eugene Debs case, Holmes underwent a mysterious metamorphosis. [7] Holmes had sent Debs to jail with apparently guiltless dispatch, but shortly after the *Debs* case Holmes's thinking seemed to undergo a deep change. As the next group of World War I protest cases reached the Court, Holmes defected from the consensus on the Court that such convictions were valid and began to write eloquently in dissent. His masterpiece was his dissent in *Abrams v. United States,*[8] in which he wrote words so haunting and powerful that they have become part of the literature of the nation. The case involved five Russian immigrants who had printed five thousand leaflets written in English and Yiddish protesting the combination of "German militarism" and "allied capitalism" to "crush the Russian revolution." The leaflets were distributed by tossing them out the upper-story window of the building in which one of the defendants worked in New York. For this the defendants were convicted under the Espionage Act and sentenced to twenty years in prison. As in all of the other cases from this period, the Supreme Court expeditiously affirmed. But for the first time there were voices calling out from the Court in protest, in the figures of Oliver Wendell Holmes and Louis Brandeis.

Over the next decade Holmes and Brandeis became famous for their dissents in First Amendment cases, but the philosophy expressed in those opinions was not truly embraced by the Court until five decades later. In *Abrams* Holmes almost seemed to have undergone a conversion; his eyes saw what they could not see in the Debs case. The defendants were being punished not for any real threat their words posed to the nation, for not enough could be squeezed from their "poor and puny anonymities to turn the color of legal litmus paper" to justify *twenty years* worth of prison time. No, transparently, they were being persecuted for the unpopularity of their creed, for the fear and loathing felt by a jury of New Yorkers in 1918 for the radical philosophy of five Russian troublemakers. For Holmes "persecution for the expression of opinion seems to me perfectly logical." This natural human tendency, however, is not the theory of our Constitution. For "when men have realized that time has upset many fighting faiths," Holmes says, "they may come to believe even more than they believe the foundations of their own conduct that the best test of truth is the power of the thought to get itself accepted in the competition of the market." And then in one of the most eloquent passages ever to emerge from Holmes's pen, he admonishes that the idea of a free marketplace of ideas

> . . . is an experiment, as all life is an experiment. Every year, if not every day, we have to wager our salvation upon some prophecy based upon imperfect knowledge. While that experiment is part of our system, I think that we should be eternally vigilant against attempts to check the expression of opinions that we loath and believe to be

fraught with death, unless they so imminently threaten immediate
interference with the lawful and pressing purposes of the law that an
immediate check is required to save the country.

Holmes had come a long way from his earlier reliance on the lame
truism that the First Amendment does not authorize shouting
"Fire!" in a crowded theater. Now his message was at once more
poetic and extreme: Even speech *fraught with death* must be tolerated unless it imminently threatens *immediate interference* with
pressing purposes. It was decades, however, before the free speech
philosophy of Holmes and his intellectual compatriot, Justice Louis
Brandeis, commanded the acceptance of a majority of the Supreme
Court.

Chapter 31

T he Holmes-Brandeis tradition was vital to *Hustler*'s defense. It was *Hustler*'s good fortune that to counter cases such as *Chaplinsky, Beauharnais,* and *Pacifica,* it could point to a number of modern cases that stand against the notion that speech may be penalized merely for its offensiveness, shock value, or bad tendencies.

One of the most important decisions in this line is *Brandenburg v. Ohio,*[1] a case that arose from a Ku Klux Klan rally in Hamilton County, Ohio. A reporter for a Cincinnati television station was invited to attend a Klan rally on a farm outside Cincinnati. The reporter and a cameraman filmed the rally, portions of which were later broadcast on the Cincinnati station and on a national network. The film footage shows hooded figures carrying a large wooden cross, a Bible, shotguns, pistols, and rifles. The sound quality of the film is poor, and much of the language used by various speakers is incomprehensible. It is, however, possible to make out some portions of the speeches. They are viciously and hysterically racist, with statements such as "the nigger should be returned to Africa, the Jew to Israel" and "if our President, our Congress, our Supreme Court, continues to suppress the white, Caucasian race, it's possible that there might have to be some revengence [sic] taken."

The state of Ohio prosecuted the leader of the Klan group under the Ohio Criminal Syndicalism Statute, which makes it illegal to advocate "the duty, necessity, or propriety of crime, sabotage, violence, or unlawful methods of terrorism as a means of accomplishing industrial or political reform" or to assemble "with any group, or assemblage of persons formed to teach or advocate the doctrines of criminal syndicalism." The defendant Brandenburg was convicted, fined $1,000, and sentenced to one to ten years' imprisonment.

In a 1969 decision the Supreme Court unanimously reversed the conviction. "The constitutional guarantees of free speech and free press," according to the Court, "do not permit a State to forbid or proscribe advocacy of the use of force or of law violation except where such advocacy is directed to inciting or producing imminent lawless action and is likely to incite or produce such action." The mere "abstract teaching" of the "moral propriety" of violence is not the same as steeling a group actually to engage in violent action.

No one was present at the Klan rally except the Klan members, the reporter, and his cameraman. There was no proof that the wild-eyed orgy of racism on the Hamilton County farm posed any actual threat to anyone else. However ugly and sickening the race-hate of the Klan members may have been, it posed no imminent danger of lawless action.

The Court reaffirmed this principle in a 1973 decision, *Hess v. Indiana*.[2] Gregory Hess was convicted of violating Indiana's disorderly conduct statute in an anti-Vietnam War demonstration on the campus of Indiana University. About one hundred to one-hundred fifty demonstrators had moved onto a public street, blocking traffic. After refusing to obey the sheriff's command to clear the street, the demonstrators were moved to the curbs by the sheriff and his deputies. As the sheriff passed by Hess, Hess said, "We'll take the fucking street later." The sheriff immediately arrested Hess for disorderly conduct. Hess was convicted.

The Supreme Court overturned the conviction by a six-to-three vote. The majority held that Hess could not be convicted merely for having used the word "fuck" since that word standing alone did not satisfy the legal definition of obscenity. Nor could Hess's statement be seen as a direct verbal challenge to fight the sheriff or his deputies—witnesses testified that he was facing the crowd, not the street, when he made the statement and that his words did not appear to be addressed to any particular person or group.

Finally, the Court held that the statement did not satisfy the *Brandenburg* requirement of an incitement to *imminent* lawless action. The words "We'll take the fucking street later," the Court maintained, could be taken as a counsel for "present moderation" or as advocacy of illegal action "at some indefinite future time." This was not enough to constitute a threat of imminent disorder, and thus Hess's right to freedom of speech made it impermissible for the state to charge him with disorderly conduct.

Perhaps no case, however, is more vital to Flynt's defense than *Cohen v. California.* On April 28, 1968, Paul Robert Cohen was observed in the corridor outside of the municipal court of the Los Angeles County Courthouse wearing a jacket bearing the words "Fuck the Draft." Women and children were present in the corridor. Cohen did not engage in any act of violence, he did not threaten any act of violence, and no other person engaged in or threatened violence in reaction to his jacket. Cohen said nothing and made no unusual noise of any kind. He wore the words "Fuck the Draft" on his jacket as a means of informing the public of the depth of his feelings against the Vietnam War and the draft. Cohen was arrested for wearing the jacket with the offending words and convicted of disturbing the peace. He was given thirty days' imprisonment.

Cohen challenged the conviction, and his case reached the United States Supreme Court in 1970. Cohen was represented by Melville Nimmer, acting on behalf of the ACLU. Nimmer, a professor at the U. C. L. A. Law School, was one of the nation's foremost experts on the First Amendment. As Nimmer approached the podium and prepared to commence his argument, Chief Justice Burger tried to signal him not to use the " 'F'-word," stating that "the Court is thoroughly familiar with the factual setting of this case and it will not be necessary . . . for you to dwell on the *facts.*"

The Chief Justice's hint at restraint, however, was no mere trifling request for decorum. To Nimmer it threatened to set precisely the wrong psychological tone in the courtroom. Nimmer, ever the courageous advocate, thought it essential that there be no tacit concession that the word is unspeakable. And so Melville Nimmer began his argument: "At the Chief Justice's suggestion," he stated, "I certainly will keep very brief the statement of facts. . . . What this young man did was to walk through the courthouse corridor . . . wearing a jacket on which were inscribed the words 'Fuck the Draft.' "

Nimmer won the case for his client; Cohen's conviction was reversed by the Supreme Court in a decision written by Justice John Marshall Harlan. Harlan opens his opinion by remarking that "This case may seem, at first blush, too inconsequential to find its way into our books, but the issue it presents is of no small constitutional significance."

Harlan begins his analysis by stripping away "various matters which this record does *not* present." Cohen's conviction, he first emphasizes, was based purely on the three words "Fuck the Draft" and not on any *conduct* on the part of Cohen. Cohen had done nothing to hurt anyone, nor anyone him; he was punished purely for the content of his communication. Nor could Cohen have been plausibly convicted for disobedience or disruption of the draft, for he had done no more than express his view on the immorality of the draft, a view he is perfectly entitled to express under the First Amendment. Nor was this an obscenity case. Obscene speech must be, in some significant way, erotic. "It cannot plausibly be maintained," Harlan writes, "that this vulgar allusion to the Selective Service System could conjure up such psychic stimulation in anyone likely to be confronted with Cohen's crudely defaced jacket."

Most significantly, Cohen's use of the words "Fuck the Draft" does not come within the definition of the "fighting words" in *Chaplinsky v. New Hampshire*. While the phrase "fuck you" could be employed in a personally provocative fashion calculated to incite a fight, there was no evidence that Cohen's use of the phrase "Fuck the Draft" was "directed to the person of the hearer." No one could have regarded Cohen's jacket as a direct *personal* insult. Nor was this a situation in which it was necessary to remove Cohen because an angry and uncontrollable crowd was on the verge of reflexive violence.

Finally, Harlan emphasizes that this was not a "captive audience" case, a situation in which distasteful speech is thrust upon unwitting and unwilling viewers, who have no ability to avert exposure. All that anyone offended by Cohen's jacket had to do was look the other way. Government cannot shut down discourse solely to protect those to whom it is objectionable from enduring a fleeting glimpse.

Having cleared away this brush, Justice Harlan gets to the heart of the matter. The question is "whether California can excise, as 'offensive conduct,' one particular scurrilous epithet from the public discourse," either on the theory "that its use is inherently likely to cause violent reaction or upon a more general assertion that the States, acting as guardians of public morality, may properly remove this offensive word from the public vocabulary."

The first theory, Harlan argues, is plainly untenable. Under this theory, the fact that there was no violence in the Los Angeles courthouse in response to Cohen's jacket is immaterial; it is enough that the words used automatically carry the high likelihood of triggering such violence. California was asserting that *any* use of the word "fuck" is *inherently* likely to foment violence. There is a world of constitutional difference, however, between the "violent effect" of language and its proclivity to *cause violence.* "We have been shown no evidence that substantial numbers of citizens are standing ready to strike out physically at whomever may assault their sensibilities with execrations like that uttered by Cohen" states Harlan.

The second theory, concedes Harlan, poses a tougher question. Does the Constitution "disable states from punishing public utterance of this unseemly expletive in order to maintain what they regard as a suitable level of discourse within the body politic" or must the state stay entirely out of the language-cleansing business?

Harlan admits that to many the immediate consequence of freedom of speech "may often appear to be only verbal tumult, discord, and even offensive utterance." But he insists that this should be seen as endemic to a free society. "That the air may at times seem filled with verbal cacophony is, in this sense, not a sign of weakness but of strength."

Against this perception of the constitutional policies involved, Harlan's analysis emerges in bold relief. The argument of the state of California seems boundless: If the state could ban this word, it could ban other words. In one of the most famous passages of the opinion Harlan writes:

> How is one to distinguish this from any other offensive word? Surely the state has no legal right to cleanse public debate to the point where it is grammatically palatable to the most squeamish among us. . . . For, while the particular "four-letter word" being litigated here is perhaps more distasteful than most others of its genre, it is nevertheless often true that one man's vulgarity is another's lyric.[3]

Harlan then points out that much linguistic expression involves a dual communicative function: Words are chosen for their emotive as well as for their cognitive force. "Oppose the draft" does not communicate quite the same thing as "screw the draft," which in turn does not communicate quite the same thing as "fuck the draft." Each of the phrases escalates the emotional intensity of the underlying thought, and that emotional intensity counts as speech, too. Harlan concludes that "we cannot indulge the facile assumption that one can forbid particular words without also running a substantial risk of suppressing ideas in the process. Indeed, governments might soon seize upon the censorship of particular words as a convenient guise for banning the expression of unpopular views."

Hustler and Flynt could also point to a series of cases that stand for the proposition that when a speaker's message, while repugnant to mainstream sensibilities, is not itself causing violence, it is impermissible to penalize that speech because of the reflexively violent response of others to that speech.

In *Terminiello v. Chicago,* a 1949 decision, the defendant Terminiello had delivered a speech in an auditorium in Chicago under the auspices of the Christian Veterans of America. The speech vigorously criticized various political and racial groups in the city. Outside of the auditorium, a crowd of over one thousand persons gathered to protest against the meeting. A cordon of police was assigned to keep order outside the auditorium, but disturbances still broke out. So the Chicago police arrested Terminiello and charged him with disorderly conduct. Terminiello was convicted.

The case poses the "heckler's veto" problem. When a speaker is not urging others to engage in violence but rather others reacting *against* the message of the speaker becomes violent, is it permissible to arrest the speaker? If it were a matter of simple mathematics, removing the speaker, instead of removing the thousand hecklers, clearly would be the rational choice. It is far cheaper and far safer to arrest one person than to arrest a hundred or a thousand in an angry mob. Why not take out the single agitator of the riot?

Obviously, however, it is not just a matter of simple mathematics. If hecklers can by their own reactive disorder force the state to arrest someone lawfully engaged in the exercise of free speech rights, then we have countenanced a "heckler's veto." The rule of the mob has overcome the rule of law; violence now pays. Nothing more clearly illustrates the social cost of free speech. A society truly committed to free speech will choose the more expensive and dangerous alternative of arresting the many violent hecklers instead of the one nonviolent speaker. And it will make that choice consistently, even when by consensus the speaker's message is hateful and repugnant.

The Supreme Court in *Terminiello* reversed the disorderly conduct conviction, striking a blow against the heckler's veto. Justice William O. Douglas, writing for the Court, argues:

A function of free speech under our system of government is to invite dispute. It may indeed best serve its high purpose when it induces a condition of unrest, creates dissatisfaction with conditions as they are, or even stirs people to anger. Speech is often provocative and challenging. It may strike at prejudices and preconceptions and have profound unsettling effects as it presses for acceptance of an idea. That is why freedom of speech . . . is nevertheless protected against censorship or punishment, unless shown likely to produce a clear and present danger of a serious substantive evil that rises far above public inconvenience, annoyance, or unrest.[4]

This idea is also prominent in *Street v. New York,* a 1969 decision arising out of reaction to the assassination of civil rights leader James Meredith by a sniper in Mississippi on June 6, 1966. Street, a black, heard the radio report of the tragic shooting on his radio in Brooklyn and was outraged, saying to himself, "They didn't protect him." He took from his drawer a neatly folded, forty-eight-star American flag, which he had always displayed proudly on national holidays. He carried the still-folded flag from his apartment to the nearby intersection of St. James Place and Lafayette Avenue. He stood on the northeast corner of the intersection, lighted the flag with a match, and dropped the burning flag to the pavement.

A police officer approached the scene, where thirty or forty persons had gathered, listening to Street saying, "We don't need no damn flag." When the officer questioned him, Street said, "Yes; that is my flag; I burned it. If they let that happen to Meredith, we don't need an American flag." Street was tried and convicted of the crime of "malicious mischief in that he did willfully and unlawfully defile, cast contempt upon, and burn an American flag . . . and shout, 'If they did that to Meredith, we don't need an American flag.' "

The Supreme Court overturned Street's conviction. The act of burning the flag is clearly a form of symbolic speech, and the words he uttered further explain its meaning. The Court admonishes that "disrespect for our flag is to be deplored no less in these vexed times than in calmer periods of our history." But the Court holds that freedom of speech includes the right to differ on things that "touch the heart of the existing order" and that it encompasses "the freedom to express publicly one's opinion about our flag, including these opinions which are defiant or contemptuous." Most significantly, the Court writes that the offensive shock value of Street's speech was not enough to justify its abridgement:

Any shock effect of appellant's speech must be attributed to the content of the ideas expressed. It is firmly settled that under our Constitution the public expression of ideas may not be prohibited merely because the ideas themselves are offensive to some of their hearers.[5]

Like the act of flag desecration in *Street, Hustler*'s Campari ad parody is neither gentle nor genteel; its shock is purposeful and, to most, offensive. But cases such as *Street, Terminiello, Cohen, Hess,* and *Brandenburg* instruct that the shock value of speech is not itself enough to permit its censorship.

Chapter 32

J erry Falwell and Larry Flynt thus presented the Supreme Court with dramatically opposing visions of what the First Amendment is all about. These competing visions are largely wrapped up in an ongoing debate over the function of the First Amendment. Is all speech of equal value in the eyes of the Constitution, or is it permissible to rank speech according to perceptions as to its relative importance?

One of America's great pioneers for freedom of speech, Professor Zechariah Chafee of Harvard,[1] identifies two distinct interests protected by the First Amendment: "There is an individual interest, the need of many men to express their opinions on matters vital to them if life is to be worth living, and a social interest in the attainment of truth, so that the country may not only adopt the wisest course of action but carry it out in the wisest way." Chafee thus points to two quite different purposes for promoting freedom of speech, one concerned primarily with the speaker's own self-realization or self-fulfillment, the other concerned primarily with society's interest in enlightenment. The "enlightenment" function of free speech can in turn be subdivided into two different First Amendment conceptualizations: the first and narrower, defining "enlightenment" in the limited sense of political self-governance, and the second and broader, treating the enlightenment function as designed to explore truths across a much wider spectrum of ideas and topics, both political and nonpolitical.[2]

Both the self-fulfillment and the enlightenment functions have often been recognized by the Supreme Court. In a 1984 libel decision, *Bose Corp. v. Consumers Union of United States, Inc.,*[3] the Court states that "the First Amendment presupposes that the freedom to speak one's mind is not only an aspect of individual liberty—and thus a good unto itself—but also is essential to the common quest for truth and the vitality of society as a whole." The Court has tended to emphasize the social interest in free speech more heavily, however, as seen in statements that the First Amendment "rests on the assumption that the widest possible dissemination of information from diverse and antagonistic sources is essential to the welfare of the public." In the context of *Falwell v. Flynt* Falwell's strategy was to emphasize a narrow conception of the enlightenment function, for it was quite possible that a number of the Supreme Court justices would find it highly implausible that the *Hustler* ad could possibly serve any useful function in the process of democratic self-governance.

The function of free speech as an aid to social self-governance has been emphasized repeatedly by the Supreme Court and by First Amendment theorists. According to Justice Brandeis, "freedom to think as you will and to speak as you think are means indispensible to the discovery and spread of political truth." For the Court, "Whatever differences may exist about interpretations of the First Amendment, there is practically universal agreement that a major purpose of that Amendment was to protect the free discussion of governmental affairs."

Perhaps the most famous exponent of the view that the primary purpose of free speech is political self-governance was Dr. Alexander Meiklejohn.[4] In Meiklejohn's words, "What is essential is not that everyone shall be heard, but that everything worth saying shall be said." The essential purpose of freedom of speech "is to give every voting member of the body politic the fullest possible participation in the understanding of these problems with which the citizens of a self-governing society must deal." For Meiklejohn, it is the "mutilation of the thinking process of the community" against which the First Amendment is directed; the "principle of the freedom of speech springs from the necessities of the program of self-government." If this view were adopted, *Hustler's* ad might be disqualified from constitutional protection on the grounds that it is a "mutilation" of public discourse.

Hustler's strategy was to stress a much broader notion of the enlightenment function of the First Amendment. In his later writing, for example, Alexander Meiklejohn departs from his original emphasis on the political function of free speech, acknowledging that free expression serves social interests in enlightenment that go beyond the purely political. Although still giving primacy to political speech, he recognizes that "there are many forms of thought and expression within the range of human communications from which the voter derives knowledge, intelligence, and sensitivity to human values: the capacity for sane and objective judgment which, so far as possible, a ballot should express." Meiklejohn then lists four such forms of speech: "education, in all its phases," the "achievements of philosophy and the sciences in creating knowledge and understanding of men," "literature and the arts," and "public discussions of public issues."

Although there is no question that political speech is well within the core of the First Amendment's protection, it is equally clear that the Supreme Court squarely rejects the suggestion that the Amendment's protection is limited to speech related to self-government: Nonpolitical speech covering an almost infinite variety of issues and topics also falls within the ambit of First Amendment protection.[5] In *Time, Inc. v. Hill*,[6] for example, an important invasion of privacy case decided under the *New York Times* standard, the Court states that "guarantees for speech and press are not the preserve of political expression or comment upon public affairs, essential as those are to healthy government." The First Amendment confers a "right of the public to receive suitable access to social, political, esthetic, moral, and other ideas and experiences." The free speech and free press guarantees "are not confined to any field of human interest," and it is "immaterial whether the beliefs sought to be advanced by association pertain to political, economic, religious or cultural matters." As the Court puts it in *West Virginia State Board of Education v. Barnette*,[7] "If there is any fixed star in our constitutional constellation, it is that no official, high or petty, can prescribe what shall be orthodox in politics, nationalism, religion, or other matters of opinion."

Hustler also sought to advance the self-fulfillment function of the First Amendment. In Justice Thurgood Marshall's words, "The First Amendment serves not only the needs of the polity but also those of the human spirit—a spirit that demands self-expression." This "achievement of self-realization" makes free expression valuable even when the speaker has no realistic hope that the audience will be persuaded to his or her viewpoint, for it nonetheless provides the speaker with an inner satisfaction and realization of self-identity essential to individual human autonomy and dignity. As Professor Alfred Hill, a distinguished member of the Columbia University School of Law, notes, the value of the First Amendment "is not merely the cultivation of uninhibited expression with a view to the potential contribution of such expression to the common good, but, more fundamentally, the protection of the speaker from governmental restraint—a sense that the speaker has a right to be let alone in the absence of a compelling reason to the contrary."

Chapter 33

I n attempting to parse out these competing visions of the First
Amendment in the context of *Falwell v. Flynt,* the Supreme Court
once again had to face an issue it had been forced to reconsider
periodically ever since it decided *New York Times Co. v. Sullivan.*
The Court had made it clear that it placed a high First Amendment
value on speech concerning public figures on issues of public concern, but the problem was somehow to define the boundary between
public and private life. Just how much invasion of privacy and psychic tranquility must a public figure accept as part of the Faustian
bargain for fame and glory?

As *Falwell v. Flynt* was being briefed by the parties, political and
religious events were unfolding that brought out the problem of
drawing the line between public and private life. These events
weighed on the minds of the justices—several justices, indeed, later
made open reference to them during the oral argument in the case.
The first of these events, the PTL scandal, carries mixed messages.
On the one hand, it seems to show that speech concerning the sexual
misadventures of ministers is per se "newsworthy" in America. On
the other hand, it emphasizes just how devastating such speech can
be.

In the spring of 1987 Falwell found himself in the midst of the
biggest American church scandal since *The Scarlet Letter.* Television evangelist Jim Bakker, who along with his wife Tammy led the
PTL Club (for "Praise the Lord" or "People That Love"), publicly

confessed that he had been sexually involved with another woman, Jessica Hahn. Hahn had been paid $265,000 by Bakker's lawyers as a "settlement." Her lawyer claimed that she had been lured to a hotel, drugged, and forcibly seduced. Bakker's camp had a different version; Hahn, then twenty-one, was in their account a seasoned temptress who knew all the tricks of the trade.

Hahn's story was that she was flown to Florida to meet Bakker by another evangelist, John Wesley Fletcher. At a hotel in Florida, she was given drugged wine. Bakker appeared, clad only in a white terrycloth swimsuit, and asked Hahn for a back rub. This soon escalated precipitously, and Hahn was too dazed to resist Bakker's sexual advances. She said she felt like a piece of hamburger thrown into the street.

After brooding over the experience for years, in 1984 Hahn contacted Richard Dortch, Bakker's second-in-command. Dortch could not persuade her to let matters drop, and Hahn had a lawyer draw up a lawsuit. Under the threat of the suit Bakker's lawyers agreed to pay Hahn $115,000—which would be divided to give $95,000 to Hahn's attorneys for fees, with $20,000 remaining for her. An additional $150,000 was placed in trust; Hahn would get an income of $800 to $1,000 per month and, if she kept quiet for twenty years, would then get the $150,000 principal.

The story was leaked to *The Charlotte Observer* by someone inside PTL. After an investigation by *The Observer,* including the uncovering of extravagant spending by Jim and Tammy Bakker and dubious bait-and-switch fundraising tactics, the paper ran the story, and Bakker's ministry unraveled. American comics had a field day; Jim and Tammy jokes swept the nation ("What do Tammy Bakker and Vail, Colorado, have in common? Ten inches of powder and forty inches of base"), as the initials PTL were transformed from "Praise the Lord" to "Pay the Lady." The bloodletting was vicious. Rival televangelist Jimmy Swaggart reported to the Assemblies of God, the group through which both Swaggart and Bakker were ordained, that he had evidence of sexual misconduct by Bakker with others. Swaggart drove home the jagged knife and twisted it with born-again vengeance, saying that he was cutting a cancer from "the Body of Christ." (These words would later come to haunt Swaggart, as he tearfully confessed to sexual sins of his own.)

Jerry Falwell came riding in on a white horse to save the day for PTL—and to add to his estimable credentials as America's impeccable evangelist ambassador-at-large. But the intrigues were too complicated; Falwell himself soon began to get sucked into an increasingly unseemly internecine battle. Falwell went to see Bakker, telling Bakker to admit his sin and resign his ministry. Falwell allegedly recommended that his lawyer from the Larry Flynt case, Grutman, represent the Bakkers, while Falwell himself would take over the PTL ministry, along with a new board. Grutman began aggressively, by publicly accusing Jimmy Swaggart of attempting to engineer "a hostile takeover" of PTL. Falwell and his new fundamentalist board of directors made Grutman general counsel of PTL. (This was surely one of the great ironies of the whole business: Here was the career lawyer for pornography king Bob Guccione and *Penthouse* being named General Counsel of the Praise the Lord Club by a newly installed fundamentalist board of directors seeking to salvage the ministry from a sex scandal.)

Jim and Tammy Bakker were soon out on the street, sharing with Gary Hart the full hypocritical wrath of American puritanical scandal-savorers, a wrath no less strong than that visited on Hawthorne's Hester Prynne. Things had apparently not gone down quite as Jim and Tammy had planned; they began to see Falwell and Grutman as the real takeover artists. (Could the whole plot have been hatched by a devious Bob Guccione, setting out to conquer and divide the Christian Right and make the world safe for *Penthouse* by infiltrating Norman Roy Grutman into their midst, like some master Russian mole in a John Le Carré spy novel? No . . . it's too fantastic to imagine!)

Falwell was, of course, right about the devastating power of allegations of sexual impropriety. Nathaniel Hawthorne, in *The Scarlet Letter*, [1] used the adulterous tale of the Massachusetts Puritan Reverend Arthur Dimmesdale and the beautiful Hester Prynne to lay bare the dark truths of America's heart: a nation of robust free individuals seeking libertine gratification, but forever torn by equally powerful puritan impulses toward moral austerity and civic propriety. Hester Prynne was forced to wear the scarlet letter "A" embroidered on her breast, and when Reverend Dimmesdale, overwhelmed by guilt, finally revealed that it was he who had gotten Hester pregnant, he fell dead.

In the 1880s America did manage to forgive the dalliance of presidential candidate Grover Cleveland. A Buffalo, New York, newspaper discovered that Cleveland had fathered an illegitimate child with a woman named Maria. Tales about Cleveland spread around the country as fast as they did one hundred years later about

Gary Hart and Donna Rice. One little Cleveland ditty was a catchy jingle:

Ma, Ma, where's my Pa?
Gone to the White House!
Ha! Ha! Ha![2]

But the public forgave old Grover. He was elected President in 1884, skipped a term, and was elected again in 1892.

About the same time the famous American abolitionist and clergyman Henry Ward Beecher was accused of seducing the wife of his protegé, Theodore Tilton. Beecher was an early-day Jim Bakker, at least in style. He earned $40,000 a year from his preaching—a princely sum for the time—shamelessly endorsed products for commissions, and ostentatiously carried uncut gems in his pockets to display his wealth. The trial over the sex charges against Beecher was such hot stuff that admission tickets were sold. The jury could not reach a verdict, and Beecher, like Grover Cleveland, continued on as popular as ever.

Sex scandals in the twentieth century have tended to be more destructive. Revelations concerning the extramarital affairs of presidents such as Franklin Roosevelt, John Kennedy, or Lyndon Johnson, it is true, never really did much to alter historical perceptions about those men. Perhaps, once a person dies, history tends to judge matters only on the merits—there is little currency in gossip about dead people. But allegations of sexual trysts have mortally wounded many others.

In the 1920s a Pentecostal evangelist Aimee Semple McPherson caught the public imagination; beautiful and flamboyant, she was known as the "Queen of Heaven," preaching in a $1.5 million Los Angeles church in flowing white robes, surrounded by choirs. McPherson disappeared suddenly in 1926 for thirty-six days. She later surfaced in a Mexican border town with a wild story of having been kidnapped and, after escaping from her captors, wandered aimlessly through the desert. The police ultimately discovered that she had spent the time with a lover, a married man, in a seaside cottage in Carmel, California. McPherson died at the age of fifty-three of an overdose of barbiturates.

More recently, the conservative Oklahoma television preacher, Billy James Hargis, was brought down by stories of former female and male students of his American Christian College in Tulsa that

Hargis had had sexual encounters with them. Hargis denied the allegations, but his career was ruined.

One of Falwell's credibility problems came from the embarrassing fact that he and Jim Bakker are not of the same religious sect. Falwell's brand of fundamentalism emphasizes the literal inerrancy of Scripture and has no brook for miraculous theatrics. Bakker is a Pentacostal in the Assemblies of God, a denomination emphasizing ecstatic personal revelation, talking in tongues, and faith-healing. Bakker's peculiar approach also associates faith in Jesus with financial rewards. (Since, for Bakker, this is in fact true, one can see where he got the idea.) All this business is way out of Falwell's line; he once dismissed people who spoke in tongues as people who "ate too much pizza last night." Falwell's entry into the PTL ministry, therefore, appeared to say that differences in religious doctrine are less important than what Bakker and Falwell *do* have in common: "stardom" as television preachers. One television evangelist was suddenly as good as another and could take over as smoothly as a guest host sitting in for Johnny Carson on *The Tonight Show*.

The PTL scandal was not the only story in 1987 to make an issue of the uneasy relation between public figure status and personal privacy. Revelations by the press that Pat Robertson's first child was conceived prior to his marriage, that Joe Biden had plagiarized material in speeches and misrepresented his law school career, and that Gary Hart had spent most of a fateful weekend with Donna Rice in his Washington apartment generated intense debate over where to draw the proper boundary between public and private life. The debate was carried on in three spheres: Journalists argued over what the self-imposed standards of their profession ought to be; lawyers argued over what standards the legal system ought to impose on journalists; and the general public debated whether either journalistic practices or legal doctrines comported with public expectations and the prevailing sensibilities of the culture. These political events, particularly the Gary Hart episode, challenged the nation to explore the dichotomy between public and private life from something more than a visceral, seat-of-the-pants, gut-reaction perspective. The time had come, it seemed, to engage in more disciplined, objective analysis.

The starting point for such an analysis is deceptively simple. Journalists, lawyers, and members of the general public virtually all agree with the basic proposition that for a public figure a matter ostensibly private, such as sexual conduct, becomes public (and thus a legitimate story for the press) only if there is some connection between the private activity and matters of public concern. The issue then becomes what will satisfy the requirement of a connection? There are at least seven standard nominees. The connection may be satisfied: (1) If the private activity is manifest in some event that is independently newsworthy, such as a congressman arrested drunk in the Tidal Basin with a female companion, or a senator driving off a bridge and killing a woman passenger, or a president having a sexual liaison with a woman with Mafia connections in a matter related to CIA activity; (2) if the private activity creates some demonstrable impairment of actual performance in public office; (3) if the private activity confirms preexisting rumors or legends about that same type of private activity; (4) if the public figure has "opened the door" to otherwise private activity by inviting or challenging the press to investigate; (5) if the private activity, even if not demonstrably an impairment of actual performance, is nevertheless probative of flaws in professional judgment; (6) if the private activity, even if not demonstrably an impairment of actual performance, is nevertheless revealing of flaws in moral character; and (7) if the private activity is such that a story about it will command sales in the market—that is, if it is clear that a segment of the public will savor the scandal. Under this last possible condition the mere fact that the story is something the "public is interested in" qualifies it as a "matter of public interest."

The Gary Hart episode is a useful working text for critically examining the legitimacy of these various nominees and their application in action. (Justice Sandra Day O'Connor, in fact, referred to the Hart story during the oral argument in *Falwell v. Flynt.*) The first two grounds are not controversial: If either of these two conditions exist—a connection to an independent news event or evidence of actual impairment of performance—then virtually everyone agrees that the press may run the story. In Hart's case, however, neither of these two conditions existed, and the next several possibilities were far more problematic. The third purported condition—the confirmation of preexisting rumors—is analytically suspect. Unless the rumors have become so ubiquitous that they are themselves independently newsworthy, it is sheer bootstrapping to use them to legitimate a story. When the rumors, for example, are circulating exclusively among reporters and other political insiders, what does actual knowledge of the private activity "confirm" and to whom?

How do rumors about a private activity somehow add to the event itself, if neither the event nor the rumors are independently newsworthy?

The fourth possible condition—the opening of the door by a challenge to the press—may be valid, but it is of limited utility as precedent. Gary Hart, frustrated at the bombardment of questions generated by the pervasive rumors, did issue the infamous "tail me" challenge. Few candidates are likely to make such an invitation in the future. More importantly, the press should not be permitted to treat the mere fact of entry into public life, such as a declaration of political candidacy, as a blanket invitation to investigate and print all things private—for that would be to throw off entirely the basic dichotomy between public and private life.

Condition number five—that private activity is fair public game if it is probative of flaws in judgment—is legitimate, but *only* if we are honest, and not hypocritical, about what we mean by "judgment." The term "judgment" should be kept distinct from "moral character," the topic of condition six. Judgment is amoral; in Gary Hart's case, the purported flaws in judgment are either that the candidate should not have taken the risk or should not have gotten caught. We should be circumspect about this condition, however, for, if a candidate has been misled into believing that his sexual affairs are not public domain as long as they do not become part of some other newsworthy event or do not impair public performance, then there *is* no exercise of bad judgment, because by all prior indications the behavior was risk-free.

Gary Hart's judgment was bad, therefore, only in a narrower sense: It was bad judgment to believe the press could be trusted. From an amoral perspective Hart's judgment was not bad in failing to follow the rules of the game but in failing to perceive how the rules of the game had changed. Hart could very persuasively argue that the press did not have the right to change the rules of the game and go with the story, unless one of the previously accepted requirements had been satisfied. Hart's judgment was thus bad, but it was bad only because he knew or should have known that the press was, at least for his candidacy, going to run the story if it caught him. He was on notice of that from the rumors, from the constant questions, and ultimately from his own "tail me" challenge. The press, however, should take little solace from condition five, for Hart's bad judgment is somewhat analogous to the bad judgment of the victim of police entrapment: If the press had no right to change the rules, it was again bootstrapping to legitimate going public with what otherwise would have been a private matter.

The sixth possible condition poses a very difficult puzzle. "Thou shalt not commit adultery" happens to be one of the most powerful moral commands of Western culture. But is apparent violation of that moral norm by a public figure a matter of public interest? A clue as to whether an alleged violation of that command is *per se* to be treated as newsworthy may be found in the daily behavior of most Americans. In our private lives all of us are constantly faced with the question of how adultery will affect our personal assessments of other human beings. There is an overwhelming consensus in American society that as a general proposition adultery, *standing alone*, without the existence of one of the other factors listed above, is *not* a disqualifier from business, political, or social acceptance. Even though people within a business, church, school, or political community may think less of an adulterer, they usually will not allow this estimation of the person's private morality to interfere with their esteem for that person in daily public interaction. Unless the entire dichotomy between public life and private life is to be dissolved, this habit of American behavior should not be abandoned merely because the scale is writ large: Private and public derelictions in morality should be kept separate in the absence of some palpable nexus between them, even for would-be presidents. Further, the fact that a candidate tries to hide the truth should not be deemed a legitimate trigger for publication of private facts. For, if the event is otherwise not newsworthy, the candidate has a *right* to hide it. Pat Robertson is justified in lying about his marriage date if he is justified in treating the time of his child's conception as private. Since it is highly implausible that many Americans would treat their private assessment of the morality of conceiving a child prior to marriage with the person who will be one's spouse as providing any serious nexus to Robertson's public morality thirty years later, neither the event nor the cover-up are legitimate stories.

This brings the analysis full circle to the seventh condition. Perhaps the rule should be that the press may publish an ostensibly private matter whenever in its judgment the public would find the matter interesting. This condition is different in kind from the first six for it is actually the antithesis of the idea of a nexus requirement. What sells, under this theory, is news. If, in candor, there is no doubt that much of the public would be interested in the relationship between Gary Hart and Donna Rice, the press may guiltlessly run the story without worrying about whether it is a matter of public interest in some analytically abstract sense.

Gossip attracts us all to some degree; it is not the exclusive preoccupation of the readers of checkout-counter publications. We differ, individually, in our affinity for gossip, in our hunger or distaste for it, in our willingness to spread it. But we all, to some extent, seek its nourishment. Gossip is the junk food of knowledge and endemic to social life. We are all "enquiring minds who want to know." If a story's gossip titillation value is all that is required to justify publication of an ostensibly private matter, then the search for an anchor in a traditionally accepted nexus between the story and matters of public interest is naive and unnecessary.

Acceptance of the seventh condition however, should be resisted. Neither journalists evolving their own norms of conduct, nor lawyers articulating First Amendment doctrines, nor the general public expressing its expectations and values has ever yet been willing to abandon the notion that even public persons are entitled to some spheres of privacy. In a robust, open culture with a vigorous First Amendment public figures must, of course, surrender much of the privacy they would otherwise enjoy—but not all of it. Ostensibly private matters should remain private, unless a nexus to public life actually exists, and the nexus should be more than the press's own bootstrap, more than the vague and shadowy invocation of words like "rumors," "judgment," or "character," and more than juicy but analytically irrelevant gossip.

How did this division between public and private life play itself out in Falwell's case against Flynt? As in every other aspect of the suit, the parties vigorously disagreed. Falwell's briefs conceded that he is an influential public figure. That fact, however, does not mean that Falwell is automatically fair game for the type of vicious attack contained in *Hustler*'s ad. For while revelations of sexual misconduct would be relevant to Falwell's fitness for his position as a preacher and moral leader, the Campari ad's bizarre fantasy does not contain information of actual sexual misconduct. This speech is not a matter of legitimate public concern, Falwell argued, because, as *Hustler* freely admitted, the sexual conduct it portrays never happened.

Flynt's team tried to turn this very argument around on Falwell and use it to Flynt's and *Hustler*'s advantage. If the ad satire is not factual, it is opinion. And therein, Flynt argued, lay the single most convincing rationale for overturning the Fourth Circuit's decision.

Chapter 34

A ll Americans, even those not schooled in the fine niceties of First Amendment history and theory, are familiar with an idea central to the free speech tradition: The Constitution creates special protection for the expression of opinion. When Americans get into hot-and-heavy verbal disputes, nothing is more commonplace than phrases like "I'm sorry, but I'm entitled to my opinion."

In many respects, however, the reverence for the free expression of opinion of the common man is more advanced than the common law. The majority common-law position prior to *New York Times Co. v. Sullivan* did not immunize all expressions of opinion. Rather, an expression of opinion could be defamatory, at least if it implied the existence of unstated underlying facts that were false. Though many opinions are inherently incapable of being proved or disproved, the common law deemed actionable some expressions of opinion that would tend to be injurious to reputation. This position was adhered to even though the truth or falsity of the opinion at issue might not be objectively determinable at all and even though the common law simultaneously maintained the position that truth was a complete defense in a civil action for defamation.

In the tentative, piecemeal fashion characteristic of decisions concerning the common law, courts gradually began to acknowledge the contradictions of the early position and to recognize that "valuable discourse might be furthered by intuitive, evaluative statements that could not be proved either true or false by the rigorous deductive reasoning of the judicial process." Concern for the need to give some shelter to these evaluative statements was vented through limited protection for opinion, primarily through the gradual recognition of a "fair comment" privilege.

The original coverage of the fair comment privilege was quite modest. Opinions were protected only if based on "true facts" that "fully and fairly justified" the opinion. Over time, however, the privilege embraced opinions about matters of public concern based on true facts, whether the opinion was "reasonable" or not. This common-law "safety valve" for fair comment emerged for much the same reasons that ultimately came to inform modern First Amendment jurisprudence. As early as the 1808 English case *Tagart v. Tipper*,[1] for example, it was explained that "Liberty of criticism must be allowed, or we should have neither purity of taste nor of morals. Fair discussion is essentially necessary to the truth of history, and the advancement of science." The majority position was that the fair comment privilege protected only expressions of opinion and not false facts expressly stated or implied from the expression of the opinion. The fair comment privilege was lost if the statement was published with "malice," in the common-law sense of "spite" or "ill will," or if the opinion was not "sincerely" held. The traditional majority position was that the fair comment privilege existed only if based on facts "truly stated," and even then, the comment had to be "fair." Courts thus inquired into whether a "reasonable man may honestly entertain such an opinion." Other courts emphasized full factual disclosure, holding that the comment must be "fair in the sense that the reader can understand the factual basis for the opinions containing the criticism." The "fairness" or "reasonableness" of the comment was usually left to the relatively unguided judgment of the jury. Since this practice permitted juries to pass judgment on the "worth" of the speaker's opinion, it carried the potential for being quite inimical to free expression. In the context of *Falwell v. Flynt,* the old common-law rule provided virtually no protection whatsoever for Flynt and *Hustler,* for the Campari ad is anything but "fair."

A series of Supreme Court opinions, however, gradually had come to give the common-law protection of opinion a constitutional gloss. This emerging constitutional protection for opinion is far more liberal than the fair comment doctrine of the common law. It protects even unfair opinions on the logic that the very essence of freedom of speech dictates that in matters of opinion it is not the business of courts to declare what is fair or unfair.

The Supreme Court had decided three cases prior to the Falwell litigation that involved the fact/opinion distinction. The first is a 1970 decision, *Greenbelt Cooperative Publishing Association v. Bresler.* The case involved Charles S. Bresler, a prominent real estate developer in Greenbelt, Maryland. Bresler was the owner of land that the city of Greenbelt wanted to purchase as the site for construction of a new high school. Bresler also owned other land in Greenbelt and was negotiating with the city for a zoning change on that other land. Bresler had the city in a negotiating vise of sorts: If the city would not give him the zoning changes he desired, then it would have to engage in protracted condemnation proceedings to obtain the site it wanted for the high school. Bresler's negotiating position was highly controversial, and during city council meetings he was vigorously attacked. In covering the story, *The Greenbelt News Review* reported in two articles that Bresler was guilty of "blackmail" in his negotiating position with the city.

Bresler sued the paper for libel and won $5,000 in compensatory damages and $12,500 in punitive damages. In a unanimous opinion the Supreme Court overturned the jury's verdict. The Court's analysis focuses on the context in which the word "blackmail" had been used and includes a passage of particular significance for *Falwell v. Flynt*:

It is simply impossible to believe that a reader who reached the word "blackmail" in either article would not have understood exactly what was meant: it was Bresler's public and wholly legal negotiating proposals that were being criticized. No reader could have thought that either the speakers at the meetings or the newspaper articles reporting their words were charging Bresler with the commission of a criminal offense. On the contrary, even the most careless reader must have perceived that the word was no more than rhetorical hyperbole, a vigorous epithet used by those who considered Bresler's negotiating position extremely unreasonable.[2]

The passage in *Bresler* does not invoke the terminology of "fact" versus "opinion," but the Court's use of the phrases "rhetorical hyperbole" and "vigorous epithet" are aimed at exactly the same principle as the fact/opinion distinction. No one was literally accusing Bresler of the crime of blackmail; the real message communicated by the use of the word is that Bresler was using his economic leverage to extort from the city zoning concessions he did not deserve on the merits. This is a mean thing to say about Bresler, to be sure, but it involves no factual misrepresentations. The cutting edge of the statement is in the opinion that what Bresler was doing was unfair; the facts were there, however, for anyone to see for themselves, and they could make up their own minds. *Hustler*'s position was that just as it is "simply impossible" for any reader to mistake the word "blackmail" as a literal accusation of a crime, it is simply impossible that any reader would take the Campari ad literally.

The Supreme Court's most important statements on the fact/opinion distinction appear in *Gertz v. Robert Welch, Inc.,* where the Court *in dicta* seems to provide absolute First Amendment immunity from defamation actions for all opinions. The Court begins its analysis of the case by stating:

> Under the First Amendment, there is no such thing as a false idea. However pernicious an opinion may seem, we depend for its correction not on the conscience of judges and juries but on the competition of other ideas. But there is no constitutional value in false statements of fact. Neither the intentional lie nor the careless error materially advances society's interest in "uninhibited, robust, and wide-open" debate on public issues. . . . They belong to that category of utterances which "are no essential part of any exposition of ideas, and are of such slight value as a step to truth that any benefit that may be derived from them is clearly outweighed by the social interest in order and morality."[3]

By this statement, *Gertz* apparently elevates to constitutional status the distinction between fact and opinion, which in common law had formed the basis of the fair comment privilege. *Gertz*'s command thus imposes on both state and federal courts the constitutional duty to distinguish facts from opinions in order to provide opinions with the requisite absolute First Amendment protection. As a number of lower courts have noted, however, the Supreme Court provides little guidance in *Gertz* itself as to the manner in which the distinction between fact and opinion is to be discerned.

In truth, *Gertz* does not focus on the fact/opinion distinction at all. Rather, assuming without lengthy discussion that the statements in that case could be construed as statements of fact, the Court ruled that the plaintiff, who was held to be a private rather than a public figure, need prove only that the statements at issue were negligently made. In the 1984 case of *Bose Corporation v. Consumers Union of the United States, Inc.* [4] the Supreme Court referred to the *Gertz* dicta with approval. But two members of the Court—Justices White and Rehnquist—have noted that "the problem of defamatory opinion was not remotely an issue in *Gertz* and there is no evidence that the Court was speaking with an awareness of the rich and complex history of the struggle of the common law to deal with this problem."

On the same day that the Supreme Court handed down its historic decision in *Gertz,* it decided a case entitled *Old Dominion Branch No. 96, National Association of Letter Carriers v. Austin.* This case, *Letter Carriers,* was technically not a First Amendment case, but rather a labor decision under the rubric of the National Labor Relations Act. Nevertheless, the Court interpreted the National Labor Relations Act in such a way as to avoid any possible First Amendment problems, and the decision has come to be understood as representing the Court's First Amendment thinking. The Supreme Court had before it in *Letter Carriers* language that was calculated to be emotionally incendiary. In the midst of a heated labor dispute a union newsletter printed a "list of Scabs" who were trying to break the union. This was no placid National Football League player's strike with substitutes crossing the picket line; it was an old-fashioned, knock-down, drag-out American labor dispute in which scabs were held in ultimate contempt by the union. Lest anyone doubt the union's view of scabs, a union newsletter explained in graphic detail what a scab was, quoting from a famous passage written by Jack London:

> After God had finished the rattlesnake, the toad, and the vampire, He had some awful substance left with which He made a scab.
>
> A scab is a two-legged animal with a corkscrew soul, a water brain, a combination backbone of jelly and glue. Where others have hearts, he carries a tumor of rotten principles.
>
> When a scab comes down the street, men turn their backs and Angels weep in Heaven, and the Devil shuts the gates of Hell to keep him out.
>
> No man (or woman) has a right to scab so long as there is a pool of water to drown his carcass in, or a rope long enough to hang his body with. Judas was a gentleman compared with a scab. For betraying his master, he had character enough to hang himself. A scab has not.
>
> Esau sold his birthright for a mess of pottage. Judas sold his

Savior for thirty pieces of silver. Benedict Arnold sold his country for a promise of commission in the British Army. The scab will sell his birthright, country, his wife, his children, and his fellow men for an unfulfilled promise from his employer.

Esau was a traitor to himself; Judas was a traitor to his God; Benedict Arnold was a traitor to his country; a SCAB is a traitor to his God, his country, his family, and his class.[5]

That definition, according to the Court, is "merely rhetorical hyperbole, a lusty and imaginative expression of the contempt felt by union members towards those who refuse to join." The Court in *Letter Carriers* obviously believes that this "lusty and imaginative expression of contempt" was designed to inflict distress—to express disgust and contempt—and yet it was nonetheless protected because it could not reasonably be understood as a literal misstatement of fact. *Letter Carriers* was an enormously important guide to the resolution of the Falwell case. In the rough-and-tumble controversies of American life, *Letter Carriers* instructs, vicious insults designed to cause severe distress will be hurled about. But unless that emotionally laden speech carries with it some harm other than its capacity to outrage, such as factual misstatements, it is legally protected.

An outrageous opinion directed against a public figure is virtually by definition intentionally or recklessly designed to generate severe emotional distress. Opinions are always "intentional"; they are designed to have an effect. But opinions are not true or false; they are only bad or good. Thus the ad satire in *Hustler* is neither true nor false. The jury, however, clearly thought it a bad opinion, bad to the point of being outrageous. The use of the Virginia cause of action for emotional distress to punish Flynt and *Hustler* for speech that the *jury found* could not be understood as factual, the defendants argued, was thus nothing more than the resuscitation of the discredited cause of action for outrageous opinion. The second element of the cause of action, the requirement that the conduct "offends generally accepted standards of decency or morality," requires that the judge and jury do what *Gertz* forbids—examine their consciences to determine if Flynt's opinion was "indecent" or "immoral."

Significantly, Virginia's own courts had interpreted the protection for opinion quite expansively. In *Crawford v. United Steelworkers, AFL-CIO,* the Virginia Supreme Court engaged in an analysis of the Supreme Court's decision in *Bresler* that contrasts sharply with the Court of Appeals' analysis in *Falwell*:

> By the same token, the words upon which the trial court fashioned liability here will not support recovery. The words are disgusting, abusive, repulsive, and are in no way condoned by this Court. Nevertheless, they cannot reasonably be understood, under the circumstances of this labor dispute, to convey a false representation of fact. To call a person a "cocksucker" does not, under the circumstances of this labor dispute, convey the false representation that the individual engaged in sodomy. Nor does calling a person a "motherfucker," under the circumstances of this case, convey the false representation that the person engaged in incest. Because this was a labor dispute and considering the way in which the words were used, these repulsive words will not support liability.[6]

Norman Roy Grutman's counter to this line of precedent was valiant, considering what he was up against. For it seemed highly unlikely that the Supreme Court would dismiss the fact/opinion distinction entirely, repudiating all special First Amendment protection for opinion. The Fourth Circuit, he argued, had correctly reasoned that the absolute protection for opinion was irrelevant when the purpose of the tort is not to vindicate the victim's reputation but to compensate for emotional injury. Grutman tried to convince the Court to define "opinion" narrowly to exclude from its coverage the content of the Campari ad. He also urged the Court to adopt the view that opinion is not absolutely but only conditionally privileged. The "right to one's own opinion" could be forfeited if exercised in an offensive and indecent manner. What Grutman effectively urged the Court to do was resuscitate the old common-law requirement that the comment be "fair" in order to be protected. "Fair" in this context apparently meant "decent." Grutman secondarily appeared to assert that opinion is protected only when the reader is aware of the facts underlying the publisher's opinion. Only "conclusory" statements are fully shielded. Grutman thus sought to distinguish holdings, such as *Bresler* and *Letter Carriers*, in which such scurrilous epithets as "blackmailer," "scab," and "corkscrew soul" were hurled about in the midst of controversies in which everyone was aware of the underlying facts. In the Campari ad, however, the underlying facts are themselves manipulated: Falwell is made to appear incestuous and drunk when he is not. This line of argument, however, could not escape being slammed full-force against the hardest underlying fact of all—the jury's decision that the ad is incapable of being perceived as having serious factual content.

Against this rich backdrop of fundamentally conflicting First Amendment philosophies the date for oral argument of *Jerry Falwell v. Larry Flynt and Hustler Magazine* quickly approached.

Chapter 35

More than any other institution of American government, the Supreme Court tends to be shrouded in mystery. Press reportage on the work of the Supreme Court often seems to bounce between two extremes: The Court is either portrayed romantically as an awe-inspiring repository of wisdom and justice or cynically as a seedy institution, tainted by politics and power struggles. Americans too often seem capable of viewing the Supreme Court justice only as the majesterial Wizard of Oz or as the pathetic phoney little man cranking the power handle behind the curtain, with Toto nipping at his heels.

The Supreme Court set the time for oral argument of *Falwell v. Flynt* for the morning of December 2, 1987. While Alan Isaacman and Norman Roy Grutman are seasoned lawyers, they could not help but feel butterflies as the date for argument approached. For Grutman and Isaacman surely understood, as most intelligent lawyers do, that the truth concerning the Supreme Court is actually midway between the two typical extremes in public perceptions.

An argument before the United States Supreme Court is a great event for any American lawyer not just because it is before the highest court on the judicial flow chart but because the Court does indeed partake of a very special form of majesty. No other nation in the history of the world has ever set out so self-consciously to embody its hopes and dreams in a written constitution as America. The United States Constitution is a ringing manifesto of human dignity, a charter embodying the wonderful promise of American life. The document incessantly vexes and cajoles the American spirit, embracing that peculiarly American combination of idealism and pragmatism. (Thus, the story of two pilgrims approaching the New World on a ship, with one saying to the other: "My immediate objective is religious freedom, but my long-term goal is to go into real estate.") Of the three branches of government, the Supreme Court has always been the principal expositor and guardian of the Constitution. The Court's majesty is the Constitution's majesty, and Americans take the Constitution quite seriously; it is the sacred text of our national life.

Even if we are a government of laws and not men, our laws are made, interpreted, and enforced by men. American constitutional law is an ongoing debate over principle, tempered by the fact that principle can never be emancipated from the flesh and blood perceptions of the human beings who are charged with interpreting it. In preparing for the argument in *Falwell v. Flynt*, Grutman and Isaacman had to do what they could intelligently to size up the human beings who then comprised the Supreme Court of the United States.

The Supreme Court was shorthanded for the *Falwell v. Flynt* decision. Justice Lewis Powell resigned from the Court in the spring of 1987, leaving the Court with only eight members. An intense firefight over Ronald Reagan's first replacement nominee, Judge Robert Bork, ended with a Senate vote denying confirmation. That defeat was followed by a second debacle, as Judge Douglas Ginsburg was forced to withdraw after revelations that he had smoked marijuana while a professor at Harvard Law School. President Reagan finally chose Judge Anthony Kennedy as Powell's replacement, and Kennedy was confirmed. Kennedy's elevation to the Court, however, did not come until well after *Falwell v. Flynt* was presented for argument.

The mathematics of Lewis Powell's resignation are quite significant for two reasons. First, Powell was often the swing vote in close cases. Many of the critical First Amendment cases of the last fifteen years (including both press victories and defeats) had been decided by five-to-four votes, with Lewis Powell in the majority. Second, Powell's absence raised the specter of a possible four-to-four deadlock. Under the Court's procedures, ties go to the winner in the court below. A four-to-four vote results in what is known as an "affirmance by an equally divided Court," and no opinion is rendered in such instances. The decision of the lower court is simply affirmed, but that affirmance has no significant precedential value. Thus Jerry Falwell could win his case two ways. If he could persuade at least five justices, he would have a solid victory, no worse than five-to-three, and would have established a landmark new precedent. Falwell could also sneak by, however, with a four-to-four tie. While such a victory would lack the precedential importance of a victory accompanied by a majority opinion, it would nevertheless end the litigation with a victory over Larry Flynt.

Flynt's odds, on the other hand, were clearly hurt by Powell's resignation, for Flynt would lose in a four-to-four tie. Furthermore, Lewis Powell was one of the justices whom Flynt might plausibly have hoped to persuade to reverse the Fourth Circuit. With Powell gone, Flynt would have to fight hard to find the five votes he needed to avoid a loss.

The eight justices comprising the Supreme Court for *Falwell v. Flynt* are a diverse mixture of personalities and judicial philosophies. On the whole, the Court was quite old—many of the justices were in their seventies or eighties. (There is, however, quite a tradition of justices serving with distinction well into their golden years. A story is told of Justice Holmes, aged ninety, walking through a park near the Court with Justice Brandeis, aged eighty-five. A beautiful woman passed by, and Holmes said to Brandeis, "Oh, to be eighty again!") *Falwell v. Flynt* was an extremely difficult case, and it was not at all an easy matter to predict how many of the justices would initially react to the case.

The lead batter in the starting line-up was Chief Justice William H. Rehnquist.[1] In September of 1986, Rehnquist was elevated to replace Chief Justice Warren Burger, becoming the sixteenth Chief Justice of the United States. Rehnquist was born and raised in Milwaukee, served in the Air Force during World War II, received a B.A. and an M.A. from Stanford, a second M.A. from Harvard in political science, and finally a law degree from Stanford in 1952, where he graduated first in his class. After law school, Rehnquist served as the law clerk to Supreme Court Justice Robert Jackson. During that clerkship, he wrote a memo defending the constitutionality of "separate but equal" for blacks. When the embarrassing memorandum surfaced years later during his confirmation hearings, Rehnquist explained that the views in the memorandum were those of Justice Jackson and not his own. After clerking, Rehnquist moved to Phoenix, Arizona, where he was a strong supporter of Barry Goldwater. During the 1964 Goldwater presidential campaign

Rehnquist met Richard G. Kleindienst, who, as President Richard Nixon's deputy attorney general, named Rehnquist to head the Justice Department's office of legal counsel, as an assistant attorney general. Rehnquist quickly gained a reputation as one of the Nixon administration's most articulate spokesmen; he was a master of tightly reasoned arguments defending the administration's conservative philosophies.

President Nixon named Rehnquist to the Supreme Court in 1971. His reputation as a brilliant legal mind flowered on the Court along with a reputation as an ardent conservative. In civil rights and free speech areas, for example, Rehnquist consistently votes for a narrow construction of constitutional liberties, and he has become the American liberals most love to hate. Although he was confirmed by the Senate as Chief Justice in 1986, his conservative record drew considerable flak during his confirmation hearings, and a substantial block of negative votes in the Senate.

Rehnquist virtually always votes against the press in First Amendment cases. In the twenty libel and invasion of privacy cases that had come before the Court since he joined it, Rehnquist had voted against the press twenty times. Did *Hustler* and Flynt have any chance at all of getting his vote, or would he be squarely in Jerry Falwell's camp? There is one striking facet of Rehnquist's personality that gave *Hustler* at least a scintilla of hope: Rehnquist likes to laugh. Through all Rehnquist has been through, he has managed to remain strikingly unstuffy and easygoing. He is always affable and good-natured toward his colleagues on the bench, even those with whom he fiercely disagrees. Rehnquist's book *The Supreme Court* is a good window on his personality—it is a warm, anecdotal history of the Court, in which Rehnquist does not have one harsh word to say about anybody.

Rehnquist can laugh at himself—he enjoys the idea that Harvard Law School had a "Rehnquist Club," in which the leader was called the "Grand Rehnquisitor" and weekly discussions were known as "Rehnquisitions." Rehnquist also has a reputation as a practical joker. One of his law school classmates remembers him as someone who loves to party and pull pranks. One of his routines was the "midnight troop review": Rehnquist would roll into the law school dorm with his drinking buddies and order everyone in the hall to "stand out."

"Like Charlie Chaplin," his friend recalls, "Bill would play the role of the Great Dictator—Adolf Hitler himself—and strut up and down in front of us shouting orders in a fractured Deutsch that no resident in the spring of '48 shall ever forget. Ultimately, the whole wild performance would dissolve into gales of laughter, and a group of us would cluster around Bill, telling ribald jokes, each trying to outdo the other." On the Supreme Court Rehnquist once played a joke on his colleagues by circulating a mock attack on a dissenting opinion of Justice Thurgood Marshall. Marshall, also known for his sense of humor, played along. Rehnquist and Marshall had some of the law clerks fooled over their mock feud until Rehnquist wrote a "Dear Thurgood" letter explaining that his opinion had been written in honor of the anniversary of an obscure Swedish-American. While everything in William Rehnquist's judicial philosophy pointed toward a vote for Falwell, there was always the possibility that the *Hustler* ad would appeal to the joker in the Chief Justice and that he would treat it as merely part of what a famous person must endure.

The most senior associate justice on the Supreme Court is William J. Brennan, Jr.[2] Brennan was born in Newark in 1906, the second of eight children of Irish immigrant parents. He attended the University of Pennsylvania and then graduated near the top of his Harvard Law School class. He practiced law in Newark from 1931 to 1949, with a break for army service during World War II. Brennan served on the New Jersey Supreme Court and was then appointed by President Dwight Eisenhower to the United States Supreme Court in 1952. Brennan evolved into the leader of the liberal wing of the Court. On any given issue, he is the justice most likely to be diametrically opposed to William Rehnquist. Like Rehnquist, however, Brennan is known for a buoyant, optimistic, friendly warmth, and he gets along well with his colleagues. Brennan is deeply committed to the First Amendment; he is the most ardent defender of speech on the Court and the author of *New York Times Co. v. Sullivan.* Brennan's was one vote almost certainly to go to *Hustler* and Flynt.

Next in seniority on the Court is Justice Byron R. White. White was born in 1917 in Fort Collins, Colorado. He went to the University of Colorado, where, as "Whizzer White," he became an outstanding scholar-athlete, receiving nine varsity letters. After graduation White played pro football for Pittsburgh for a year, but then quit to attend Oxford University as a Rhodes Scholar. After Oxford White returned to the United States and enrolled in the Yale Law School, alternating between Yale and a career as a professional football player for the Detroit Lions. White is a member of the Pro Football Hall of Fame.

White served as a law clerk to Supreme Court Chief Justice Fred Vinson and then went to a prominent Denver law firm to practice law. A long-time friend of John Kennedy, White campaigned for Kennedy for president in 1960. Kennedy named him a deputy attorney general and in 1962 appointed him to the Supreme Court. White is one of the Court's centrists and a tough pragmatist. He is a relatively gruff, sharp questioner during oral argument and has been known still to delight in muscling out his law clerks under the boards during pick-up basketball games with Court personnel. He is known as a strong advocate of school desegregation and a defender of minority rights, but tends to be conservative in other areas, such as the rights of criminals. On the whole, White is relatively conservative on press issues and has openly questioned the wisdom of both the *Gertz* and *New York Times* decisions in the libel area. He seemed more likely to side with Falwell than Flynt.

Justice Thurgood Marshall was born in 1908 in Baltimore, Maryland. He is the first black to serve on the Supreme Court. Marshall attended Lincoln University in Chester, Pennsylvania, an all-black school, and then graduated from the Howard University Law School. In the 1930s Marshall began a long and historic association with the civil rights struggles of the National Association for the Advancement of Colored People, becoming director and counsel of the NAACP Legal Defense and Education Fund. Marshall was a principal architect of the civil rights litigation strategy that changed the face of American life, culminating in the 1954 decision in *Brown v. Board of Education*. Marshall's leadership in this process was a characteristic mixture of legal acumen and salty common sense. The NAACP made a deliberate strategy choice to begin its assault at the graduate and law school levels. The NAACP thus laid the groundwork for the historic decision in *Brown v. Board of Education* through a series of cases prior to *Brown* in which the Supreme Court ruled that law school and graduate school facilities for black students in Texas, Oklahoma, and Missouri were not equal to the facilities available for white students. Why did the NAACP start at the highest levels of education in its desegregation effort instead of high school or grade school? There are a number of explanations. Inequality in the South was easier to document at the higher levels of education, where blacks had little or no graduate and professional school opportunities and the financial burden on the states would

make the achievement of genuinely equal facilities for blacks imprac-
ticable. The numbers of black students involved would be relatively
small, thus decreasing the intensity of resistance, and leadership
throughout the black community would be immediately enhanced
through such upper-level advances. But perhaps the best explanation
was supplied by Thurgood Marshall, who put it in simple, earthy,
human terms: "Those racial supremacy boys somehow think that
little kids of six or seven are going to get funny ideas about sex and
marriage just from going to school together, but for some equally
funny reasons, youngsters in law school aren't supposed to feel that
way. We didn't get it, but we decided that if that was what the South
believed, then the best thing for the moment was to go along."

President Kennedy nominated Marshall to the United States
Court of Appeals for the Second Circuit in 1961. Southern senators
opposed Marshall's nomination and delayed his confirmation until
1962. In 1965 President Lyndon Johnson appointed Marshall solici-
tor general, and in 1967 he appointed Marshall to the Supreme
Court. Like William Brennan, Marshall is a stalwart member of the
liberal wing of the Court, known for his unflinching commitment to
civil rights and his expansive interpretation of free speech and press
guarantees. Marshall was expected to favor Flynt.

Justice Harry A. Blackmun was born in Nashville, Illinois, in
1908, but grew up in the Minneapolis-St. Paul area. Blackmun went
to Harvard for both his undergraduate degree and law school, taught
as a law professor for a year after graduation, and then entered
private practice in Minneapolis. In 1950 he accepted the position of
house counsel for the Mayo Clinic in Rochester, Minnesota, one of
the nation's most prestigious medical complexes. In 1959 he was
appointed to the Eighth Circuit Court of Appeals and in 1970 to the
Supreme Court by Richard Nixon. Nixon had tried unsuccessfully
to nominate first Clement Haynsworth of South Carolina and then
G. Harold Carswell of Florida to the Court, but then, realizing that
the Senate in 1970 would not confirm a conservative southerner, he
picked Blackmun on his third try. Blackmun is a boyhood friend of
Warren Burger, and when he was first elevated to the Court to serve
with Burger, the two were dubbed "The Minnesota Twins." In his
early years on the Court, Blackmun tended to vote with Burger. He
steadily migrated, however, to the liberal wing of the Court and by
the 1980s usually joined with Brennan and Marshall. His most famous opinion is the 1973 abortion decision, *Roe v. Wade*. Blackmun
had to be counted as leaning toward Flynt.

Justice John Paul Stevens was born in 1920 in Chicago, Illinois. He went to college at the University of Chicago and law school at Northwestern. Stevens clerked for Supreme Court Justice Wiley B. Rutledge after law school. He then joined a well-known antitrust law firm in Chicago and taught part-time at the Northwestern and Chicago Law Schools. He was appointed by Richard Nixon in 1970 to the Court of Appeals for the Seventh Circuit, and in 1975 President Gerald Ford elevated him to the Supreme Court. Stevens is the Court's ultimate independent. He tends to reject rigid legal formulation in favor of pragmatic case-by-case analysis. His record in First Amendment cases is mixed, so it was difficult to get any firm handle on how he would treat *Falwell v. Flynt.*

Justice Sandra Day O'Connor was born in El Paso, Texas, in 1930. She received both her undergraduate and law degrees from Stanford. At the Stanford Law School, she was a classmate of William Rehnquist. O'Connor encountered sex discrimination when she applied for her first job after law school. "I interviewed with law firms in Los Angeles and San Francisco," she recalls, "but no one had ever hired a woman before as a lawyer, and they were not prepared to do so." One Los Angeles firm, of which William French Smith, later attorney general, was a partner, did offer to hire her— as a legal secretary. She served as a deputy county attorney for San Mateo County in California and as a civilian attorney for the army. She then spent eight years as homemaker with her three children. She resumed her legal career as an assistant attorney general in Arizona. In 1970 she was elected to the Arizona Senate and ultimately became majority leader. She served on the Maricopa County superior court and then the Arizona Court of Appeals until President Ronald Reagan nominated her to the Supreme Court in 1981. She is the first woman appointed to the Supreme Court. O'Connor's early years on the Court were marked by a reputation for extremely incisive questions during oral argument and carefully crafted opinions. While generally a conservative, O'Connor has shown a significant streak of independence and often appears to be staking out a centrist position, looking for areas of consensus between the left and right wings of the Court. In this respect, her jurisprudence seems to be evolving toward the sort of swing-vote role characteristic of Justice Lewis Powell. O'Connor had authored a significant pro-press decision in 1986, holding in a libel suit against the *Philadelphia Inquirer* that the plaintiff had the burden of proving that the allegedly libelous story was false. Like Justice Stevens, however,

O'Connor's ambiguous track record in First Amendment cases made her inclinations in *Falwell v. Flynt* too close to call.

The Court's most junior member is Justice Antonin Scalia. Scalia was nominated to the Supreme Court in 1986 by Ronald Reagan, when Reagan nominated Rehnquist to move over to the Chief Justice's position vacated by Warren Burger. Scalia was born in New Jersey, grew up in New York, and went to Georgetown as an undergraduate and then to Harvard Law School. Scalia taught at the University of Chicago and University of Virginia Law Schools and was later appointed to the United States Court of Appeals for the District of Columbia.

Scalia, a father of nine ("He always said he was going to have a baseball team," confides his aunt), bases his conservative judicial philosophy on strict separation of powers and a disdain for far-reaching federal remedies for social problems. He has a peppery prose style and an acid pen: He once called the Freedom of Information Act "the Taj Mahal of the Doctrine of Unanticipated Consequences, the Sistine Chapel of Cost-Benefit Analysis Ignored." In a caustic critique of affirmative action, he facetiously proposed a system he dubbed "R.J.H.S.—the Restorative Justice Handicapping System," in which individuals would be awarded points based on their ethnic backgrounds to determine how much they owed society. Justice Rehnquist and Scalia are regular players in a monthly nickel-and-dime poker game. Rehnquist's style of play is described by *The Wall Street Journal* as "subdued and canny," Scalia's as "intuitive and ebullient." Scalia's conservative leanings tend to place him in alliance with Rehnquist. He was expected to favor Falwell.

No one could possibly predict how the Supreme Court would actually vote in *Falwell v. Flynt,* but the preliminary guesstimates pointed toward an extremely close vote. Leaning to Falwell were probably Rehnquist, White, and Scalia, leaning to Flynt, Brennan, Marshall, and Blackmun; too close to call, Stevens and O'Connor. The legal and factual issues in *Falwell v. Flynt,* however, are so explosive that as many as five or six votes on the Court might actually be up for grabs. It was up to Alan Isaacman and Norman Roy Grutman to persuade the undecided.

Chapter 36

I t was a cold, blustery, December day in Washington. Two hours before the oral argument began, a large crowd gathered in the spectator waiting line on the front steps of the Supreme Court building.

As the entourages of Alan Isaacman and Norman Roy Grutman arrived separately at the Supreme Court building, the entrance of each lawyer epitomized their very different styles. Alan Isaacman was confident and happy, with a hint of a cocky, loosey-goosey swagger in his step. Among the group waiting in the cold were eleven members of Alan Isaacman's family, including his mother, his siblings, and other relatives—it's not every day that a member of the family argues his first case in the United States Supreme Court. The family was beaming with pride over Isaacman, and they showed their moral support by cheering as Isaacman and David Carson got out of their car and walked past the line toward the door for attorneys. Isaacman's mother gave him a hug and kiss for good luck.

Norman Roy Grutman arrived at the Supreme Court building with his wife and associates. Grutman was every bit as confident as Isaacman, but his was not the confidence of the swaggering all-American boy; he instead exuded the serene self-assurance of a sophisticated New York lawyer convinced of the righteousness of his cause. Everything about his long walk up the majestic steps of the Supreme Court building fit the part—he was dressed elegantly, and he moved with the studied dignified presence of a distinguished barrister. He seemed to glide more than walk past the long line of spectators with the easy grace of a seasoned ambassador reviewing the ceremonial troops in a foreign capital.

As the time for the oral argument approached, the nervous excitement in the courtroom increased by the minute. Among those in the crowded courtroom was a class of high school students there to see the Supreme Court of the United States in action. How much did they understand? Did they really know who Larry Flynt and Jerry Falwell were? Could they appreciate what the case represents? Whether they understood the nuances or not, they clearly perceived the drama of the moment; they were on the edge of their seats, craning their necks not to miss a thing.

Also present in the courtroom was a class far more attuned to the legal and cultural battle they were about to witness. *New York Times* correspondent Anthony Lewis teaches a class at the Harvard Law School on the press and the Constitution. A seasoned student of the Court and an expert on the First Amendment, he was the *Times* correspondent assigned to cover the Court earlier in his career and has won two Pulitzer prizes for his writing on legal issues. Lewis brought his class of law and graduate students down from Harvard to watch the oral argument. His students had the rare opportunity to witness firsthand a landmark decision in the making.

With thirty minutes to go before the argument was scheduled to begin, the courtroom was already packed. Jerry Falwell had arrived early and had a seat with his wife in the front row of the spectator section. Impeccably dressed and sporting a smart red, white, and blue striped tie, he smiled politely to others in the courtroom as they caught his eye, but he was far from casual. Falwell appeared intense and alert, anxious for the case to begin; he betrayed the nervous excitement of someone who cared deeply about the dramatic events about to unfold. Norman Roy Grutman glanced back from the counsel table at the front of the courtroom and saw Falwell. Grutman immediately got up and, with his wife, walked back to the spectator area to exchange greetings with Reverend and Mrs. Falwell. And then, in one of those unpretentious, touching gestures that only a mother can provide, Alan Isaacman's mother walked over to where the Falwells were seated and introduced herself. Reverend Falwell was the perfect gentleman; he shook hands warmly with Mrs. Isaacman and exchanged pleasantries with her for several minutes.

Jerry Falwell had come to the Supreme Court. Would Larry

Flynt show up also? Flynt's last personal appearance during the oral argument in *Keeton v. Hustler* in 1983 had been a disaster: It was on that occasion that he had shouted obscenities at the justices and been dragged away, under arrest for contempt of Court. Among the law clerks to the justices, rumors had been circulating for days over whether Flynt would appear again. One rumor had it that Isaacman had attempted to keep Flynt from learning of the oral argument date so that he would not try to attend. In fact, Isaacman had written a letter a few weeks before to Chief Justice Rehnquist, asking whether members of the Court would allow his client to appear. Chief Justice Rehnquist replied that Flynt's appearance would not be a problem for the justices.

With less than ten minutes to go before the argument was scheduled to begin, the conventional wisdom in the gallery was that Flynt would not show up. And then suddenly, he appeared, rolled in discreetly in his custom gold-plated wheelchair through a side-rear entrance in the courtroom. His chair was positioned only twenty feet from where Falwell was sitting with his wife. Dressed in a conservative business suit, Flynt seemed composed and content, exchanging pleasantries with a number of the students sitting near him. But when the Court came out, would he behave?

In the special seating area reserved for lawyers who are members of the Supreme Court Bar, two attorneys, Roslyn Mazer (the author of the *amicus curiae* brief for the Cartoonist's Association) and Harriette Dorsen (vice president and general counsel for the Bantam, Doubleday, Dell Publishing Group and a legal expert on satire and parody), struck up a conversation with one of the Supreme Court marshals. Mazer was curious about whether it was permissible to take notes on the argument. The marshal explained that members of the general public seated in the spectator section are not permitted to take notes, but that lawyers seated in the Supreme Court Bar section could. Mazer asked why the Court had such a rule—what if members of the general public wanted to write about what they had seen? "Well," said the marshal politely, "we're just afraid they'll write the wrong thing." Mazer and Dorsen chuckled; the marshal's comment was a curious prologue to a Supreme Court oral argument in one of the most important First Amendment cases in years.

Isaacman and Grutman were reviewing their arguments for the final time. Both men knew that an argument before the Supreme Court is not a speech, but a dialogue. The justices constantly interrupt the advocate with questions. The success of the advocate turns on how well he or she is able to manage that give-and-take. Isaacman particularly wanted that give-and-take to be loose and free-spirited. "My view of this case," said Isaacman, "is that we run into problems with this ad parody if people aren't prepared to look at it as an attempt at humor. If somebody will look at it and laugh at it, then we've come a long way towards saying, 'Hey, this thing is acceptable, it's permissible.' "

"*Hustler* readers will look at this ad parody, and they'll laugh at it," explained Isaacman. "If you take this ad parody and you put it in front of a Virginia jury composed of twelve fundamentalists who aren't *Hustler* readers, who have a high regard for Jerry Falwell, and are in an imposing courtroom, you can take Johnny Carson and try to make these people laugh, and they're not going to laugh." As Isaacman mulled things over in the Court's lounge for attorneys before the argument, he was thinking, "If I can get humor into this somehow—if I can get them relaxing a bit and laughing a little bit and then, maybe, thinking 'This is not that terrible, that outrageous!' "

But Isaacman had been warned that the Supreme Court was not *The Tonight Show* or *Late Night with David Letterman.* The Court was not particularly hospitable to lawyer-comedians. And to joke openly about Falwell would be particularly risky, for it could easily backfire—here were *Hustler*'s people, still hounding and hooting Reverend Falwell in the United States Supreme Court.

Isaacman still wanted to introduce at least a little levity, however, and he hit on the strategy of using the safest of all forms of humor—self-deprecation. If *Hustler* could laugh at itself, perhaps all could laugh together. If he had an opening, he would use it.

Chapter 37

The eight justices filed out from behind the red velvet curtain in back of the bench and stood behind their seats. "All rise!" said the marshal. As everyone in the courtroom rose to their feet, the Court's marshal proclaimed the traditional opening announcement: "Oyez, oyez, oyez. The Honorable, the Chief Justice and the Associate Justices of the Supreme Court of the United States. All persons having business before this honorable Court are admonished to draw nigh and give their attention, for the Court is now sitting. God save the United States and this honorable Court." As always, this was a moving ceremony, one of the most solemn and dignified known in American government.

Traditionally, the first order of business is to swear in new attorneys who have just been admitted to the Supreme Court Bar. There were several such ceremonial swearings-in, followed by a few remarks by Chief Justice Rehnquist warmly welcoming the new attorneys to the Bar of the Supreme Court.

Chief Justice Rehnquist then announced, "We'll hear the argument first this morning in number 86–1278, *Hustler Magazine and Larry C. Flynt versus Jerry Falwell.*" (While the case had been entitled *Falwell v. Flynt* in the lower courts, the title of the case was changed in the Supreme Court, in which *Hustler* and Flynt, the two "petitioners" seeking reversal of the lower court judgment, were listed first.)

The Chief Justice then nodded at Alan Isaacman, who had al-

264 RODNEY A. SMOLLA

ready taken his position. "Mr. Isaacman, you may proceed whenever you're ready."[1]

"Mr. Chief Justice, and may it please the Court," began Isaacman. "The First Amendment protects all speech except for certain narrowly drawn categories. For example, the First Amendment does not protect false statements of fact made with requisite fault. The First Amendment doesn't protect obscene speech. The First Amendment doesn't protect fighting words made in the presence of the person to whom the words are addressed and likely to incite violence. This case raises as a general question whether the Court should expand the areas left unprotected by the First Amendment and create another exception to protected speech. And in this situation, the new area that is sought to be protected is satiric or critical commentary of a public figure which does not contain any assertions of fact."

Chief Justice Rehnquist interrupted, "Are you suggesting that would be a change in our constitutional jurisprudence to protect that?"

"Yes, sir, I am," replied Isaacman. "I am suggesting that. In a specific way, the question becomes: Is rhetorical hyperbole, satire, parody, or opinion protected by the First Amendment when it doesn't contain assertions of fact and when the subject of the rhetorical hyperbole is a public figure? Another way of putting this case is: Can the First Amendment limitations which have been set out in *New York Times v. Sullivan* and its progeny be evaded by a public figure who, instead of alleging libel or instead of alleging invasion of privacy, seeks recovery for an allegedly injurious falsehood by labeling his cause of action intentional infliction of emotional distress?

"In judging the publication that's at issue here," continued Isaacman, "I think it's important to look at the context in which it appeared. The speaker, of course, was *Hustler Magazine,* and *Hustler Magazine* is known by its readers as a magazine that contains sexually explicit pictures and contains irreverent humor. As an editorial policy, it takes on the sacred cows and the sanctimonious in our society. It focuses on three subject areas primarily. It focuses on sex, it focuses on politics, and it focuses on religion.

"*Hustler Magazine* has been the target of attacks and critical commentary by Jerry Falwell for years and years prior to this ad publication. *Hustler Magazine* is at the other end of the political spectrum from Jerry Falwell. On the other hand, Jerry Falwell, to fill out the context of this speech, is the quintessential public figure.

It's hard to imagine a person in this country who doesn't hold political office who can have more publicity associated with his name than Jerry Falwell. Jerry Falwell is the head of the Moral Majority. The Moral Majority, he testified at the trial, numbers some six million people. It's a political organization, he indicates. It was set up to advance certain political views. One of the foremost views is to attack what he considers to be pornography and to attack kings of porn, in his words. And foremost among those kings of porn in his mind is Larry Flynt. He includes in that group others as well, such as Bob Guccione of *Penthouse* and such as Hugh Hefner of *Playboy.*

"The *Moral Majority* and Jerry Falwell also attack sexual conduct that they don't consider appropriate. He has spoken on the subject of extramarital and premarital sex. He doesn't approve of heterosexuals living together outside of wedlock. He also doesn't approve [of] and condemns homosexuality. Now, these aren't private views he has kept to himself or just shared with his family. These are views that he's gone on the political stump and tried to convince other people about.

"He has been known in his words, as he testified, by the *Good Housekeeping* magazine, which did a survey, as the second-most admired man in the United States, next to the president."

Justice Sandra Day O'Connor impatiently interrupted. "Well, Mr. Isaacman, is the fact that you claim Mr. Falwell is a public figure in dispute in this case?"

"It isn't in dispute at all."

"Well then, I guess we could move on to the arguments, because apparently your remarks are for the purpose of demonstrating he's a public figure. Is that right?"

"Justice O'Connor, it's really to fill out the political context and the fact that what we have here are people who are at opposite ends of the political spectrum, engaging in the uninhibited robust and wide open debate of *New York Times v. Sullivan.* "

"Does the State have an interest in protecting its citizens from emotional distress, do you suppose?"

"Clearly, the State has an interest in protecting its citizens from emotional distress."

"And perhaps that's an even greater interest than protecting reputation," suggested Justice O'Connor.

"I would submit that it is not a greater interest than protecting reputation," replied Isaacman, "because in the area of reputational injury, libel as we know it, for example, when it's in written form, emotional distress is an element of recovery as well as damage to reputation, and reputation affects what other people think of you. It affects what goes on in the minds of other people as well, and not just the minds of one citizen. So reputation in a sense covers a lot more territory than emotional distress does."

Isaacman then returned to his argument concerning *New York Times Co. v. Sullivan.* In less than a minute, however, he was interrupted again, this time by Justice White.

"Would this be a different case if the jury had found that the allegations could be considered factual?" White wanted to know.

"It certainly would be a different case," replied Isaacman. He then argued that the jury's determination that the Campari ad could not be understood as factual was a determination the Supreme Court was not free to overturn. The Court was bound by the jury's decision on that issue; it was to be treated as a given in analyzing the case.

This argument piqued Justice O'Connor. Why should the Supreme Court be bound by the jury on this point, she wanted to know? She referred Isaacman to a Supreme Court decision in a libel case entitled *Bose Corp. v. Consumers Union of United States, Inc.,*[2] a decision that holds that the Supreme Court has a duty in First Amendment cases to examine factual issues independently, without treating the jury's findings as binding.

Isaacman was ready with a counterargument. "Justice O'Connor, I suggest that in the First Amendment context, when a determination is made by a jury that's adverse to speech, and when a jury finds that the speaker made statements that could be construed as statements of fact and were knowingly false, then it is incumbent upon the Court to take that review for the purpose of protecting the speaker. And that's what the First Amendment says, that you have to protect the speaker."

Now Chief Justice Rehnquist entered the discussion. "You think *Bose* is a one-way street, then?" he asked.

"Your Honor," Isaacman replied, "I do think it is a one-way street. *Bose* is intended to protect the speaker; it's not intended to protect the emotional distress interest that the State is seeking to protect in the area of intentional infliction of emotional stress or in the area of libel." Isaacman further pointed out that the question of whether the ad is capable of being understood as factual is part of the libel count submitted to the jury. The libel count, however, was not appealed by Norman Roy Grutman, and so that question was technically not before the Court for review.

These preliminary skirmishes with the justices were quite important to Isaacman. However dismal the sordid trial record in his case might appear to be, he came to the Supreme Court armed with one powerful point in his favor: The jury had held that the ad cannot be understood as factual. Isaacman could not risk losing that point; it was the best thing he had going for him. So any suggestion by the justices that they were free to *decide for themselves* whether the Campari ad could be taken seriously had to be tenaciously fought. Since the Supreme Court normally is permitted to reexamine jury determinations in First Amendment cases, Isaacman had to make a "one-way door" argument. Such searching review, he had to claim, is only warranted when the Court is reviewing a lower court verdict against the press. When the ruling of the court below is in favor of the press, however, the Supreme Court must not intervene. This is a risky argument—it smacks of press duplicity and arrogance, of wanting to have all legal rules break the media's way. If the rule of independent appellate review is good for the goose, why not for the gander?

Isaacman was arguing, however, that the "one-way door" notion makes sense under the First Amendment. The Court reopens jury determinations, he claimed, so that the jury is not permitted to abuse its fact-finding power and penalize a speaker's First Amendment rights. A jury might find, for example, that a soapbox orator was guilty of "incitement to riot," even though the speaker had in fact posed no threat of stirring the crowd to violence. A jury might make such a finding out of prejudice against the speaker's point of view. A jury could thus penalize a defendant for his or her creed, but disguise that prejudice by "burying" it in a trumped-up finding that the defendant actually posed a "clear and present danger" of violence. The only way to guard against the danger that juries might trample on First Amendment rights by disingenuously interpreting the facts is to permit appellate courts independently to scrutinize the factual record to insure that the jury's verdict is justified. The integrity of a sacred principle such as freedom of speech may be compromised if appellate courts are not vigilant in guarding against manipulation of the underlying focus.

This is the rationale underlying "independent appellate review" of jury determinations in First Amendment cases. Alan Isaacman was arguing before the Supreme Court that this rationale makes sense only when the Court is reviewing a decision by a jury antagonistic to First Amendment values. Such review is not warranted, however, when the jury has acted in favor of speech, as it did on the libel count in the Falwell case.

Isaacman had only just barely made his point when the justices changed the subject. In the pressure cooker of a thirty-minute Supreme Court argument, there is no time to dwell—a lawyer has to get in and get out, make his point and move on. It was Justice Scalia who pushed matters to the next level of difficulty, with a question that went for the jugular of *New York Times v. Sullivan.* [3]

"Mr. Isaacman," stated Scalia, "what the *New York Times* rule provides is not an absolute protection, but a knowing element, an element of specific intent to create a falsehood. It doesn't give an absolute privilege to state falsehood. It just says the falsehood is okay unless there's an intent. Now, here we have a state tort that is specifically an intentional tort. There must be an intent to create the emotional distress, so it really is not quite in the same category that you're making it out to be. The issue is whether the intent element, which is enough to provide a major exception from *New York Times,* is also enough to make a major exception for purposes of this tort action. Isn't that right?"

"Justice Scalia," replied Isaacman, "We have a lot of cases, including *New York Times v. Sullivan,* including *Garrison v. Louisiana,* [4] that say it's not the intent to cause harm. It's not the hatred, it's not the ill will, it's not the spite that the First Amendment is directed at. It's intent to cause harm through knowing falsehood or reckless falsehood."

"I understand you can draw the line there," said Scalia. "But all *New York Times* says is if you state falsehood with knowledge of the falsehood, the First Amendment does prevent it. All I'm asking you is why can't that principle be extended to say you can cause emotional harm to your heart's content, just as you can state falsity to your heart's content, but where you intend to create that emotional harm, we have a different situation? Isn't that a possible line?"

"I don't think that any reasonable reader of any of the speech that has occurred in the cases, including *New York Times v. Sullivan, Garrison,* and all the other cases that have come down—*Letter Carriers* I gave as an example—could ever say that the speaker did not intend to cause harm. When you say that somebody has a corkscrew soul and has tortured principles for a heart and is a traitor, who can believe that person doesn't intend to cause harm? People intend the natural consequences of their actions. And they intend when they say something critical that that's going to cause some harm or some distress. And that speech has to be protected, or all we're going to have is a bland, milquetoast kind of speech in this country."

"That may well be. My only point is *New York Times,* it seems to me, doesn't speak to it. *New York Times* says intent is okay, is enough to get you out of it. What you're saying is, this kind of intent shouldn't be enough, intent to cause harm shouldn't be."

"That's correct. Knowing falsity may be enough."

Justice Stevens then joined in. "But even in the *New York Times* sense," he said, "If the asserted facts here were known to be untrue— I mean, one who knew nothing about Mr. Falwell or anything about the background could read this and think *there might be* some individual that this was a factually correct statement about—so that these are statements that *were* knowingly false—they really satisfied the *New York Times* standard, in that sense."

"Justice Stevens," Isaacman rejoined, "the response to that is really that there were no facts asserted."

"Well, I understand what your argument is, but to the extent that there are factual statements, they satisfy the *New York Times* standard because everybody knows they're false, including the speaker."

"If you change what this article means, and you say this article's capable of being interpreted as an assertion of fact, then you've kind of set the stage differently from what it is, and from what the jury determined. If you say that in *Letter Carriers,* that the person who made that comment was really saying—"

"Really," Stevens cut him off. "All I'm suggesting is pretty much the same thing Justice Scalia is. I'm not sure *New York Times* speaks to the problem we have before us in this case."

These questions seemed to be heading the argument into an area not completely hospitable to *Hustler.* Several of the justices seemed to be flirting with an analysis similar to the Fourth Circuit's. A prior Supreme Court decision, known as *Time, Inc. v. Firestone,*[5] holds that in a libel suit brought by a private figure, in which the private figure demonstrated negligence, it is permissible to allow a jury to award damages solely for the emotional distress caused by the libel. No separate proof of damage to reputation is necessary. Falwell, of course, is a public figure, and his jury award is not for libel but for emotional distress alone. But if he established the higher level of fault—intent to cause harm—why shouldn't he be able to recover?

Building on this theory, Justice White set out to pin Isaacman down. "Well, even accepting what the jury found, that there was no reputational injury here because there was no believable fact asserted, for you to win, you have to say that opinion or parody is never actionable, even though it's done intentionally for the purpose of inflicting emotional distress. That's your proposition, isn't it?"

"Well, Justice White, my proposition is—"

"Isn't it, or not?"

"No, no. As you stated it, Your Honor, no, it isn't."

"What is it, then?"

"Because what that leaves out is opinion or parody that does not contain anything that can be reasonably understood as a statement of fact."

"All right. I agree with that, because that's what the jury found."

"The second thing that your hypothetical left out—your proposition left out—was that this is a public figure who is bringing this action, somebody who's supposed to have a thick skin."

"All right. Include that, and then you say, parody or opinion about a public figure is never actionable even though it's done intentionally for the purpose of causing emotional distress—that's your proposition."

"And even though it contains nothing that can be understood as a false statement of fact."

"Sure, sure," said White.

"Including that, I agree, yes. That's my proposition."

"That's your proposition."

"You cross the line when you say something that can be understood as a false statement of fact. Otherwise, you're not going to have the uninhibited, robust—"

"Well, I take it certainly it's arguable that we must judge this case on the basis that there was no fact involved. You say the jury said there wasn't," interrupted White.

"The jury said there was nothing that could be perceived, could be understood as a fact."

"If we judge the case on that basis, then your proposition is there can't be any liability here at all—"

"That's correct."

"—if there's a public figure involved. Would you say if there wasn't a public figure involved, that we could sustain this judgment? Let's assume it was not a public figure. No believable statement was said that could be interpreted as a fact, and so there would be no libel, no reputational injury. If there was not a public figure involved, would you say the judgment would stand, or not?"

"Fortunately, that's not my case. But I will answer that. We don't have to deal with that case in resolving this one."

"Well, you haven't answered it, yet."

"I would say that if it does not contain a false statement of fact, or something that can be perceived as a false statement of fact, then even if it's a private figure, it's protected speech."

Justice O'Connor then interjected, "At common law, I suppose the exception was just for fair comment, wasn't it?"

O'Connor's point here was potentially explosive. She was suggesting that the common-law tradition did not protect all opinion, but only "fair" opinion. If this Supreme Court were to go back and revisit the fact/opinion distinction, it might choose to revert back to the common-law view. This would be disastrous for Flynt. How could Isaacman persuade Justice O'Connor not to pursue the "fair comment" theory? In one of those accidents of litigation, he was spared having to give an in-depth answer. Before he could say much at all to O'Connor, Justice Stevens cut him off and steered the argument back toward an inquiry into the social value of the Campari ad compared to the social interest in protecting the public from emotional distress.

"Mr. Isaacman," asked Stevens, "you puzzled me with your answer to Justice White, and, assuming there's no public figure involved—and you've admitted there's a public interest in protecting the citizenry from emotional distress—what's the public interest in protecting speech that does nothing else?"

"There is a public interest in allowing every citizen of this country to express his views," replied Isaacman. "That's one of the most cherished interests that we have as a nation."

"Well, what view was expressed by this?"

"By this ad parody, or your example?"

"Well, either one, other than something that just upsets the target of the comment?"

"What view is expressed by the ad parody is really a couple-fold view, two views or more. In the first place, we have to understand that we're talking about one page out of 150 pages in the magazine."

"I understand."

"So it's not a treatise or a novel that's gone into a long development. It is a parody of a Campari ad, number one—it does that."

"I understand."

"And that's a legitimate view for it to express. And we all can understand how it parodied the ad. It is also also a satire of Jerry Falwell, and he is in many respects the perfect candidate to put in this Campari ad, because he's such a ridiculous figure to be in this ad. Somebody who has campaigned against alcohol, campaigned against sex and that kind of thing."

"Well," pressed Stevens, "What is the public interest that you're describing, that you're building up here? That there's some interest in making him look ludicrous? Or is it just that there's a public interest in doing something that people might think is funny? What is the public interest?"

Isaacman hung tough. "There are two public interests," he argued. "With respect to Jerry Falwell alone, there are two public interests. One is there is a public interest in having *Hustler* express its view that what Jerry Falwell says, as the rhetorical question at the end of the ad parody indicates, is 'B. S.' And *Hustler* has every right to say that somebody who's out there campaigning against it, saying don't read our magazine and we're poison on the minds of America and don't engage in sex outside of wedlock and don't drink alcohol—*Hustler* has every right to say that man is full of 'B. S.' And that's what this ad parody says. And what the first part of the ad parody does, it puts him in a ridiculous setting. Instead of Jerry Falwell speaking from the television with a beatific look on his face and the warmth that comes out of him, and the sincerity in his voice, and he's a terrific communicator, and he's standing on a pulpit, and he may have a Bible in his hand—instead of that situation, *Hustler* is saying, let's deflate this stuffed shirt, let's bring him down to our level, or at least to the level where you will listen to what we have to say."

Isaacman's statement "let's bring him down to our level" was a minor bit of self-deprecating humor, but the whole courtroom exploded in laughter, including the justices on the bench. It had not taken much to break the tension. Chief Justice Rehnquist laughed so hard he grabbed his side and seemed almost about to fall out of his chair.

When the laughter subsided, Isaacman wryly apologized. "I was told not to joke in the Supreme Court. I really didn't mean to do that."

Justice Stevens was ready to return to business. "That's the answer to the first half of my question," he said. "What's the public interest in the case involving a private figure?"

"In the case of a private figure, the public interest is admittedly less."

"Less? What is it?"

"There is still interest in expressing your views—there's still an interest in people being able to express their views, apart from the fact that the public may not have any great interest in hearing those views."

Justice Antonin Scalia stepped in next, engaging Isaacman in one of the most incisive exchanges in the entire oral argument. "Mr. Isaacman," Scalia said, "to contradict Vince Lombardi, the First Amendment is not everything. It's a very important value, but it's not the only value in our society, certainly. You're giving us no help in trying to balance it, it seems to me, against another value which is that good people should be able to enter public life and public service. The rule you give us says that if you stand for public office, or become a public figure in any way, you cannot protect yourself or, indeed, your mother, against a parody of your committing incest with your mother in an outhouse. Now, is that not a value that ought to be protected? Do you think George Washington would have stood for public office if that was the consequence? And there's no way to protect the values of the First Amendment and yet attract people into public service? Can't you give us some line that would balance the two?"

Scalia was making two cogent points at once. The *New York Times* decision had not given the press absolute protection in libel cases but only a qualified level of protection. The press could still be held responsible if it acted with knowing or reckless disregard for falsity. Yet Isaacman seemed to want an absolute rule immunizing the press in emotional distress cases. Couldn't he offer the Court some compromise, as in *New York Times*? Scalia's second point was even more ingenious. Free speech is an important value in American life, but it is not the only important value. Among the reasons we value free speech is that it assists us in self-governance. Robust public discourse is vital to a democracy. But Scalia was pointing out another formidable requirement for a thriving democracy: the ability of a society to attract high-quality people to public service. How will America attract the best and the brightest to public life if such an entry requires deals with devils like Larry Flynt? Is the sort of ridicule conveyed by *Hustler*'s ad parody part of the price everyone must be willing to pay in exchange for entry into the public arena?

Isaacman tried to meet Scalia's points head-on. "Well," he began, "one of the lines was suggested by a question earlier, and that is in the private figure or public figure area, if the Court really wants to balance. But take somebody whose going into public life, George Washington as an example. There's a cartoon—I think it's in the brief of the Association of American Editorial Cartoonists—that has George Washington being led on a donkey and underneath there's a caption that so and so who's leading the donkey is leading this ass, or something to that effect."

"I can handle that," Justice Scalia interrupted. "I think George could handle that." Again the courtroom burst into wild laughter. "But that's a far cry from committing incest with your mother in an outhouse." The laughter picked up again. Scalia was on a roll. "I mean, there's no line between the two? We can't protect that kind of parody and not protect this?"

"There's no line in terms of the meaning, because *Hustler* wasn't saying that he committed incest with his mother," Isaacman insisted. "Nobody could understand it to be saying that as a matter of fact. And what you're talking about, Justice Scalia, is a matter of taste. And as Justice Scalia, you said in *Pope v. Illinois,*[6] just as it's useless to argue about taste, it's useless to litigate about it. And what we're talking about here is, well, is this tasteful or not tasteful? That's really what you're talking about, because nobody believed that Jerry Falwell was being accused of committing incest. The question is, is this in good taste to put him in this, draw this image, paint a picture. If you charge a man with a crime, Your Honor, and it's an assertion that he committed a crime—"

"If it's against a public figure, it's okay?" Scalia interrupted.

"No."

"No?"

"If it's a knowing false statement of fact, if you're charging him with a crime and it's perceived that you're charging him with a crime, and you're doing it with knowledge that that's false, it's not okay against a public figure."

For the first time, Justice Thurgood Marshall jumped in, and he seemed rather pointedly hostile to *Hustler*'s actions. "Well, isn't that this case?" he asked.

"No, it isn't this case."

"You say they didn't charge him with incest?"

"Justice Marshall, they did not charge him with incest, and a jury determined—"

Marshall interrupted, "Why did they have him and his mother together?"

"They had him and his mother together to show what's called in literary form travesty to put somebody in a ridiculous, unbelievable setting for purposes of effect. They put him in this situation knowing nobody would really perceive that that's what he's actually doing, but to say we're going to deflate this man who is so self-righteous in the area of sex and telling everybody else what to do, as well as telling them what to read."

"And what public purpose does that serve?"

"It served the same public purpose, in a sense, of having Garry Trudeau in *Doonesbury* call George Bush a wimp. What public purpose does that have? It makes people look at that and maybe think of George Bush a little bit differently. And somebody who is out there telling other people how to live and being very serious and sober about it and acting as though he has more knowledge than they do about how they live their lives—*Hustler* has a right to make comments about it and make him look ridiculous as long as they don't state false statements of fact knowingly or recklessly."

"Well, it was a false statement of fact that he was in the outhouse with his mother. That was a false statement of fact."

"It was not a statement of fact, Your Honor, and the jury so found."

"Well, what was it?"

"What was it? It was hyperbole."

"Hyperbole?"

"Just as calling somebody a blackmailer was not saying he's a blackmailer. It was saying that he was engaged in—"

"If you charge somebody with, say, if you don't pay me money, I'll report you, that's blackmail."

"That's correct."

"Well, that's the same as this was."

"That's correct. But in *Greenbelt,*[7] saying that somebody was a blackmailer—"

"Oh, you mean, they had to say that he was guilty of incest, in quotes? Is that right? Is that right?"

"No, it is not right, Your Honor."

"How close would they have to get to that?"

"They would have to say it in a way that a reasonable reader would perceive that that's what *Hustler* was saying, that he is guilty of incest. And this jury—which was certainly not a jury that came from *Hustler*'s background in any way—said that no reasonable reader could perceive this as a statement of fact."

Isaacman could see that his thirty-minute time limit was about to expire. It had gone so fast! He had been peppered with questions from the first minute he had taken the podium. As oral advocates are trained to do, Isaacman tried to use his last precious moments to summarize his position. He wanted to leave the Court with one final forceful reminder: that this is much, much bigger than *Hustler*, Larry Flynt, and Jerry Falwell.

"And in summing up," he said, "what I would like to do is say this is not just a dispute between *Hustler* and Jerry Falwell, and a rule that's applied in this case is not just that *Hustler Magazine* can no longer perform what it does for its readers, and that is produce this type of irreverent humor or other types of irreverent humor. It affects everything that goes on in our national life. And we have a long tradition, as Judge Wilkinson said, of satiric commentary, and you can't pick up a newspaper in this country without seeing cartoons or editorials that have critical comments about people. And if Jerry Falwell can sue because he suffered emotional distress, anybody else who is in public would be able to sue because they suffered emotional distress. And the standard that was used in this case— does it offend generally accepted standards of decency and morality? —is no standard at all. All it does is allow the punishment of unpopular speech."

Isaacman's peroration had been snappy and effective. The argument had gone reasonably well. He was ready to sit down. But Justice Scalia wasn't quite through with Isaacman yet. Before Isaacman could retreat to the safety of the counsel table, Scalia hit him with a final intriguing question: "How often do you think you're going to be able to get a jury to find that it was done with the intent of creating emotional distress?" Scalia asked. "I mean, there is that finding here."

Scalia was suggesting that the rest of the press need not worry about the verdict against *Hustler* because it would be quite rare for a jury to find, as it did in this case, that the publication set out deliberately to inflict emotional distress.

Isaacman was equal to the challenge. His final answer was as important as any statement he had made to the Court. "Every time," Isaacman replied. "Almost every time that something critical is said about somebody. Because, how can any speaker come in and say, 'I didn't intend to cause any emotional distress,' and be believed? If you say something critical about another person, and if it's very critical, it's going to cause emotional distress. We all know that. That's just common sense. So it's going to be an easy thing to show, intent to harm. That's why that's a meaningless standard." Isaacman paused a moment for effect, and sat down.

"Thank you, Mr. Isaacman," said Chief Justice Rehnquist.

Isaacman had made great mileage from his own natural personality during his argument. He was himself—a little bit "aw shucks, ma'am," a little bit prankish, a little bit familiar, a little bit cocky. He showed great respect for the justices and intense feelings for the gravity of the issues in the case, but he exuded a relaxed sense of perspective—he was casual and even *friendly* toward the justices; he seemed to be winking at them, saying we all know that this is a crazy case—it's okay to laugh a little about it. He set that tone by his own demeanor more than by anything else. He was having fun. "Ask me anything you want," Isaacman was communicating, "because I have the answers." Isaacman could also be thankful that, throughout the entire argument, his client Larry Flynt had behaved. No sudden outbursts had marred the proceedings.

Isaacman clearly savored every moment of his performance. Professionally and personally, he had gotten all he could have hoped for. "I loved it. When I was up there, I loved it," he said later. "I was outside myself watching myself, which is a strange feeling. I'm watching my hands move and I'm listening to what I'm saying and watching. I didn't want to sit down, I really didn't—I could have stayed there another two hours, I was enjoying it so much."

Chapter 38

As Norman Roy Grutman came to the podium, one could see before he even uttered his first word that his style and tone would contrast sharply with Isaacman's. A master of oration, he had just seen his opponent argue effectively for thirty minutes. Grutman set out, characteristically, to dispel Isaacman's momentum, to alter the psychology of the courtroom.

"Mr. Chief Justice, may it please the Court," Grutman began, in his deep, melodic voice. "Deliberate, malicious character assassination is not protected by the First Amendment to the Constitution. Deliberate, malicious character assassination is what was proven in this case. By the defendant's own explicit admission, the publication before this Court was the product of a deliberate plan to assassinate, to upset the character and integrity of the plaintiff, and to cause him severe emotional disturbance with total indifference then and now to the severity of the injury caused. When the publication was protested by the bringing of this lawsuit, the unregenerate defendant published it again."

This was a powerful start. The mood in the room was changing. Grutman had the Court's attention. He proceeded to play one of the advocate's favorite tricks: He took up as his first specific point the very last question Justice Scalia had asked of Isaacman and tried to turn it to Falwell's advantage. "I'd like to answer a question that you raised with my adversary. 'How often are you going to be able to get proof like this?' I dare say, very infrequently, and I dare say, that the kind of behavior with which the Court is confronted is aberrational. This is not the responsible publisher. This is the wanton, reckless, deliberately malicious publisher who sets out for the sheer perverse joy of simply causing injury to abuse the power that he has as a publisher."

Justice O'Connor quickly interrupted. "Mr. Grutman, I guess there are those who think that the conduct of certain newspapers in pursuing Mr. Hart recently was of the same unwarranted character. Should that result in some kind of liability?"

"I don't think so in that case," responded Grutman, "because what was being done by the newspapers in that case was reporting the truth, the truth about a public figure who was a candidate for public office. The context in which the publications about Gary Hart appeared cannot really be compared favorably with what was done here."

"So you would limit the recovery for the tort of emotional distress to recovery for a falsehood?" O'Connor pressed.

"No."

"No?"

"Under the theory of the intentional infliction of emotional distress, even the truth can be used in such a way, if it is used in some outrageous way, it must be something which is so repellent—"

"And what if the jury were to determine that what the newspapers did with regard to Mr. Hart fell in that category? Is that recoverable?"

"If the jury were able to find from the evidence, Justice O'Connor, that the publication was outrageous—and I would doubt that they *would* find that, because it is not that kind of conduct, reporting the truth—"

"But you would say it's open to a jury determination?" O'Connor interrupted.

"Only in a highly theoretical sense, if the animating purpose behind the publisher was simply to inflict intense and severe emotional distress upon Gary Hart. But I think that's really not the issue. The focus in this Court, which is not the Court of libel, the focus is on the harm which is inflicted on the victim."

"Well," O'Connor asked, "do you think a vicious cartoon should subject the drawer of that cartoon to potential liability?"

"Only in the event that the cartoon constitutes that kind of depiction which would be regarded by the average member of the community as so intolerable that no civilized person should have to bear it. That's the definition of the Court."

Justice White seemed to think Grutman was overstating his position. "Well, Mr. Grutman," White said, "you're certainly posing a much broader proposition than is necessary for you to win this case."

"Indeed, but I was answering the question of Justice O'Connor."

"Well, the way you put it from the very outset, you put it the same way. We're judging this case on the basis that the jury found that no one could reasonably have believed that this was a statement of fact. That's the way we judge this case."

"No. I'd like to address that point, Justice White, because I think a kind of semantic conundrum has been presented here when counsel says that there was no statement of fact. There was a statement of fact. Just as we argued in our brief, you could state gravity causes things to fly upward. That is a statement of fact. It's just a false statement of fact. And if one consults the record—"

"What do you make out of the special verdict the jury returned?" interrupted White.

"I make out of it the fact that the jury said that this was not describing actual facts about the plaintiff or actual events in which the plaintiff participated. That is a finding that the statement in the publication was false. Perhaps we should have appealed that. That's a finding of falsity which is all that we needed to prove to sustain libel. But we did not appeal that, and that question is not before the Court. But, in answer to your question, I find that the meaning of the answer to that question only goes to the issue of whether the jury thought that Reverend Falwell—"

White impatiently cut Grutman off. "I don't know why you insist on this, because if there's anything factual about this statement, you certainly have to contend with *New York Times*. And if there's nothing factual about it, you don't have to contend with it at all. All you have to say to win, which is plenty, is that using opinion or parody to inflict emotional distress is not protected by the First Amendment, which is a considerably different proposition than what you've been pushing."

"I agree that parody or so-called satire, whatever it calls itself," Grutman replied, "is not necessarily protected speech when the purpose of the publisher is to inflict severe emotional distress. And while the contention is made in the argument that you've heard this morning that this was a parody, I think that the jury could properly examine this and recognize it for what it is. A fig leaf isn't going to protect this kind of a publication from being recognized as the kind of behavior with which the tort of the intentional infliction of emotional distress is intended to deal."

Chief Justice Rehnquist followed up on White's inquiry. "But you would subject, though, the range of political cartoonists, for example, to that kind of jury inquiry, whether it was vicious enough to warrant recovery?"

"No," insisted Grutman. "Two things must conjoin. What you have to have is an irresponsible intention on the part of the defendant to inflict injury. That's only one half of it. The other is that what the cartoonist, the writer, or the speaker does constitutes in the mind of the community an utterance of such enormity, such a heinous kind of utterance, usually false, that nobody should have to bear that if the purpose was to inflict severe emotional injury and severe emotional injury results."

"What about a cartoonist who sits down at his easel, or whatever cartoonists sit down at," asked Rehnquist, "and thinks to himself that a candidate running for the presidency is just a big windbag, a pompous turkey, and thinks 'I'm going to draw this cartoon showing him as such'? You know, part of his intent, is that he enjoys cartooning and just likes to make people look less than they are, to show up the dark side of people. But he knows perfectly well that's going to create emotional distress in this particular person. Now, does that meet your test?"

"No. It does not, unless what he depicts is something like showing the man committing incest with his mother when that's not true, or molesting children, or running a bordello, or selling narcotics."

"What about the state of mind required from the defendant?"

"Well, the state of mind is precisely what we're concerned with."

"What about the state of mind I've hypothesized to you? Does that satisfy your test for the Constitution, or not?"

"No, it would not. If the man sets out with the purpose of simply making a legitimate aesthetic, political, or some other kind of comment about the person about whom he was writing or drawing, and that is not an outrageous comment, then there's no liability."

"Even though he knows it will inflict emotional distress?" asked Justice Stevens.

"It has to be—correct, because you cannot have emotional distress for mere slights, for the kinds of things which people in an imperfect world have got to put up with, calling somebody some of the epithets that were mentioned in the opposing argument, black-mailer, or some other conclusory and highly pejorative terms, an epithet, but when you say not that you are some foul conclusory term, but when you depict someone in the way in which Jerry Falwell was depicted with all of the hallmarks of reality, including the pirated copyright and the pirated trademark, so that the casual reader looking at it could think this is for real, that rises to the level of—"

Both Justices Scalia and Stevens jumped in simultaneously.

"That's a different argument," said Scalia.

"Yeah," said Stevens, "That doesn't go to the question of intent. What about a case in which another magazine publisher today decided 'I think I could sell a lot of magazines by reprinting this very parody here, because it's gotten so much publicity and some people may think it's funny and so forth; I don't care if it hurts Mr. Falwell, but it will cause precisely the same harm as this one'? Is there recovery in that case or not?" Stevens asked.

"I do not think so, or it's a much harder case." The justices were hitting Grutman harder and harder, and he seemed to be backpeddling.

"So it's free game now. Anybody can publish this other than Mr. Flynt?"

"Justice Stevens, Mr. Flynt republished it for a third time after the jury verdict."

"I understand. But what you're telling me under your test, anybody else may publish it without incurring liability?"

"Liability requires an intent."

"But you agree with what I said?"

"I do, I do, Mr. Justice Stevens. I agree that intent—this is why this is such a rare tort. This is, as I've suggested, an interstitial tort."

"Mr. Grutman," said Justice Scalia, "you've given us a lot of words to describe this: outrageous, heinous—"

"Repulsive and loathsome," finished Grutman.

" 'Repulsive and loathsome.' I don't know," continued Scalia, "maybe you haven't looked at the same political cartoons that I have, but some of them, and a long tradition of this, not just in this country but back into English history—I mean, politicians depicted as *horrible-looking beasts*—and you talk about portraying someone as committing some immoral act? I would be very surprised if there were not a number of cartoons depicting one or another political figure as at least the *piano player* in a bordello." The spectators in the courtroom laughed.

"Justice Scalia, we don't shoot the piano player. I understand that," said Grutman, playing along.

"But can you give us something that the cartoonist or the political figure can adhere to, other than such general words as 'heinous' and what not. I mean, does it depend on how ugly the beast is, or what?" Again the crowd laughed. Scalia could make it on *David Letterman* at this rate.

"No, it's not the amount of hair the beast has or how long his claws may be, said Grutman. "I believe that this is a matter of an evolving social sensibility. Between the 1700s and today, I would suggest, that people have become more acclimatized to the use of the kinds of language or the kinds of things that, had they been depicted at an earlier age, would have been regarded as socially unacceptable. And while that evolutionary change is taking place, and it's a salutory thing, there are certain kinds of things. It's difficult to describe them. This Court struggled for years to put a legal definition on obscenity, and Justice Stewart could say no more than, 'I know what it is when I see it.' Well, this kind of rare aberrational and anomalous behavior, whatever it is, whatever the verbal formulation that the nine of you may come upon, clearly it can be condensed in the form of words that I used, which are not mine—they belong to the oracles of the Restatement [a legal text]—who have tried to say that it is for the jury to decide whether or not what is being depicted is done in so offensive, so awful, and so horrible a way, that it constitutes the kind of behavior that nobody should have to put up with."

Justice O'Connor wasn't satisfied with this answer. "Well, Mr. Grutman," she said, "In today's world, people don't want to have to take these things to a jury. They want to have some kind of a rule to follow so that when they utter it or write it or draw it in the first place, they're comfortable in the knowledge that it isn't going to subject them to a suit."

"I frankly think that it isn't too much to expect, Justice O'Connor, that a responsible author, artist, or anyone would understand that attempting to falsely depict as a representational fact that someone is committing incest with his mother in an outhouse and saying that she's a whore, and that when the person involved is an abstemious Baptist minister, that he always gets drunk before he goes into the pulpit—it isn't too much to say that anybody who would do that ought to take the consequences for casting that into the stream."

The justices were giving Grutman no quarter. His answer to Justice O'Connor's question seemed to be grounded in the assumption that the ad parody could be understood as factual. Justice White jumped in immediately, as he had with Isaacman, to explore this point.

"Well, the way you put it, we don't need any new law for that," White pointed out. "That's just—*New York Times*[1] wouldn't insulate any statement of fact like that."

"Justice White," replied Grutman, "I don't think this case is governed by the *New York Times* rule. When I tried this case, we were living in the heyday of *Gertz*,[2] and we had not yet had this Court's decision in *Dun & Bradstreet*[3] or in *Philadelphia Newspapers v. Hepps*.[4] I would suggest to this Court that we are covered by your decisions in those cases. This is not speech that matters. This is not the kind of speech that is to be protected. The *New York Times* rule is not a universal nostrum. It is a rule that you formulated to meet a constitutional crisis involving truth, which is irrelevant here."

"Well, if these were factual statements as you mentioned, you could win under *New York Times* any time," said White.

"Yes, we could win under *New York Times,* but I'm suggesting that, as a jurisprudential matter, the *New York Times* formulation of actual malice is inappropriate and irrelevant for this tort for the reason that when you're dealing with the tort of libel, the focus of inquiry, the gravamen, is on the issue of truth or falsity in which facts become the measure of what is true or false, or something which has been dealt with recklessly. The gravamen of this, as I say, interstitial tort is on the harm that was inflicted on the victim, and the constitutional measure here is intentionality. It's what this Court said in the dissent of Chief Justice Rehnquist, we're really dealing with *scienter* or *mens rea.*" (Grutman was using technical legal terms for "knowing intent.")

"Well, Mr. Grutman," pointed out Justice O'Connor, "there's plenty of malice here all right. I mean, I don't think that's your problem. But the jury said this can't be reasonably viewed as making a factual allegation."

"I disagree, Justice O'Connor, and if you'll give me a moment— that is the easy way of looking at it, but that's not what they said. The question they answered is, can this be understood as describing actual—meaning truth—actual facts about the plaintiff or actual events in which the plaintiff participated? And they said no. That to me means that they said this is not a true statement of fact, but it's nonetheless a statement of fact for the purposes of *New York Times* or for the purposes of this case."

Grutman was making a strange point. The Campari ad, he seemed to be saying, is not a "true statement of fact" but is nevertheless a "statement of fact." This linguistic distinction clearly engaged the academic mind of Justice Scalia. "Give me a statement that isn't a statement of fact," he challenged Grutman.

"Pardon?" said Grutman.

"Give me a statement that isn't a statement of fact in your interpretation of what 'statement of fact' means. I mean, when you say, 'statement of fact,' it means true fact, or it means nothing at all."

"No. That is the Aristotelian interpretation of a statement of fact as propounded by Professors Wechsler and Michael in their famous monograph, but in the common parlance in which we speak, a statement of fact is an utterance about either an event or a thing or a person which can be proven either true or false. If it's true, then it's a true fact, but if it's false, like gravity causes things to float upward—that's a statement of fact, but it's manifestly false."

(This case had everything! A lawsuit that began with a depiction of Jerry Falwell in an outhouse with his mother now included a lawyer expounding on "the Aristotelian interpretation of a statement of fact as propounded by Professors Wechsler and Michael in their famous monograph." Even Norman Roy Grutman must have bitten his cheeks a little with that one. As it turns out, in the heat of the argument, Grutman had made an inadvertent error. The "famous monograph" was a text he remembered from his days at Columbia Law School, from Columbia Professor Herbert Wechsler's class— but Wechsler had not been the author.)

Justice Scalia wasn't going to bite at all. "So there's no statement that is not a statement of fact is what you're saying?"

"That's correct. However, there may be statements—that's an interesting philosophical question that we could explore endlessly, but—"

"Mr. Grutman, that's not the way the Fourth Circuit interpreted the finding in this case," pointed out Justice Scalia, trying to bring the argument back down to earth. "They interpreted it, as I read their opinion, the majority, to mean that the jury understood it was not a factual statement about him. They didn't admit that they thought the statement was false. So you're urging on us a meaning that's not been accepted by any of the courts that have had the case so far."

"Candidly, I must say that I do not think that the Fourth Circuit made the point which I first tried to make to Justice O'Connor, and which I am making to you: in retrospect, I believe we could have appealed this as a proper basis for libel with that finding."

"You could, but you didn't," said Justice Stevens.

"But I didn't, and therefore it wasn't before the Fourth Circuit, and it's not before you now."

"Not only that, but the purpose in the jury instruction was to ask *that* question as a predicate to the *second* jury question—which related to *malice*—which wouldn't have had any purpose to it unless it's interpreted the way—"

"That is the way it looks in the cold light in the Supreme Court today. I remember that at the time that those jury instructions were being fought over in the pit of the trial, it really had to do with a certain contention that Judge Turk was flirting with about the meaning of *Pring* as to whether or not what was done in *Pring* constituted some basis."

"Yes, but your second question all goes to the *New York Times* malice standard, and that just isn't even implicated unless it's a false statement of fact."

"Justice Stevens, I agree that maybe I should have done something different, but I thought at the time that the damages we were seeking to recover were equally recoverable under the intentional infliction of emotional stress."

This was the lowest moment of the argument for Grutman. The justices seemed fixated on the jury's finding that no one could understand the ad as factual, and Grutman was now being impaled by that finding. The more Grutman was questioned on that finding, the more his argument seemed to founder. As he was forced to concede that "maybe I should have done something different," he appeared to be backpeddling, and was in danger of being caught on the ropes. He tried to fight his way out of peril by engaging in a dialogue with Justices Stevens and Marshall over the history of the tort of intentional infliction of emotional distress. This is not a new tort, he insisted. "It's been in existence for a hundred years."

Chief Justice Rehnquist challenged Grutman on this assertion. "It's certainly a new tort when applied to the press," he maintained.

"No, it is not a new tort, because there have been cases that have been decided in a number of states in which the press has been held liable for this tort, not only for the intentional infliction—"

"Yes, but how recent are those cases?"

"Well, the Florida case that I speak of is a 1984 case."

"What I said was it's only recently, isn't it, that the courts have been bringing activities of the press within this expanding tort of intentional infliction of emotional distress?"

"To that extent, I agree with you, Mr. Chief Justice. This is for this Court a tabula rasa, not exactly, however, terra incognita, because, in this connection, you are guided by the principles that the Court has developed in constitutional interpretations certainly over the last twenty-three years, when what has been described as the federalization of the law of libel first began in a commendable context, and has now spread to the point where I believe you are considering either dismantling or discarding *Gertz*. And the reason for that is that the press, the press that clamors here for a *universal exemption* so that they may have license to do what these people have done, now argues that it should be condoned and considered just a trivial or trifling matter, an incident of being a public figure. In Mr. Justice Powell's decision in *Gertz*, he talked about protecting speech that mattered."

"Wasn't that before the Court?" interjected Justice Harry Blackmun.

"Yes, it was," replied Grutman. "But in the opinion that Mr. Justice Powell wrote for the Court—"

"Lawyers always personalize these opinions, and they are Court opinions," protested Blackmun.

"I apologize to the other members of the Court to whom I meant no slight, but it's an opinion I'm sure—"

"Of course, I was in dissent," Justice White said. The spectators laughed.

"In my view, Mr. Justice White, that dissent either is, or may become, or should become the law of the land."

"I doubt it," quipped White.

"Mr. Grutman," said Justice Scalia, "I think it would be a different—you know, if there was a Virginia statute saying, you know, it's tortious to depict someone as committing incest, then you know, the cartoonist knows what he's up against. But, just to say 'heinous' and just leave it to the jury. . . . You think, for example, it isn't only the incest that offends you; you think that portraying a Baptist minister as having taken a shot or two before he went on to the pulpit, that that would qualify in your notion as heinous?"

"I think particularly it would satisfy. All these questions are debatable. That's why they go to juries for determination. But I think it is highly unrealistic that a legislature should sit down and write a decalogue or a catalogue of prohibitions to constitute guidelines for people exercising free speech. As a judge said in another case, the common law has been sufficient not to muzzle the press, and the common law is already—"

"The common law hasn't had this tort."

"This is a common-law tort. *Downton v. Wilkinson*[5] was a common-law tort."

"Since 1984, as applied to this field, do you tell us?"

"No. I said in 1984, when I started to quote these cases to Mr. Chief Justice Rehnquist, there was a Florida case in 1984, there was a Missouri case in 1982, there was a case in Wisconsin in 1970, another in 1982, and there have been cases in New Hampshire, Ohio, and the District of Columbia, including one in 1929, which is *Perry v. Capital Traction Corporation*, in which this Court denied *cert.*"

"This isn't *Blackstone*, I mean, this is pretty new, all of it, isn't it?"

"The memory of man runneth contrary perhaps to a time when this was a tort. I think the tort originated in the early 1900s. It originated in England. It's present here. Perhaps it's something that becomes more prevalent in our society because of the irresponsibility of certain aberrant publishers. This is an established tort under the law of Virginia and under most of the states. And I believe, as a constitutional rule, the protection of the individual's interest in his own sense of worth and dignity and to be free from this kind of gratuitous onslaught and damage to his feelings is something that ought properly to be left to the states. *Hustler* and Judge Wilkinson argued that there is some new kind of category that this Court ought to establish called the 'political public figure.' That is a figure unknown in any other decision and certainly not in this Court, and I would surely argue against it. Because this Court has said that, by becoming a public figure, a person does not abdicate his rights as a human being. And if libel will not protect someone who is subjected to this utterly worthless kind of verbal assault, then the tort of intentional infliction of emotional distress which Virginia recognizes is a tort which deserves support and endorsement in this case and in this Court."

The lights on the podium showed that Grutman's time was up. He was ending strongly and chose to finish by attempting to refute the closing theme that Alan Isaacman had sounded. To decide in favor of Falwell, Grutman wanted to convince the Court, would not threaten the legitimate press.

"This case is no threat to the media. It will be the rare case indeed where this kind of behavior will ever be replicated, but where it occurs, it deserves the condemnation which the jury gave it, which the Fourth Circuit found, and which I respectfully submit this Court should affirm. Thank you."

"Thank you, Mr. Grutman," said Chief Justice Rehnquist.

And with that, oral argument in *Hustler Magazine and Larry C. Flynt v. Jerry Falwell,* no. 86–1278, was completed in the United States Supreme Court.

Chapter 39

No ritual in American government has more majesty than an argument in the United State Supreme Court, and no exercise in American government is shrouded in more mystery than the deliberative processes of the justices following an argument. The sense of mystery seems to permeate even the architecture of the Supreme Court building. Justice Harlan F. Stone once wrote his sons, "The place is almost bombastically pretentious, and thus it seems to me wholly inappropriate for a quiet group of old boys such as the Supreme Court." He told his friends that the justices were like "nine black beetles in the Temple of Karnak."

Chief Justice Rehnquist has noted the inherent monasticism of the Supreme Court; for justices who do not venture out a bit to make speeches, write books, or conduct law school classes, it can become an oppressively two-dimensional world. Justices have developed a variety of strategies for coping with life on the Court. Legend has it that in the early years of the republic, during the tenure of the great Chief Justice John Marshall, there had even been talk of the justices' drinking a bit too much, particularly on "conference days," when the justices would gather to discuss and vote on cases. Marshall responded to the rumors by establishing a new rule, forbidding drink on decision days—except when it was raining. On the first scheduled conference day following the imposition of this new rule, the justices assembled in their conference room, and Chief Justice Marshall instructed Associate Justice Joseph Story to "please step to the window to see if there is any sign of rain." Story dutifully looked out the window, but there was no sign of rain. He came back and seriously said to the Chief Justice, "Mr. Chief Justice, I have very carefully examined this case, and I have to give it as my opinion that there is not the slightest sign of rain." Marshall replied, "Justice Story, I think that is the shallowest and most illogical opinion I have ever heard you deliver. You forget that our jurisdiction extends to all the states and territories of the United States. By the laws of nature, it must be raining *somewhere.* Bring on the rum."

One of the greatest challenges to a Supreme Court justice is to attempt to separate sharp ideological differences of opinion from personal relationships with other justices. Bitter personal feuds have been known to erupt from time to time. One of the hallmarks of an effective chief justice is his ability to convince fellow justices to leave their rivalries "on the playing field"—in conference and in the pages of their written opinions. One of the traditions of the Court, developed during the nineteenth century by Chief Justice Melville Fuller, was for each justice to greet and shake hands with the other justices before sitting down for the Court's conference.

What actually takes place in the conference room of the Supreme Court when a case is to be discussed and decided has rarely been revealed. No one other than the justices themselves are in the room during conference—no secretaries and no law clerks. (One of the few recurring "breaches" of this protocol comes during the World Series. Chief Justice Earl Warren first permitted pages periodically to update the scores at the end of each inning during the confrontation between the New York Yankees and Brooklyn Dodgers. The love of many of the justices for baseball continues to result in such "bulletins" when conference sessions in October fall on World Series game days.)

While the substance of the Supreme Court's discussions of individual cases remain among the few well-kept secrets in the City of Leaks, the basic procedure of the meetings is clear. The justices by tradition "speak down and vote up." The chief justice leads off, giving his views of the case, and is followed by each associate justice, in order of seniority. On *Falwell v. Flynt* this meant that William Rehnquist was the first to express his views, followed by the most senior associate justice, William Brennan. The most junior justice, Antonin Scalia, spoke last. Theoretically, after the justices have each spoken their piece, there is some opportunity for free give-and-take, and then a formal vote, cast in reverse order of seniority, is taken.

(The justices "vote up" from most junior to the senior so as not to put the most junior justice on the hotseat of the last vote in close cases.) In practice, however, the justices tend to reveal their positions clearly during their remarks, and no formal "vote" is taken. The justices thus actually "talk down" and "vote down," and, by the time the turn of the more junior justices comes around, there is often little new left to say.

When the views of all the justices have been registered, the task of writing the opinion is assigned. If the chief justice is among the majority of voters on a case, the chief assigns the job of writing the Court's opinion. The chief justice may assign the opinion to himself or to any of the other justices in the majority. If the chief justice is not in the majority, the responsibility for assigning the opinion devolves on the most senior associate justice. When the justices are split, a dissenting opinion is usually written. Once again, if the chief justice is in the majority of the dissenting justices, he assigns the dissenting opinion; if not, it is assigned by the most senior of the dissenters. No justice, however, is ever required to "join" in the opinion of another justice. Each justice is free to write his or her own opinion, either "concurring" or "dissenting" from the majority result. In some particularly anguishing cases, such as decisions over issues like the death penalty or affirmative action, all nine justices may issue individual opinions.

How would the justices approach *Falwell v. Flynt*?

The eight justices had been clearly "up" for the oral argument in the case. *New York Times* correspondent Anthony Lewis, a seasoned Court-watcher, remarked that he had not seen the justices so involved in "playing the game" in years. They were animated and aggressive in their questioning; the packed courtroom was filled with an electric crackle of excitement that could mark the argument of only a truly great case. The justices obviously saw the case as a major First Amendment decision. Freedom of speech disputes have a charisma few other areas of the law can match, and that charisma was reflected in the heightened response of the justices. What their decision would be, however, was anyone's guess.

Chapter 40

On the morning of February 24, 1988, the Supreme Court of the United States announced its decision in case no. 86–1278, *Hustler Magazine and Larry C. Flynt, Petitioners v. Jerry Falwell.*[1] The opinion of the Court was written by Chief Justice William Rehnquist.

Chief Justice Rehnquist begins his opinion by reviewing the history of the case, including the jury's verdict and the decision of the Fourth Circuit Court of Appeals affirming the $200,000 jury award. He then summarizes the issues facing the Supreme Court. "This case," writes Rehnquist, "presents us with a novel question involving First Amendment limitations upon a State's authority to protect its citizens from the intentional infliction of emotional distress." Rehnquist describes the Campari ad satire as offensive to Jerry Falwell, and "doubtless gross and repugnant in the eyes of most."

Rehnquist provides an essay on the purposes of the First Amendment. According to him, "At the heart of the First Amendment is the recognition of the fundamental importance of the free flow of ideas and opinions on matters of public interest and concern." He then recognizes the two principal functions of free speech, the self-fulfillment of the individual speaker and the broader social search for enlightenment. Quoting from the Court's 1984 decision, *Bose v. Consumers Union,*[2] he notes that " 'the freedom to speak one's mind is not only an aspect of individual liberty—and thus a good unto itself—but also is essential to the common quest for truth and the vitality of society as a whole.' " The Court has been particularly vigilant, he observes, to ensure that ideas remain free from governmentally imposed sanctions because the "First Amendment recognizes no such thing as a 'false' idea." Rehnquist caps off his introductory remarks by invoking one of the most sacred passages in the First Amendment tradition, the haunting appeal for tolerance by Justice Oliver Wendell Holmes in his dissent in *Abrams v. United States*:[3] " 'When men have realized that time has upset many fighting faiths, they may come to believe even more than they believe the very foundations of their own conduct that the ultimate good desired is better reached by a free trade in ideas—that the best test of truth is the power of the thought to get itself accepted in the competition of the market.' "

Chief Justice Rehnquist's philosophical base is decidedly not grounded in Allan Bloom's thesis that society must regulate public discourse in order to elevate it. Rehnquist instead begins with the antithesis of the Bloom philosophy, with a ringing endorsement of the classic Holmes-Brandeis view of free speech. Rehnquist endorses the marketplace of ideas metaphor not grudgingly but with positive enthusiasm.

If the marketplace of ideas is to be robust and wide-open, what does that bode for public figures? The next section of Rehnquist's analysis goes to great lengths to establish that in America the prevailing ethos is not to encourage people to enter the public arena by guaranteeing them shelter from caustic and virulent attack; it is rather to require as a cost of entering the public arena a certain toughening of the hide. Good but sensitive people may be discouraged in America from stepping forward into public life but that is part of the price of an open society and a spirited democracy. In this nation a public figure must be able to take as well as give.

Public figures, observes Chief Justice Rehnquist, have a substantial capacity to shape events. Quoting Felix Frankfurter, he notes that one " 'of the prerogatives of American citizenship is the right to criticize public men and measures.' " And in this country, such criticism will not always be reasoned and moderate. Quoting again from a prior Supreme Court decision, Rehnquist makes a point that seemed aimed personally at Jerry Falwell: " 'The candidate who vaunts his spotless record and sterling integrity cannot convincingly cry 'Foul' when an opponent or an industrious reporter attempts to demonstrate the contrary.' " The use of quotation is a diplomatic way of stating to Reverend Falwell that moralists must expect attacks on their morality.

This does not mean, cautions Rehnquist, "that *any* speech about a public figure is immune from sanction in the form of damages." Speech that is libelous in the conventional sense—speech that contains genuine misstatements of fact and that injures reputation—may be penalized in some circumstances. But even here, Rehnquist admonishes, the Constitution requires that the rules of libel be fashioned to provide sufficient breathing space for free speech. In what is a remarkable paragraph, Chief Justice Rehnquist proceeds wholeheartedly to endorse *New York Times Co. v. Sullivan* and its progeny. It is critical that public figures and public officials prove *both* that the offending statement was false and made with actual malice. If the Chief Justice has any doubts about the wisdom of the *New York Times* ruling, they are not apparent here; in both letter and spirit, he reaffirms *New York Times* with relish.

The argument of Norman Roy Grutman and the Fourth Circuit, however, was that the rules emanating from *New York Times* do not apply to the emotional distress tort and that the state's interest in protecting its citizens from emotional distress far outweighs any interest the speaker may have in propagating vulgar and shocking speech. It should adequately protect First Amendment interests, they argued, to require that the plaintiff prove intent to inflict the distress and to prove that the speech is offensive and outrageous.

But in the world of debate over public affairs, Rehnquist points out, people do many things with less than admirable motives, but they do not for that reason alone forfeit their First Amendment protection. That an utterance is spoken out of hatred does not mean it is false. Larry Flynt may hate Jerry Falwell as much as Jerry Falwell hates Satan, but it does not follow that the hate-filled speech of either man is not in its own way a contribution to the free interchange of ideas. Rehnquist thus writes that "while such a bad motive may be deemed controlling for purposes of tort liability in other areas of the law, we think the First Amendment prohibits such a result in the area of public debate about public figures."

This conclusion, the Chief Justice argues, is necessary in order to avoid censoring the work of political cartoonists and satirists. The art of caricature, he argues, is based on deliberate distortion or exaggeration for satirical effect. The cartoonist's method is often not reasoned or evenhanded, but slashing and one-sided, full of black scorn and ridicule. Rehnquist then engages in a moving tribute to the great American tradition of spirited satire and parody of public figures. He describes the cartoons of Thomas Nast, who published in *Harper's Weekly* in the post-Civil War era. Nast engaged in a graphic vendetta against William M. "Boss" Tweed and his corrupt "Tweed Ring" in New York City. Nast was effective because he constantly went beyond the bounds of good manners and taste. Rehnquist recalls caricatures of George Washington, James G. Blaine, and Abraham Lincoln and cartoonists' renditions of "Teddy Roosevelt's glasses and teeth and Franklin D. Roosevelt's jutting jaw and cigarette holder." From the viewpoint of history, he argues, "it is clear that our political discourse would have been considerably poorer without them."

But cannot these famous caricatures in political cartoons be distinguished from the coarse *Hustler* satire? Rehnquist concedes that the *Hustler* satire is at best a distant cousin of the conventional political cartoon, "and a rather poor relation at that." In what may be the single most important analytic step in his opinion, however, Rehnquist argues that there is no way to draw a principled distinction between the *Hustler* ad and other satiric efforts. The statement "I know it when I see it" is simply not good enough. "If it were possible," states Rehnquist, "by laying down a principled standard to separate the one from the other, public discourse would probably suffer little or no harm." But the Supreme Court was doubtful, Rehnquist explains, that any reasonably concrete standard could ever be articulated. One thing is certainly clear: The amorphous pejorative "outrageous" is too subjective to withstand First Amendment requirements. To permit a jury to impose liability for mere "outrageousness" would invite jurors to judge liability on the basis of their tastes and prejudices.

Chief Justice Rehnquist then makes it clear that the mere capacity of speech to embarrass or offend does not strip it of its protected character. In citing the holdings in *FCC v. Pacifica*,[4] the George Carlin "seven dirty words" case, and *Chaplinsky v. New Hampshire*,[5] the "fighting words" case, Rehnquist emphasizes that those holdings represent narrow exceptions to the general First Amendment rule that the government must remain neutral in the marketplace of ideas. While the Court has recognized that all speech is not of equal First Amendment importance, Rehnquist explains, the speech in this case simply does not fit into the precisely drawn categories in which lower levels of protection have been permitted. "We conclude," writes Rehnquist, "that public figures and public officials may not recover for the tort of intentional infliction of emotional distress by reason of publications such as the one here at issue without showing in addition that the publication contains a false statement of fact which was made with 'actual malice,' *i.e.*, with knowledge that the statement was false or with reckless disregard as to whether it was true." Here, the jury explicitly had found that the statement is not factual. Thus, in the absence of or misstatement of fact, Falwell could not recover for the mere intentional infliction of emotional distress. The last sentence of the opinion pronounces, "The judgment of the Court of Appeals is accordingly: *Reversed.*"

Chapter 41

Larry Flynt and *Hustler* had won! The vote was eight to zero. Six other Justices joined in the Chief Justice's opinion—Justices Brennan, Marshall, Blackmun, Stevens, O'Connor, and Scalia. Only Justice Byron White failed to join the Rehnquist opinion, instead filing a brief, two-sentence, separate concurring opinion. "As I see it, the decision in *New York Times v. Sullivan* has little to do with this case, for here the jury found that the ad contained no assertion of fact," writes Justice White. "But I agree with the Court that the judgment below, which penalized the publication of the parody, cannot be squared with the First Amendment." Justice Anthony Kennedy, who had only just been sworn in days before, did not participate in the consideration or decision of the case.

The result is stunning. It is as striking for its technical merit as its artistic impression. Not only had Jerry Falwell lost, he had lost in a unanimous decision. And not only had the decision been unanimous, it had been written by the Chief Justice of the United States, a justice known for conservative views on the First Amendment. It seemed to be a case in which the role made the man; Rehnquist had written a decision as *Chief* Justice. Given Rehnquist's strongly conservative anti-press record, and the strong emotional temptation to side with Falwell, Rehnquist's eloquent endorsement of freedom of speech ranks as one of the most striking events in his career.

The reactions of the two principals were predictable. Larry Flynt proclaimed the decision a victory not just for *Hustler* but for all satirists and all members of the press. Jerry Falwell echoed the words he had spoken throughout the case: "No sleaze merchant like Larry Flynt," he said, "should be able to use the First Amendment as an excuse for maliciously attacking public figures. The Supreme Court has given the green light to Larry Flynt and his ilk." Reacting to the Court's unanimous endorsement of the *New York Times* line of precedent, Norman Roy Grutman stated, "The question is, why doesn't the Supreme Court scrap *Gertz* and abolish it, because the differences and distinctions no longer matter?"

Did Grutman and Falwell regret all the effort and expense? They clearly did not. For Grutman, the case had been one of the proudest of his professional accomplishments. Summing it all up, he stated, "If we left the field vanquished, we did not leave with dishonor. We left with glory."

Even the timing of the decision, however, seemed to underscore the thoroughness of the defeat. It had not been a good week for fundamentalist televangelists. Jimmy Swaggart confessed to having sexually sinned, apparently with a prostitute from a no-tell motel sleaze strip in Louisiana. He was suspended from his ministry. After a strong start in the Iowa caucuses, Pat Robertson had begun to galvanize support from his followers but undercut hopes of broader support with a series of dubious, shoot-from-the-hip assertions, including the allegation that his Christian Broadcasting Network had information about the whereabouts of American hostages in Lebanon—though he could not interest anyone within the Reagan administration with the information. And to top it off, Jerry Falwell had been unanimously rebuffed by the Supreme Court.

What, in the end, does it all mean? The precise technical meaning of a landmark decision is not always readily apparent. It may take years for lawyers and lower courts to puzzle out all of the ramifications of *Hustler v. Falwell*. According to Justice Rehnquist, public figures and public officials may not recover for the tort of intentional infliction of emotional distress without showing in addition that the publication contains a false statement of fact made with actual malice. Does this statement mean that Rehnquist was trying to do the illogical—to force the square peg of *New York Times* into the round hole of infliction of emotional distress?

The soundest answer is no. While the Chief Justice heavily emphasizes the *Times* holding, in fact, his opinion goes well beyond the *Times* standard by arguing that the expression of opinion, as opposed to a misstatement of fact, is absolutely protected by the First

Amendment. Rehnquist's invocation of the *New York Times* standard makes perfect sense against the broader First Amendment backdrop of the case, for, while the *New York Times* standard is cited by Rehnquist, what his opinion actually establishes is the rule that public figures and public officials are *absolutely barred* from recovery when nothing factual is communicated and the *only* thing they can demonstrate is that the speech hurts their feelings.

The most intriguing technical legal issue posed by the opinion, however, is its express limitation to public figures and public officials. What if *Hustler* were to run a similar satire concerning a private person? Chief Justice Rehnquist's insistence that all speech is not of equal First Amendment value suggests that a different rule might obtain in such cases.

Rehnquist's opinion appears to invite lower courts to embark on a more complex analysis in private figure cases.[1] One possibility would be to borrow from the sort of multi-tiered rules that have evolved in the context of libel. The universe of tort recovery for emotional distress might be schematically arranged according to five variables: (1) whether the underlying tortious conduct is expressive (relating to communication of thoughts or emotions using language or symbols) or nonexpressive; (2) whether, if the conduct is expressive, the plaintiff is a public figure or official or a private figure; (3) whether, if the conduct is expressive, the communication involves matters of public interest; (4) whether the victim's emotional distress is coupled with injury *other* than emotional distress; and (5) whether the actor's conduct may be fairly characterized as satisfying all of the elements of some tort other than emotional distress or, instead, must be challenged exclusively under the rubric of emotional distress.

The Rehnquist opinion establishes absolute immunity at the "high end" of the scale suggested by these variables when public plaintiffs sue to recover for injuries caused by expressive conduct involving issues of public concern and when the only actual injury or legal interest implicated is emotional distress. When public plaintiffs sue to recover for injuries caused by public speech, the capacity of the speech to cause emotional disturbance is never enough, standing alone, to justify its abridgement.

No absolute immunity is mandated, however, when the case implicates some interest of the plaintiff other than the disturbing quality of the speech; in such cases, the regulation of speech is incidental to the protection of some palpable social interest distinct from the capacity of the speech to disturb. The test for whether speech is being restricted because of a state interest other than the disturbing quality of the speech is whether one can identify, either factually or legally, some nonemotional injury to the plaintiff. Thus, the fact that the plaintiff can prove nonemotional injury or that the plaintiff can point to some independently cognizable nonemotional distress tort, such as assault, battery, defamation, or invasion of privacy, is evidence that such a palpable state interest exists. Even in such cases, however, the sacrifice of First Amendment freedom must be meticulously balanced against the strength of the state interest. When the plaintiff and the speech are both public, the First Amendment interest is at its highest level. Abridgement of that interest through tort liability is thus permitted only when there is intentional or reckless conduct with regard to a risk other than the distress-inducing potential of the speech. It is critical that the intentional or reckless conduct be in relation to the other palpable interest being protected and not simply to the risk of causing distress; if the risk is only related to distress, the case must fall within the Supreme Court's holding in *Falwell*, in which the expressive conduct is absolutely protected.

This rationale remains applicable as one moves down the scale to speech that involves public figures but no public issues or public issues but no public figures. Because First Amendment concerns for penalizing speech for its disturbance potential alone still exist in these cases, it remains essential that the fault standard applied be in relation to risks other than the emotional distress evoked by the speech. On the other hand, because prior Supreme Court opinions inform us that private figures are in greater need and more deserving of tort remedies for injurious speech, the balance in these suits swings toward negligence rather than reckless or intentional conduct. The defendant must thus demonstrate both the public status of the plaintiff and the public status of the speech to receive the benefit of the "knowing or reckless" test. Showing only one of the two would drop the minimum First Amendment standard to negligence. In all of these cases, however, the First Amendment requires that the risk be in relation to something *other* than the emotional content of the speech.

No one, of course, can be sure exactly how lower courts will handle the technical implications of *Hustler v. Falwell* in all its applications. For the moment, however, the future legal technicalities are not what really matter. To decipher the meaning of the case only in terms of its technical ramifications is to sap the decision of its true resonance and power, like treating *Moby Dick* as a simple whaling adventure.

What is most important about Chief Justice Rehnquist's opinion is its larger meaning in reaffirming the role of freedom of speech in American life. Oliver Wendell Holmes once wrote that "The law is the witness and external deposit of our moral life. Its history is the history of the moral development of the race." The most powerful assaults on freedom of speech in America have always come not from bad people but from good people, people who would sanitize our speech to make it less sexist or sexual, less racist, less vulgar, less stinging. To many, the Supreme Court's decision must symbolize an accelerating disintegration of our moral life, the moral regression, not development, of the race.

That view of the Supreme Court's decision, however, entirely misses Chief Justice Rehnquist's point. More than that, it misses the central point of America's constitutional experience. The freedoms enshrined in the Constitution are not reducible to neatly organized abstract legal doctrines. They are more human, more emotional, more fluid and dynamic, more sensitive and sentient than that. Our constitutional freedoms are part of an ongoing evolution of a living tradition, as each generation engages in a continuing dialogue over what it means to be American. What endures is not so much the collection of answers supplied by each generation as the dialogue itself.

Just as T. S. Eliot admonished the fledgling young poet to bring discipline to his creativity by steeping himself in English poetry so as to develop " 'The historical sense'—a perception, not only of the pastness of the past, but of its presence"—any American who wishes to understand the First Amendment must be willing to relive the history of the hard-fought battles through which freedom of conscience and expression have been purchased. As William Faulkner put it, "The past is never dead. It isn't even past."

History reveals that, as often as not, the great First Amendment battles have been fought by our cultural rejects and misfits, by our communist-agitators, our civil rights activists, our Ku Klux Klanners, our Jehovah's Witnesses, our Larry Flynts.

The year 1988 was the year of *Falwell v. Flynt* and the bicentennial anniversary of the ratification of the United States Constitution. We are the oldest constitutional democracy in the world. The great resiliency of the American Constitution is its capacity for growth, and that capacity is nourished by our abiding faith in tolerance, even for the intolerant. We have wagered our salvation not on our collective capacity to elevate public discourse by controlling it but on our collective capacity to discover truth through the free, unregulated trade of ideas.

The Supreme Court's opinion in *Falwell v. Flynt* is a triumphant celebration of freedom of speech. Far from signalling the disintegration of America's moral gyroscope, the opinion reaffirms the most powerful magnetic force in our constitutional compass: that essential optimism of the American spirit, an optimism unafraid of wild-eyed, pluralistic, free-wheeling debate. We are a good and generous people, but we are not particularly gentle or genteel; we prefer to speak our minds. When all is said and done, Americans have the good common sense to distinguish the hustler from the real thing, and we have established as a first principle the censorship of neither. Thomas Jefferson taught that a little rebellion now and then is a good thing. Rebellion is often raucous and disturbing, indecorous and indecent. But it can also ring true, in the way that only George Carlin, Garry Trudeau, Richard Pryor, or Robin Williams can ring true. That Jeffersonian side of us is good for the soul.

Notes

CHAPTER 1

1. Harry Kalven, Jr., *A Worthy Tradition: Freedom of Speech in America* (New York: Harper & Row, 1988), p. 6.

CHAPTER 2

1. See generally, Jerry Falwell, *Strength for the Journey* (New York: Simon and Schuster, 1987).
2. Hustler Magazine, Inc. v. Moral Majority, Inc., 796 F.2d 1148 (9th Cir. 1986).
3. Ibid.
4. Ibid.
5. Ibid.
6. Ibid.

CHAPTER 3

1. Falwell v. Penthouse, 7 Med. L. Rep. (BNA) 1981 (D. W. Va. 1981).
2. Pring v. Penthouse International, Ltd., 695 F.2d 438 (10th Cir. 1982), *cert. denied,* 462 U.S. 1132 (1983).
3. See generally, Gerry Spence, *Trial by Fire* (New York: William Morrow, 1986).

CHAPTER 4

1. Reverend Jerry Falwell, Plaintiff, v. Larry C. Flynt, Hustler Magazine, Inc., and Flynt Distributing Company, Inc., Civil Action No. 83–0155–L–R, United States District Court for the Western District of Virginia, Roanoke Division.

CHAPTER 6
1. Allan Bloom, *The Closing of the American Mind* (New York: Simon and Schuster, 1987).

CHAPTER 7
1. The sentence which Larry Flynt was serving at the time of his deposition was imposed by the Honorable Manuel Real, Chief U.S. District Judge for the Central District of California. Judge Real imposed the sentence for contempt of court. The conviction was reversed in U.S. v. Flynt, 756 F.2d 1352 (9th Cir. 1985). The sentence was imposed on January 30, 1984, although Mr. Flynt had been in custody since December, 1983 on charges related to his wearing of the American flag to court in the *DeLorean* case. Mr. Flynt was released pending his appeal in July, 1984, upon the order of the U.S. Court of Appeals for the Ninth Circuit.
2. The material quoted throughout the account of Larry Flynt's deposition is from the trial transcript of that deposition, which was also part of the record on appeal. Joint Appendix, p. 91.

CHAPTER 8
1. Bob Colacello, "Larry Flynt, 'Hustling the American Dream,' " *Vanity Fair,* Feb. 1984, pp. 44–49.
2. Ibid.
3. Ibid.

CHAPTER 10
1. See generally, Rodney A. Smolla, *Suing the Press: Libel, the Media, and Power* (New York: Oxford University Press, 1986).
2. Rodney A. Smolla, *Law of Defamation* (Clark, Boardman, 1986), pp. 2–4.
3. See generally, Randall P. Bezanson, Gilbert Cranberg, and John Soloski, *Libel Law and the Press: Myth and Reality* (New York: The Free Press, 1987); Lois G. Forer, *A Chilling Effect: The Mounting Threat of Libel and Invasion of Privacy Actions to the First Amendment* (New York: W. W. Norton and Company, 1987); Robert D. Sack, *Libel, Slander, and Related Problems* (New York: Practicing Law Institute 1980); Bruce W. Sanford, *Libel and Privacy: The Prevention and Defense of Litigation* (New York: Law and Business, 1985).
4. New York Times Co. v. Sullivan, 375 U.S. 254 (1964).
5. Anthony Lewis, "New York Times v. Sullivan Reconsidered: Time to Return to 'The Central Meaning of the First Amendment,' " *Columbia Law Review* 83, 603 (1983).
6. Gertz v. Robert Welch, Inc., 418 U.S. 323 (1974).
7. Burnett v. National Enquirer, 144 Cal. App. 3d 991, 193 Cal. Rptr. 206 (1983), *appeal dismissed* 465 U.S. 1014 (1984).
8. Wilkinson v. Downton, 2 Q.B. 57 (1897).
9. Fisher v. Carrousel Motor Hotel, Inc., 424 S.W.2d 627 (Tex. 1967).

10. Western Union Telegraph Co. v. Hill, 25 Ala. App. 540, 150 So. 709 (1933).
11. Rodney A. Smolla, "Emotional Distress and the First Amendment," *Arizona State Law Journal* (1988).
12. L. L. Bean, Inc. v. Drake Publishers, Inc., 811 F.2d 26 (1st Cir. 1987).
13. Dallas Cowboys Cheerleaders, Inc. v. Pussycat Cinema, Ltd., 604 F.2d 200 (2d Cir. 1979).

CHAPTER 11
1. Defendant's Motion to Dismiss or, In the Alternative, to Disqualify Plaintiff's Counsel, and accompanying exhibits and memoranda.
2. Ibid.
3. Ibid.
4. 18 United States Code § 201(h).
5. 18 United States Code § 201(d).
6. Virginia Code of Professional Responsibility, Ethical Consideration 7–25.
7. Rancho La Costa v. Penthouse, 8 Med. L. Rep. (BNA) 1865 1982).
8. Penthouse v. Playboy, 663 F.2d 371 (2d Cir. 1981).
9. Guccione v. Hustler Magazine, 7 Med. L. Rep. (BNA) 2077 (Ohio Ct. App., Franklin County, 1981).
10. Ibid.
11. American Bar Association Code of Professional Responsibility, Ethical Consideration 7–37.
12. Guccione v. Hustler Magazine, Inc., 800 F.2d 298 (2d Cir. 1986).
13. Keeton v. Hustler Magazine, Inc., 465 U.S. 770 (1984).
14. Lerman v. Flynt Distributing Co., 745 F.2d 123 (2d Cir. 1974), *cert. denied*, 105 S.Ct. 2114 (1985).

CHAPTER 12
1. The material quoted throughout the account of Jerry Falwell's testimony is taken from the trial transcript, Joint Appendix, p. 38.
2. See generally, Jerry Falwell, *Strength for the Journey* (New York: Simon and Schuster, 1987).
3. See generally, Frances Fitzgerald, *Cities on a Hill* (New York: Touchstone, Simon and Schuster, 1987), pp. 121–201.
4. Dinesh D'Souza, *Falwell: Before the Millenium* (Chicago: Regnery Gateway, 1984), pp. 36–64.

CHAPTER 13
1. See generally, Jerry Falwell, *Listen, America!* (New York: Doubleday, 1980); Jerry Falwell, *The Fundamentalist Phenomenon* (New York: Doubleday, 1980).

CHAPTER 14
1. A. James Reichley, *Religion in American Public Life* (Washington, D.C.: Brookings Institution, 1985), pp. 314–327.

2. Jerry Falwell, *Listen, America!* (New York: Doubleday, 1980).
3. See generally, Ralph Clark Chandler, "The Wicked Shall Not Bear Rule: The Fundamentalist Heritage of the New Christian Right," in David G. Bromley and Anson Shupe, eds., *New Christian Politics* (Macon, Georgia: Mercer University Press, 1984), pp. 41–60; Robert Booth Fowler, *Religion and Politics in America* (Metuchen, New Jersey: American Theological Library Association and Scarecrow Press, 1985), pp. 203–230; James A. Speer. "The New Christian Right and Its Parent Company: A Study in Political Contrasts," in David G. Bromley and Anson Shupe, eds., *New Christian Politics* (Macon, Georgia: Mercer University Press, 1984), pp. 19–40; Anson Shupe, "Interpreting the New Christian Right: A Commentary on the Substance and Process of Knowledge Creation," in David G. Bromley and Anson Shupe, eds., *New Christian Politics* (Macon, Georgia: Mercer University Press, 1984), pp. 1–16; "An Interview with the Lone Ranger of American Fundamentalism," *Christianity Today,* Sept. 1981, pp. 22–27.

CHAPTER 17
1. See generally, Lawrence W. Levine, *Defender of the Faith, William Jennings Bryan: The Last Decade, 1915–1925* (New York: Oxford University Press, 1965), pp. 324–357.
2. See generally, Irving Stone, *Clarence Darrow for the Defense* (New York: Doubleday, 1941).
3. A. James Reichley, *Religion in American Public Life* (Washington, D.C.: The Brookings Institute, 1985), pp. 311–331.
4. See Frances Fitzgerald, *Cities on a Hill* (New York: Touchstone, Simon and Schuster, 1987), p. 129.
5. Ibid.
6. Jeffrey K. Hadden, "Televangelism and the Future of American Politics," in David G. Bromley and Anson Shupe, eds., *New Christian Politics* (Macon, Georgia: Mercer University Press, 1984), pp. 151–165.
7. Ibid., p. 158.

CHAPTER 19
1. Bob Colacello, "Larry Flynt, 'Hustling the American Dream,' " *Vanity Fair,* Feb. 1984, pp. 44–49.

CHAPTER 20
1. Michael Gilbert, *The Oxford Book of Legal Anecdotes* (New York: Oxford University Press, 1986), p. 101.
2. William O. Douglas, *Go East, Young Man* (New York: Random House, 1974), p. 451.

CHAPTER 22
1. Falwell v. Flynt, 797 F.2d 1270 (4th Cir. 1986).
2. Womack v. Eldridge, 215 Va. 338, 210 S.E.2d 145 (1974).

CHAPTER 23

1. Palsgraf v. Long Island R.R., 248 N.Y. 339, 162 N.E. 99 (1928).
2. New York Times Co. v. Sullivan, 376 U.S. 254 (1964).
3. Falwell v. Flynt, 805 F.2d 484 (4th Cir. 1986). (Wilkinson, J., dissenting from denial of rehearing.)
4. Harriette K. Dorsen, "Satiric Appropriation and the Law of Libel, Trademark, and Copyright: Remedies Without Wrong," *Boston University Law Review* 65, 923 (1985).

CHAPTER 24

1. See generally, Anthony Lewis, *Gideon's Trumpet* (New York: Random House, 1964).
2. See generally, William H. Rehnquist, *The Supreme Court: How It Was, How It Is* (New York: William Morrow, 1987).
3. Alexander Pope, *Epistle to Dr. Arbuthnot* (Riverside, 1969).

CHAPTER 25

1. Frederick Schauer, "The Back Side of the First Amendment," in "Public Figures," *William and Mary Law Review* 25, 905 (1984).

CHAPTER 26

1. Chaplinsky v. New Hampshire, 315 U.S. 568 (1942).
2. Harry Kalven, Jr., *A Worthy Tradition: Freedom of Speech in America* (New York: Harper and Row, 1988), pp. 70–95.
3. For examples of Supreme Court cases in which Jehovah's Witnesses were victorious, see Cantwell v. Connecticut, 310 U.S. 296 (1940); West Va. St. Bd. of Educ. v. Barnette, 319 U.S. 624 (1943); Taylor v. Mississippi, 319 U.S. 583 (1943); Thomas v. Review Bd., 450 U.S. 707 (1981).
4. Beauharnais v. Illinois, 343 U.S. 250 (1952).

CHAPTER 27

1. John E. Nowak, Ronald D. Rotunda, and J. Nelson Young, *Constitutional Law*, 3rd ed. (West Publishing Company, 1986), pp. 1009–1029.
2. Roth v. United States, 354 U.S. 476 (1957).
3. See generally, Miller v. California, 413 U.S. 15 (1973); Paris Adult Theatre I v. Slaton, 413 U.S. 49 (1973); Jenkins v. Georgia, 418 U.S. 153 (1974); Pope v. Illinois, 107 S.Ct. 1918 (1987).
4. Miller v. California, 413 U.S. 15 (1973).
5. Frederick Schauer, "Speech and 'Speech'—Obscenity and 'Obscenity': An Exercise in Interpretation of Constitutional Language," *Georgetown Law Journal* 67, 899 (1979).
6. Rodney A. Smolla, *Suing the Press: Libel, the Media, and Power* (New York: Oxford University Press, 1986).
7. Bowers v. Hardwick, 106 S.Ct. 2841 (1986).
8. *Final Report of the Attorney General's Commission on Pornography* (Nashville, TN.: Rutledge Hill Press ed., 1986).

9. Bob Woodward and Scott Armstrong, *The Brethren* (New York: Simon and Schuster, 1979), p. 199.
10. Jacobellis v. Ohio, 378 U.S. 184 (1964).

CHAPTER 28
1. FCC v. Pacifica Foundation, 438 U.S. 726 (1978).
2. Red Lion Broadcasting Co. v. FCC, 395 U.S. 369 (1969).
3. Miami Herald Co. v. Tornillo, 418 U.S. 241 (1974).

CHAPTER 29
1. Jerry Falwell, *Strength for the Journey* (New York: Simon and Schuster, 1987), pp. 103–106.
2. A. James Reichley, *Religion in American Public Life* (Washington, D.C.: Brookings Institute, 1985), p. 318.
3. Ibid., p. 314–331.
4. See generally, Jerry Falwell, *Listen, America!* (New York: Doubleday, 1980); Jerry Falwell, *The Fundamentalist Phenomenon* (New York: Doubleday, 1980).
5. Jerry Falwell, *Listen, America!* (New York: Doubleday, 1980).
6. William Lee Miller, *The First Liberty: Religion and the American Republic* (New York: Alfred A. Knopf, 1986), pp. 209–210, 249–251.
7. Ibid., p. 19.
8. See generally, Ralph Clark Chandler, "The Wicked Shall Not Bear Rule: The Fundamentalist Heritage of the New Christian Right," in David G. Bromley and Anson Shupe, eds., *New Christian Politics* (Macon, Georgia: Mercer University Press, 1984), pp. 41–61; Frances Fitzgerald, *Cities on a Hill* (New York: Touchstone, Simon & Schuster, 1987), pp. 121–201; Robert Booth Fowler, *Religion and Politics in America* (Metuchen, New Jersey: American Theological Library Ass'n and Scarecrow Press, 1985), pp. 203–30; A. James Reichley, *Religion in American Public Life* (Washington, D.C.: Brookings Institute, 1985); Anson Shupe, "Interpreting the New Christian Right: A Commentary on the Substance and Process of Knowledge Creation," in David G. Bromley and Anson Shupe, eds., *New Christian Politics* (Macon, Georgia: Mercer University Press, 1984), pp. 1–16; James A. Speer, "The New Christian Right and Its Parent Company: A Study in Political Contrasts" in David G. Bromley and Anson Shupe, eds., *New Christian Politics* (Macon, Georgia: Mercer University Press, 1984), pp. 19–40.
9. Lemon v. Kurtzman, 403 U.S. 602 (1971).
10. Committee for Public Education and Religious Liberty v. Regan, 444 U.S. 646 (1980).
11. William Lee Miller, *The First Liberty: Religion and the American Republic* (New York: Alfred A. Knopf, 1986).
12. Ibid., p. 230.
13. Ibid., p. 184.
14. Ibid., p. 185.
15. Ibid.

16. Cantwell v. Connecticut, 310 U.S. 296 (1940).
17. Burstyn v. Wilson, 343 U.S. 459 (1952).

CHAPTER 30

1. Rodney A. Smolla, *Suing the Press: Libel, the Media, and Power* (New York: Oxford University Press, 1986), pp. 45–52.
2. Richard Labunski, *Libel and the First Amendment* (New Brunswick, New Jersey: Transaction Books, 1987), p. 34.
3. I. Stat. 596 (1798).
4. Debs v. United States, 249 U.S. 211 (1919).
5. Masses Publishing Co. v. Patten, 244 Fed. 535 (S.D.N.Y., 1917).
6. Harry Kalven, Jr., *A Worthy Tradition: Freedom of Speech in America* (New York: Harper and Row, 1988), pp. 506–587.
7. Donald L. Smith, *Zechariah Chafee, Jr.: Defender of Liberty and Law* (Cambridge: Harvard University Press, 1986), pp. 18–35.
8. Abrams v. United States, 250 U.S. 616 (1919).

CHAPTER 31

1. Brandenburg v. Ohio, 395 U.S. 444 (1969).
2. Hess v. Indiana, 414 U.S. 105 (1973).
3. Cohen v. California, 403 U.S. 15 (1970).
4. Terminiello v. Chicago, 337 U.S. 1 (1949).
5. Street v. New York, 394 U.S. 576 (1969).

CHAPTER 32

1. See generally, Zechariah Chafee, *Free Speech in the United States* (Cambridge: Harvard University Press, 1941).
2. Rodney A. Smolla, *Law of Defamation* (New York: Clark, Boardman, 1986), pp. 18–24.
3. Bose Corp. v. Consumers Union of United States, Inc., 466 U.S. 485 (1984).
4. See generally, Alexander Meiklejohn, *Free Speech and Its Relation to Self-Government* (New York: Harper and Row, 1948).
5. Melville Nimmer, *Nimmer on Freedom of Speech* (New York: Matthew Bender, 1984), pp. 1–53.
6. Time, Inc. v. Hill, 385 U.S. 374 (1967).
7. West Virginia State Board of Education v. Barnette, 319 U.S. 624 (1943).

CHAPTER 33

1. Nathaniel Hawthorne, *The Scarlet Letter* (1850; reprint, New York: Portland House, 1987).
2. Michael Wines, "In Bed with the Press," Washington Journalism Review, Sept. 1987, p. 16.

CHAPTER 34

1. Tagart v. Tipper, 170 Eng. Rep. 981 (1808).
2. Greenbelt Cooperative Publishing Ass'n v. Bresler, 398 U.S. 6 (1970).

3. Gertz v. Robert Welch, Inc., 418 U.S. 323 (1974).
4. Bose Corp. v. Consumers Union of United States, Inc., 466 U.S. 485 (1984).
5. Old Dominion Branch No. 96, National Ass'n of Letter Carriers v. Austin, 418 U.S. 264 (1974).
6. Crawford v. United Steelworkers, AFL-CIO, 230 Va. 217, 335 S.E.2d 828 (1985).

CHAPTER 35

1. See generally, William H. Rehnquist, *The Supreme Court: How It Was, How It Is* (New York: William Morrow, 1987).
2. For information on the Justices, see generally, Geoffrey R. Stone, Louis M. Seidman, Cass R. Sunstein, and Mark V. Tushnet, *Constitutional Law* (Boston: Little, Brown, 1986).

CHAPTER 37

1. The account of the oral argument is taken from the author's own notes, and from the Transcript of the Proceedings, no. 86–1278, December 2, 1987 (Washington, D.C.: Heritage Reporting Corporation).
2. Bose Corp. v. Consumers Union of United States, Inc., 46 U.S. 485 (1984).
3. New York Times Co. v. Sullivan, 376 U.S. 254 (1964).
4. Garrison v. Louisiana, 379 U.S. 64 (1964).
5. Time, Inc. v. Firestone, 424 U.S. 448 (1976).
6. Pope v. Illinois, 107 S.Ct. 1918 (1987).
7. Greenbelt Cooperative Publishing Ass'n v. Bresler, 389 U.S. 6 (1970).

CHAPTER 38

1. New York Times Co. v. Sullivan, 376 U.S. 254 (1964).
2. Gertz v. Robert Welch, Inc., 418 U.S. 323 (1974).
3. Dun & Bradstreet, Inc. v. Greenmoss Builders, Inc., 472 U.S. 749 (1985).
4. Philadelphia Newspapers, Inc. v. Hepps, 106 S.Ct. 1558 (1986).
5. Wilkinson v. Downton, 2 Q.B. 57 (1897).

CHAPTER 40

1. Hustler Magazine, Inc. v. Falwell, 108 S.Ct. 876 (1988).
2. Bose Corp. v. Consumers Union of United States, Inc., 466 U.S. 485 (1984).
3. Abrams v. United States, 250 U.S. 616 (1919) (Holmes, J., dissenting).
4. FCC v. Pacifica Foundation, 438 U.S. 726 (1978).
5. Chaplinsky v. New Hampshire, 315 U.S. 568 (1942).

CHAPTER 41

1. See generally, Rodney A. Smolla, "Emotional Distress and the First Amendment," *Arizona State Law Journal* 20, 423 (1988).

Appendix I

Appendix II

HUSTLER MAGAZINE AND LARRY C. FLYNT, PETITIONERS V. JERRY FALWELL

SUPREME COURT OF THE UNITED STATES

February 24, 1988

CHIEF JUSTICE REHNQUIST delivered the opinion of the Court.

Petitioner Hustler Magazine, Inc., is a magazine of nationwide circulation. Respondent Jerry Falwell, a nationally known minister who has been active as a commentator on politics and public affairs, sued petitioner and its publisher, petitioner Larry Flynt, to recover damages for invasion of privacy, libel, and intentional infliction of emotional distress. The District Court directed a verdict against respondent on the privacy claim, and submitted the other two claims to a jury. The jury found for petitioners on the defamation claim, but found for respondent on the claim for intentional infliction of emotional distress and awarded damages. We now consider whether this award is consistent with the First and Fourteenth Amendments of the United States Constitution.

The inside front cover of the November 1983 issue of *Hustler Magazine* featured a "parody" of an advertisement for Campari Liqueur that contained the name and picture of respondent and was entitled "Jerry Falwell talks about his first time." This parody was modeled after actual Campari ads that included interviews with various celebrities about their "first times." Although it was apparent by the end of each interview that this meant the first time they sampled Campari, the ads clearly played on the sexual double entendre of the general subject of "first times." Copying the form and layout of these Campari ads, *Hustler*'s editors chose respondent as the featured celebrity and drafted an alleged "interview" with him in which he states that his "first time" was during a drunken incestuous rendezvous with his mother in an outhouse. The *Hustler* parody portrays respondent and his mother as drunk and immoral, and suggests that respondent is a hypocrite who preaches only when he is drunk. In small print at the bottom of the page, the ad contains the disclaimer, "ad parody—not to be taken seriously." The magazine's table of contents also lists the ad as "Fiction; Ad and Personality Parody."

Soon after the November issue of *Hustler* became available to the public, respondent brought this diversity action in the United States District Court for the Western District of Virginia against Hustler Magazine, Inc., Larry C. Flynt, and Flynt Distributing Co. Respondent stated in his complaint that publication of the ad parody in Hustler entitled him to recover damages for libel, invasion of privacy, and intentional infliction of emotional distress. The case proceeded to trial.[1] At the close of the evidence, the District Court granted a directed verdict for petitioners on the invasion of privacy claim. The jury then found against respondent on the libel claim, specifically finding that the ad parody could not "reasonably be understood as describing actual facts about [respondent] or actual events in which [he] participated." App. to Pet. for Cert. C1. The jury ruled for respondent on the intentional infliction of emotional distress claim, however and stated that he should be awarded $100,000 in compensatory damages, as well as $50,000 each in punitive damages from petitioners.[2] Petitioners' motion for judgment notwithstanding the verdict was denied.

On appeal, the United States Court of Appeals for the Fourth Circuit affirmed the judgment against petitioners. *Falwell* v. *Flynt,* 797 F. 2d 1270 (CA4 1986). The court rejected petitioners' argument that the "actual malice" standard of *New York Times Co.* v. *Sullivan,* 376 U. S. 254 (1964), must be met before respondent can recover for emotional distress. The court agreed that because respondent is concededly a public figure, petitioners are "entitled to the same level of first amendment protection in the claim for intentional infliction of emotional distress that they received in [respondent's] claim for libel." 797 F. 2d, at 1274. But this does not mean that a literal application of the actual malice rule is appropriate in the context of an emotional distress claim. In the court's view, the *New York Times* decision emphasized the constitutional importance not of the falsity of the statement or the defendant's disregard for the truth, but of the heightened level of culpability embodied in the requirement of "knowing . . . or reckless" conduct. Here, the *New York Times* standard is satisfied by the state-law requirement, and the jury's finding, that the defendants have acted intentionally or recklessly.[3] The Court of Appeals then went on to reject the contention that because the jury found that the ad parody did not describe actual facts about respondent, the ad was an opinion that is protected by the First Amendment. As the court put it, this was "irrelevant," as the issue is "whether [the ad's] publication was sufficiently outrageous to constitute intentional infliction of emotional distress."[4] Id., at 1276. Petitioners then filed a petition for rehearing en banc, but this was denied by a divided court. Given the importance of the constitutional issues involved, we granted *certiorari*.

This case presents us with a novel question involving First Amendment limitations upon a State's authority to protect its citizens from the intentional infliction of emotional distress. We must decide whether a public figure may recover damages for emotional harm caused by the publication of an ad parody offensive to him, and doubtless gross and repugnant in the eyes of most. Respondent would have us find that a State's interest in protecting public figures from emotional distress is sufficient to deny First Amendment protection to speech that is patently offensive and is intended to inflict emotional injury, even when that speech could not reasonably have been interpreted as stating actual facts about the public figure involved. This we decline to do.

At the heart of the First Amendment is the recognition of the fundamental importance of the free flow of ideas and opinions on matters of public interest and concern. "[T]he freedom to speak one's mind is not only an aspect of individual liberty—and thus a good unto itself—but also is essential to the common quest for truth and the vitality of society as a whole." *Bose Corp.* v. *Consumers Union of United States, Inc.,* 466 U. S. 485, 503–504 (1984). We have therefore been particularly vigilant to ensure that individual expressions of ideas remain free from governmentally imposed sanctions. The First Amendment recognizes no such thing as a "false" idea. *Gertz* v. *Robert Welch, Inc.,* 418 U. S. 323, 339 (1974). As Justice Holmes wrote, "[W]hen men have realized that time has upset many fighting faiths, they may come to believe even more than they believe the very foundations of their own conduct that the ultimate good desired is better reached by free trade in ideas—that the best test of truth is the power of the thought to get itself accepted in the competition of the market. . . ." *Abrams* v. *United States,* 250 U. S. 616, 630 (1919) (dissenting opinion).

The sort of robust political debate encouraged by the First Amendment is bound to produce speech that is critical of those who hold public office or those public figures who are "intimately involved in the resolution of important public questions or, by reason of their fame, shape events in areas of concern to society at large." *Associated Press* v. *Walker,* decided with *Curtis Publishing Co.* v. *Butts,* 388 U. S. 130, 164 (1967) (Warren, C.J., concurring in result). Justice Frankfurter put it succinctly in *Baumgartner*

v. *United States,* 322 U. S. 665, 673–674 (1944), when he said that "[o]ne of the prerogatives of American citizenship is the right to criticize public men and measures." Such criticism, inevitably, will not always be reasoned or moderate; public figures as well as public officials will be subject to "vehement, caustic, and sometimes unpleasantly sharp attacks," *New York Times, supra,* at 270. "[T]he candidate who vaunts his spotless record and sterling integrity cannot convincingly cry 'Foul' when an opponent or an industrious reporter attempts to demonstrate the contrary." *Monitor Patriot Co.* v. *Roy,* 401 U. S. 265, 274 (1971).

Of course, this does not mean that *any* speech about a public figure is immune from sanction in the form of damages. Since *New York Times Co.* v. *Sullivan, supra,* we have consistently ruled that a public figure may hold a speaker liable for the damage to reputation caused by publication of a defamatory falsehood, but only if the statement was made "with knowledge that it was false or with reckless disregard of whether it was false or not." Id., at 279–280. False statements of fact are particularly valueless; they interfere with the truth-seeking function of the marketplace of ideas, and they cause damage to an individual's reputation that cannot easily be repaired by counterspeech, however persuasive or effective. See *Gertz,* 418 U. S., at 340, 344, n. 9. But even though falsehoods have little value in and of themselves, they are "nevertheless inevitable in free debate," id., at 340, and a rule that would impose strict liability on a publisher for false factual assertions would have an undoubted "chilling" effect on speech relating to public figures that does have constitutional value. "Freedoms of expression require 'breathing space.' " *Philadelphia Newspapers, Inc.* v. *Hepps,* 475 U. S. 767, 772 (1986) (quoting *New York Times,* 376 U. S., at 272). This breathing space is provided by a constitutional rule that allows public figures to recover for libel or defamation only when they can prove both that the statement was false and that the statement was made with the requisite level of culpability.

Respondent argues, however, that a different standard should apply in this case because here the State seeks to prevent not reputational damage, but the severe emotional distress suffered by the person who is the subject of an offensive publication. Cf. *Zacchini* v. *Scripps-Howard Broadcasting Co.,* 433 U. S. 562 (1977) (ruling that the "actual malice" standard does not apply to the tort of appropriation of a right of publicity). In respondent's view, and in the view of the Court of Appeals, so long as the utterance was intended to inflict emotional distress, was outrageous, and did in fact inflict serious emotional distress, it is of no constitutional import whether the statement was a fact or an opinion, or whether it was true or false. It is the intent to cause injury that is the gravamen of the tort, and the State's interest in preventing emotional harm simply outweighs whatever interest a speaker may have in speech of this type.

Generally speaking the law does not regard the intent to inflict emotional distress as one which should receive much solicitude, and it is quite understandable that most if not all jurisdictions have chosen to make it civilly culpable where the conduct in question is sufficiently "outrageous." But in the world of debate about public affairs, many things done with motives that are less than admirable are protected by the First Amendment. In *Garrison* v. *Louisiana,* 379 U. S. 64 (1964), we held that even when a speaker or writer is motivated by hatred or ill-will his expression was protected by the First Amendment:

> "Debate on public issues will not be uninhibited if the speaker must run the risk that it will be proved in court that he spoke out of hatred; even if he did speak out of hatred, utterances honestly believed contribute to the free interchange of ideas and the ascertainment of truth." Id., at 73.

Thus while such a bad motive may be deemed controlling for purposes of tort liability in other areas of the law, we think the First Amendment prohibits such a result in the area of public debate about public figures.

Were we to hold otherwise, there can be little doubt that political cartoonists and satirists would be subjected to damages awards without any showing that their work falsely defamed its subject. *Webster's* defines a caricature as "the deliberately distorted picturing or imitating of a person, literary style, etc. by exaggerating features or mannerisms for satirical effect." *Webster's New Unabridged Twentieth Century Dictionary of the English Language* 275 (2d ed. 1979). The appeal of the political cartoon or caricature is often based on exploration of unfortunate physical traits or politically embarrassing events—an exploration often calculated to injure the feelings of the subject of the portrayal. The art of the cartoonist is often not reasoned or evenhanded, but slashing and one-sided. One cartoonist expressed the nature of the art in these words:

> "The political cartoon is a weapon of attack, of scorn and ridicule and satire; it is least effective when it tries to pat some politician on the back. It is usually as welcome as a bee sting and is always controversial in some quarters." Long, *The Political Cartoon: Journalism's Strongest Weapon,* The Quill, 56, 57 (Nov. 1962).

Several famous examples of this type of intentionally injurious speech were drawn by Thomas Nast, probably the greatest American cartoonist to date, who was associated for many years during the post-Civil War era with *Harper's Weekly.* In the pages of that publication Nast conducted a graphic vendetta against William M. "Boss" Tweed and his corrupt associates in New York City's "Tweed Ring." It has been described by one historian of the subject as "a sustained attack which in its passion and effectiveness stands alone in the history of American graphic art." M. Keller, *The Art and Politics of Thomas Nast* 177 (1968). Another writer explains that the success of the Nast cartoon was achieved "because of the emotional impact of its presentation. It continuously goes beyond the bounds of good taste and conventional manners." C. Press, *The Political Cartoon* 251 (1981).

Despite their sometimes caustic nature, from the early cartoon portraying George Washington as an ass down to the present day, graphic depictions and satirical cartoons have played a prominent role in public and political debate. Nast's castigation of the Tweed Ring, Walt McDougall's characterization of presidential candidate James G. Blaine's banquet with the millionaires at Delmonico's as "The Royal Feast of Belshazzar," and numerous other efforts have undoubtedly had an effect on the course and outcome of contemporaneous debate. Lincoln's tall, gangling posture, Teddy Roosevelt's glasses and teeth, and Franklin D. Roosevelt's jutting jaw and cigarette holder have been memorialized by political cartoons with an effect that could not have been obtained by the photographer or the portrait artist. From the viewpoint of history it is clear that our political discourse would have been considerably poorer without them.

Respondent contends, however, that the caricature in question here was so "outrageous" as to distinguish it from more traditional political cartoons. There is no doubt that the caricature of respondent and his mother published in *Hustler* is at best a distant cousin of the political cartoons described above, and a rather poor relation at that. If it were possible by laying down a principled standard to separate the one from the other, public discourse would probably suffer little or no harm. But we doubt that there is any such standard, and we are quite sure that the pejorative description "outrageous" does not supply one. "Outrageousness" in the area of political and social discourse has an inherent subjectiveness about it which would allow a jury to impose liability on the basis of the jurors' tastes or views, or perhaps on the basis of their dislike of a particular expression. An "outrageousness" standard thus runs afoul of our longstanding refusal to allow damages to be awarded because the speech in question may have an adverse emotional impact on the audience. See *NAACP* v. *Claiborne Hardware Co.,* 458 U. S. 886, 910 (1982) ("Speech does not lose its protected character . . . simply because it may embarrass others or coerce them into action"). And, as we stated in *FCC* v. *Pacifica Foundation,* 438 U. S. 726 (1978):

> "[T]he fact that society may find speech offensive is not a sufficient reason for suppressing it. Indeed, if it is the speaker's opinion that gives offense, that consequence is a reason for according it constitutional protection. For it is a central tenet of the First Amendment that the government must remain neutral in the marketplace of ideas." Id., at 745–746.

See also *Street* v. *New York,* 394 U. S. 576, 592 (1969) ("It is firmly settled that . . . the public expression of ideas may not be prohibited merely because the ideas are themselves offensive to some of their hearers").

Admittedly, these oft-repeated First Amendment principles, like other principles, are subject to limitations. We recognized in Pacifica Foundation, that speech that is "vulgar," "offensive," and "shocking" is "not entitled to absolute constitutional protection under all circumstances." 438 U. S., at 747. In *Chaplinsky* v. *New Hampshire,* 315 U. S. 568 (1942), we held that a state could lawfully punish an individual for the use of insulting "fighting" words—those which by their very utterance inflict injury or tend to incite an immediate breach of the peace." Id., at 571–572. These limitations are but recognition of the observation in *Dun & Bradstreet, Inc.* v. *Greenmoss Builders, Inc.,* 472 U. S. 749, 758 (1985), that this Court has "long recognized that not all speech is of equal First Amendment importance." But the sort of expression involved in this case does not seem to us to be governed by any exception to the general First Amendment principles stated above.

We conclude that public figures and public officials may not recover for the tort of intentional infliction of emotional distress by reason of publications such as the one here at issue without showing in addition that the publication contains a false statement of fact which was made with "actual malice," i.e., with knowledge that the statement was false or with reckless disregard as to whether or not it was true. This is not merely a "blind application" of the *New York Times* standard, see *Time, Inc.* v. *Hill,* 385 U. S. 374, 390 (1967), it reflects our considered judgment that such a standard is necessary to give adequate "breathing space" to the freedoms protected by the First Amendment.

Here it is clear that respondent Falwell is a "public figure" for purposes of First Amendment law.[5] The jury found against respondent on his libel claim when it decided that the *Hustler* ad parody could not "reasonably be understood as describing actual facts about [respondent] or actual events in which [he] participated." App. to Pet. for Cert. C1. The Court of Appeals interpreted the jury's finding to be that the ad parody "was not reasonably believable," 797 F. 2d, at 1278, and in accordance with our custom we accept this finding. Respondent is thus relegated to his claim for damages awarded by the jury for the intentional infliction of emotional distress by "outrageous" conduct. But for reasons heretofore stated this claim cannot, consistently with the First Amendment, form a basis for the award of damages when the conduct in question is the publication of a caricature such as the ad parody involved here. The judgment of the Court of Appeals is accordingly Reversed.

JUSTICE KENNEDY took no part in the consideration or decision of this case.

JUSTICE WHITE, concurring in the judgment.

As I see it, the decision in *New York Times* v. *Sullivan,* 376 U. S. 254 (1964), has little to do with this case, for here the jury found that the ad contained no assertion of fact. But I agree with the Court that the judgment below, which penalized the publication of the parody, cannot be squared with the First Amendment.

NOTES

1. While the case was pending, the ad parody was published in *Hustler Magazine* a second time.
2. The jury found no liability on the part of Flynt Distributing Co., Inc. It is consequently not a party to this appeal.
3. Under Virginia law, in an action for intentional infliction of emotional distress a plaintiff must show that the defendant's conduct (1) is intentional or reckless; (2) offends generally accepted standards of decency or morality; (3) is causally connected with the plaintiff's emotional distress; and (4) caused emotional distress that was severe. 797 F. 2d, at 1275, n. 4 (citing *Womack* v. *Eldridge,* 215 Va. 338, 210 S. E. 2d 145 [1974]).
4. The court below also rejected several other contentions that petitioners do not raise in this appeal.
5. Neither party disputes this conclusion. Respondent is the host of a nationally syndicated television show and was the founder and president of a political organization formerly known as the Moral Majority. He is also the founder of Liberty University in Lynchburg, Virginia, and is the author of several books and publications. *Who's Who in America* 849 (44th ed. 1986–1987).

Index